IN SEARCH OF
THE GOLDEN WEST

EARL POMEROY

IN SEARCH OF THE
GOLDEN
WEST

THE TOURIST
IN WESTERN AMERICA

University of Nebraska Press
Lincoln and London

First Bison Book printing: 1990
Most recent printing indicated by the last digit below:
10   9   8   7   6   5   4   3   2   1

Library of Congress Cataloging-in-Publication Data
Pomeroy, Earl S. (Earl Spencer), 1915–
In search of the Golden West: the tourist in western America /
Earl Pomeroy.—1st Bison Book print.
p. cm.
Reprint, with new introd. Originally published: New York:
Knopf, 1957.
ISBN 0-8032-8725-9
1. West (U.S.)—Description and travel—1880–1950.   2. Tourist
trade—West (U.S.)—History.   3. Travelers—West (U.S.)—His-
tory.   I. Title.
F595.P78   1990
338.4'7917804—dc20
90-36467   CIP

Published by arrangement with Alfred A. Knopf, Inc.

♾

PREFACE TO THE BISON BOOK EDITION

This book came out of projects that I expected to have other consequences. Having a fellowship from the Foundation for the Advancement of Teaching in 1953–54 and so for the first time in thirteen years a change from teaching, I planned to spend the year reading widely over fields of American history for which I was responsible in the classroom, emphasizing the history of the American West but not confining myself to it. Although I had done a graduate thesis on a western American topic, it and much of my later writing for publication had been constitutional or administrative rather than social history, to the extent that members of my graduate committee said that I might have taken my degree in political science. My first nine years of teaching had been almost as much in European and Latin-American as in American history, on the American side more in naval and diplomatic history than in any other field, on the American West only during one short summer session. At the University of Oregon after 1949 I had a narrower but still varied repertoire, with courses for the first time regularly in the history of the West, which also was the field in which local and regional resources and the interests of students suggested special responsibility and opportunity. In my reading during the year of the fellowship I emphasized accounts by travelers in the West in order to gain insights in dimensions of history in which I felt deficient and to be able to recommend some to students. I also attended classes of Carl Bridenbaugh in colonial and social history and of Henry Nash Smith in transcendentalism and read widely around their lectures. The books that I then hoped to write would have drawn only slightly on my travelers (one on progressives, especially western progressives, in the 1920s, perhaps one on Senator Hiram W. Johnson, whose son during that year showed me his father's papers). I had started reading travelers' accounts and other firsthand narratives before I inherited the course on the West and for a while thought of doing a biography of Hamlin Garland, who wrote both as child of pioneers and as visitor to areas of pioneering. I vaguely considered travelers as subjects as well as sources, then put aside the idea when Robert Athearn, who like me had first emphasized politics, said that he was finishing a book on British ranchers and visitors in the Rocky Mountains.[1] But at Berkeley and at the Huntington Library at San Marino I more systematically read their accounts, ploughing along shelves and through catalogs and sets of bound periodicals. During that same year Alfred Knopf and Walter Johnson asked me to do one of a series of eight regional histories of the United States that Johnson was to edit along with a chronological series. The contract that I signed seemed to oblige me to continue with my program of reading while giving it further direction.

The idea of writing about travelers came back to me as I revised a draft of a general interpretative and historiographical article setting forth some of my prejudices about western American history and how it had become isolated from other fields and sent it to an editor.[2] When I mentioned to Bridenbaugh how proprietors of western resorts imitated eastern and European watering places, he referred me to writers on colonial counterparts and on British architecture and landscaping. Before I returned to teaching I had a draft of an article and, with Smith's encouragement, decided to expand it into a short book before writing the book for the regional series. *In Search of the Golden West* was the result, a by-product of my obligations as a teacher and of another book that I finished only seven years later. *The Pacific Slope*[3] did not extend over the whole of the West of my tourists, but most of them went to California and its neighbors, taking in the Rocky Mountains and the Southwest on the way, some of them inadvertently, as early French and German travelers had taken in the Alps and the Dolomites on the way to Italy.

Under other circumstances, with different preparation, I might have written a quite different book, as others since then have written different books on topics concerning tourists and the West. The proliferation of amusement parks after Disneyland opened in 1955 and the multiplication of visitors to them, of tourists from abroad, of visitors to national parks and wilderness areas, and of organizations dedicated to protecting and despoiling them suggest proportions for another book on tourists that I have not written. Increases in travel by motor vehicles, which more than tripled in three decades, and the reconstruction of American cities and landscapes around automobiles and highways since the 1950s have had their consequences in what tourists do and in the manners of their doing it, and pollution of air and general congestion over parts of the West that once offered above all else unspoiled space and relief from respiratory ailments. The development of airplane transportation since the 1950s would make ignoring Hawaii and giving as little attention as I did to Alaska even less justifiable now than then. I have followed such themes in other formats as aspects of the development of regions: first six states in *The Pacific Slope,* then eighteen on which I am still writing, considering how sojourners, some of whom first came as tourists, became resident westerners and in becoming changed their attitudes toward regional settings and traditions, and how residents changed their ideas of what they ought to show to tourists.[4]

Although tourists in the West now do more than they did before 1957, I think that if I had waited more than thirty years to write the book I still should have excluded much that people do on holiday away from home. In some parts of the West travelers spend so little time and see so little on the way to their destination that calling them *tourists* stretches the word badly beyond its primary sense of those who travel around, make a circuit, suggesting a case for other nomenclature. (I should be glad to find also an alternative to *tourism*. It commonly refers so indiscriminately to activity, behavior, experience, interest, industry, occupation, or any aspect of travel, vacation, and recreation away from home that it threatens to drive focus out of language as badly as *racism* and *sexism*.) Las Vegas has so many visitors that it has become second only to the New York metropolitan area in number of hotel rooms, but less than three in ten of its visitors go anywhere else in Nevada,[5] not even to Boulder Dam, thirty miles away.

Travel over long distances by public transportation has become prodigiously cheaper, ordinarily costing far less in constant dollars than the $99 that the railroads charged for the coast-to-coast round trip in the 1930s. At late-twentieth-century speeds and prices, most Americans can manage a long trip and far less often make it with the sense that it will be their one such opportunity and therefore that they should do as much as they can on it. Routine visiting and other kinds of vacationing have increased much more than touring has, and lines between touring and other kinds of travel have blurred.

Writing about tourists and the places where tourists go

also has increased, although only two general accounts of American tourist travel have appeared: John A. Jakle, *The Tourist: Travel in Twentieth-Century America* (1985),[6] and Warren James Belasco, *Americans on the Road: From Autocamp to Motel, 1910–1945* (1979).[7] Quotations from published accounts by travelers dominate most of Jakle's chapters; both authors define tourists broadly and follow them beyond the West. Others have said more about the backgrounds of tourist travel and the attitudes and expectations that tourists brought to their travels, as Robert Athearn does in some of the most suggestive chapters of *The Mythic West in Twentieth-Century America* (1986).[8] When I began my vicarious *Wanderjahr* I had the advantage of Robert Taft's *Artists and Illustrators of the Old West* (1953)[9] and of two articles that Hans Huth had published in 1948 and 1950[10] but not yet of his *Nature and the American* (1957),[11] or of William H. Goetzmann's solid and suggestive demonstrations of the possibilities of approaching Western exploration as intellectual historian rather than as antiquarian,[12] or of various fine studies of philosophers and advocates of wilderness, especially Henry Thoreau, John Muir, and Aldo Leopold.[13] Arthur A. Ekirch, Jr., has surveyed the European roots and the literary and philosophical dimensions of American attitudes toward nature in *Man and Nature in America* (1963);[14] Roderick W. Nash in *Wilderness and the American Mind* (1953 and later editions).[15] Nash emphasizes preservationist impulses but notes other recent contributions over broad swaths including the history of conservation. Keith Thomas traces English thought on which Americans drew in *Man and the Natural World* (1983),[16] Malcolm Andrews in *The Search for the Picturesque: Landscape Aesthetics and Tourism in Britain, 1760–1800* (1989).[17] David Lowenthal has surveyed changing attitudes toward the heritage of the past including attempts to change it in

The Past Is a Foreign Country (1985).[18] I remain skeptical about the new germ theory of armchair anthropologists who contend that submerged primitive memories reemerged in nineteenth-century Americans to prejudice them against forests. Most of them instead regarded trees as signs of fertile soil and indispensable sources of timber and fuel, long passing by the fertile prairies and "swamp and overflowed lands" of the Old Northwest, the Mississippi Valley, and central California. But more mainstream anthropologists have shown how tourists, as well as traders and colonizers, change societies that they visit.[19] Thomas R. Cox and others introduce the history of American forests and their uses in broad enough terms to provide useful background in *This Well-Wooded Land* (1985).[20]

I could have used other kinds of help still not available. Historians of parks and of movements and measures to protect parks and wilderness have been active,[21] but most accounts of individual parks and of park systems emphasize policy and administration, passing over visitors. Perhaps a new general history of travel extending over and beyond the ground of Seymour Dunbar's[22] and done as modern social history would be too much to expect. We seem more likely to have social and economic histories of the automobile and its passengers that move on from the suggestive pioneering volumes of John B. Rae and James J. Flink[23] and from pictorial accounts of individual highways.[24] For all the multiplication of accounts of railroads and airlines, ranging from orthodox business histories to appreciations of what cultists have called "varnish," we lack substantial and comprehensive histories of travel by rail and air and its social consequences; travel by bus is almost entirely *terra incognita*, as is the history of travel agencies.

Preoccupied with another book, I have not attempted to revise the book that I wrote over thirty-three years ago, not even to tinker with words and punctuation as I should do if they were before me on a screen. A Wyoming historian brought to my attention a misstatement that I made when I relied on an account that I did not corroborate, that the Potter Palmers had a ranch north of Laramie (p. 80); probably it has company. I hope that others will improve on what I wrote and that it may suggest some of what they might do.

NOTES

1. Robert G. Athearn, *Westward the Briton* (New York: Charles A. Scribner's Sons, 1953; Lincoln: University of Nebraska Press, 1962). Lawrence M. Woods has emphasized resident newcomers over much of the same area in *British Gentlemen in the Wild West: The Era of the Intensely English Cowboy* (New York: The Free Press, 1989).

2. "Toward a Reorientation of Western History: Continuity and Environment," *Mississippi Valley Historical Review*, 41 (March 1955): 579–600.

3. *The Pacific Slope: A History of California, Oregon, Washington, Idaho, Utah, and Nevada* (New York: Alfred A. Knopf, Inc., 1965; Seattle: University of Washington Press, 1973).

4. I pursued such themes, which first attracted me as I studied tourists, briefly in "California's Legacies from the Pioneers," in George H. Knoles, ed., *Essays and Assays: California History Reappraised* (San Francisco: California Historical Society, 1973), 79–90, 127–29; and in "Rediscovering the West," *American Quarterly*, 12 (Spring 1960): 20–30.

5. John M. Findlay, *People of Chance: Gambling in American Society from Jamestown to Las Vegas* (New York: Oxford University Press, 1986), 110, 115–16, 128; *1982 Census of Service Industries, Industry Series, Hotels, Motels, and Other Lodging Places* (Washington: Government Printing Office, 1986), 17, 18; Las Vegas Convention and Visitors Authority, *Las Vegas Visitor Profile Study 1988* (Las Vegas, 1988), 49.

6. (Lincoln: University of Nebraska Press).

7. (Cambridge, Mass.: MIT Press).

8. (Lawrence: University Press of Kansas).

9. (New York: Charles A. Scribner's Sons).

10. Hans Huth, "Yosemite: The Story of an Idea," *Sierra Club Bulletin,* 33 (March 1948): 47–78; Huth, "The American and Nature," *Journal of the Warburg and Courtauld Institute,* 12 (January 1950): 101–49.

11. *Nature and the American: Three Centuries of Changing Attitudes* (Berkeley: University of California Press, 1957).

12. Goetzmann, *Army Exploration in the American West, 1803–1863* (New Haven: Yale University Press, 1959); *Exploration and Empire: The Explorer and the Scientist in the Winning of the American West* (New York: Alfred A. Knopf, Inc., 1966); Goetzmann (with William N. Goetzmann), *The West of the Imagination* (New York: W. W. Norton, 1986); and *Looking at the Land of Promise: Pioneer Images of the Pacific Northwest* (Pullman: Washington State University Press, 1988). For Frederick Jackson Turner's comments contrasting his analytical and institutional approach with that of those who "approached the west as fighting ground, or ground for exploration history," see Turner to Constance Lindsay Skinner, 15 March 1922, in "Turner's Autobiographic Letter," *Wisconsin Magazine of History,* 59 (September 1935): 96, 101.

13. Paul Brooks, *Speaking for Nature: How Literary Naturalists from Henry Thoreau to Rachel Carson Have Shaped America* (Boston: Houghton Mifflin, 1980); Michael P. Cohen, *The Pathless Way: John Muir and the American Wilderness* (Madison: University of Wisconsin Press, 1984); Susan Flader, *Thinking Like a Mountain: Aldo Leopold and the Evolution of an Ecological Attitude toward Deer, Wolves, and Forests* (Columbia: University of Missouri Press, 1974); Stephen R. Fox, *John Muir and His Legacy: the American Conservation Movement* (Boston: Little, Brown, 1981); Holway R. Jones, *John Muir and the Sierra Club: The Battle for Yosemite* (San Francisco: Sierra Club, 1965); Lee Clark Mitchell, *Witnesses to a Vanishing America: The Nineteenth-Century Response* (Princeton: Princeton University Press, 1981); Frederick Turner, *Rediscovering America: John Muir in His Time and Ours* (New York: Viking, 1985).

14. (New York: Columbia University Press, 1963; Lincoln: University of Nebraska Press, 1973).

15. (New Haven: Yale University Press, 1953, 1973, 1982).

16. *Man and the Natural World: Changing Attitudes in England, 1500–1800* (London: Allen Lane, Penguin Books, 1983); American edition with different subtitle, *A History of the Modern Sensibility* (New York: Pantheon Press, 1983).

17. (Stanford: Stanford University Press, 1989).

18. (Cambridge [Cambridgeshire]: Cambridge University Press).

19. Valene L. Smith, ed., *Hotels and Guests: The Anthropology* ⟩ ? *of Tourism* (Philadelphia: University of Pennsylvania Press, 1977).

20. Thomas R. Cox, Robert S. Maxwell, Phillip Drennon Thomas, and Joseph J. Malone, *This Well-Wooded Land: Americans and Their Forests from Colonial Times to the Present* (Lincoln: University of Nebraska Press, 1985).

21. Richard A. Bartlett, *Nature's Yellowstone* [to 1872] (Albuquerque: University of New Mexico Press, 1974), and *Yellowstone: A Wilderness Besieged* [chiefly 1872–1920] (Tucson: University of Arizona Press, 1985); Thomas R. Cox, *The Park Builders: A History of State Parks in the Pacific Northwest* (Seattle: University of Washington Press, 1988); Michael Frome, *Battle for the Wilderness* [the Wilderness Act of 1964] (New York: Praeger, 1974); Aubrey L. Haines, *The Yellowstone Story: A History of Our First National Park* (Yellowstone National Park, Wyoming: Yellowstone Library and Museum Association, 1977); John F. Reiger, *American Sportsmen and the Origins of Conservation* (New York: Winchester Press, 1975); Elmo Richardson, *Dams, Parks and Politics; Resource Development and Preservation in the Truman-Eisenhower Era* (Lexington: University Press of Kentucky, 1973); Alfred Runte, *National Parks: The American Experience* (Lincoln: University of Nebraska Press, 1979); Susan R. Schrepfer, *The Fight to Save the Redwoods: A History of Environmental Reform, 1917–1978* (Madison: University of Wisconsin Press, 1983); Donald C. Swain, *Wilderness Defender; Horace M. Albright and Conservation* (Chicago: University of Chicago Press, 1970).

22. Dunbar, *A History of Travel in America* (4 vols.; Indianapolis: The Bobbs-Merrill Company, 1915).

23. Rae, *The Road and the Car in American Life* (Cambridge, ⟩

Mass.: MIT Press, 1971); Flink, *America Adopts the Automobile, 1895–1910* (Cambridge, Mass.: MIT Press, 1970), and *The Car Culture* (Cambridge, Mass.: MIT Press, 1975).

24. Drake Hokanson, *The Lincoln Highway: Main Street Across America* (Iowa City: University of Iowa Press, 1988); Quinta Scott and Susan Croce Kelly, *Route 66: the Highway and its People* (Norman: University of Oklahoma Press, 1988).

PREFACE

IF THOSE who write books about the West say little of the
tourist, except to quote what he says of other matters, it
may be in part because he is nearly always there. He hitch-
hikes with the explorers and soldiers of mid-nineteenth
century; he saturates the highways and parks of mid-
twentieth century. Because he continues to come, decade
after decade, he may seem to deserve literary treatment
less than some who come for only a moment and are gone,
as the forty-niner, who is the best known but the least
representative of tourists, or the Indian fighter of the
plains, who is often a special kind of merchandise manu-
factured for the tourist trade.

From the beginnings of the West the tourist has been
important to Westerners, though like other people they
sometimes resent him, or affect to wish themselves rid of
him. "And what has the tourist done," asked an English
visitor to the Far West in the 1870's, "that in the eyes of
his fellow-creatures he should be an object of loathing and
scorn?" [1] In the main they do not loathe him in the sense

[1] Earl of Dunraven: *The Great Divide: Travels in the Upper Yellowstone in the Summer of 1874* (London: Chatto and
Windus; 1876), p. vii.

that one hears of Europeans loathing him, though they
sometimes resent being dependent on him. They may sometimes mistreat him, offering him what he wants to see instead of what he should see, or what he should see instead
of what he wants to see, and even requiring him to obey
local traffic-ordinances, but in the main they welcome the
first of the species each year as they welcome spring lambs
and winter wheat. He himself is a crop, and he is more
than that; he is a link to the rest of the world that their
souls need as well as their pocketbooks. He is capital; he is
income; he is market for gasoline and ice-cream cones and
real estate, for the West itself; he is the East sitting in
judgment on the West when he comes, and conferring the
approval that Westerners crave when he comes again.

To those who want to understand the West, including
historians when that is their purpose, the tourist has additional values. Old residents may have known more about
the West, but when at last they have time to write it down,
they seldom remember much that others want to hear; and
perhaps the local pioneer cult has persuaded them that
they were more heroic, or more gentlemanly, or more flam-
boyant than anyone perceived when they were young. In
the aggregate the tourist makes up in leisure and perspective what he lacks in information. Sometimes he may be
short on information in the most limited sense but long on
the kinds of misinformation on which the West has grown.
He can tell us not only something about what the West
was, but much about what it wanted to be and pretended
to be, and about what he thought it was. What he tells
may seem to be more about himself than about the West
as we think we know it, but he and his dreams were a part

of the West that belongs in the balance along with land titles and Indian wars and boundary disputes. Even when his purpose is not ours, still it is something that we must understand along with politics and prospecting.

A great virtue of the tourist as an index to the West is this fact that he is not only recorder but ingredient, and further that he is not a pure ingredient. He pretends to be simply a tourist so that he may more easily select a cattle ranch to buy. He pretends to be a rancher so that hotel-keepers will not overcharge him as a tourist. Thus pretending, he may deceive even himself or only himself. But even when the college boys who click him off on their comptometers at Wilshire and La Brea are surest of how to classify him—1957 Ford, New York license, trailer with television, wife, mother-in-law, three children—he spills out of one category into another, as all Americans do, and all Westerners especially. He never simply tours through the West: he changes the West when he looks at it, not only because he wears out the highway pavements, but because Westerners change the West into what they think he wants it to be or, with less commercial intent, even change themselves into what they think he is. The tourist becomes a Westerner, if he is not one already, and the Westerner becomes a tourist.

The Western tourist has had a special prominence ever since the 1870's. A nation urbanized, industrialized, and free in its urban and industrial prosperity from the distractions of civil war, could afford to send more tourists west, and shortly had railroad cars to carry them. A new West offered climate and scenery unknown to the older West of the Ohio Valley, and a drama of wilderness that was too much for many Easterners until it was no longer wild and the legendary ruffians were safely dead. At all events the tourist came as he had never come before, and he continues to come in larger numbers decade by decade.

My purpose is chiefly to consider what the West has meant to tourists and to those who set out to attract tourists. The traveler as well as the novelist, the poet, the settler, and the politician reveals how Americans reacted to the newest parts of a new continent. A large part of the story appears in the shape of the tourist industry, but I have not attempted to give a complete picture of that important phase of Western economic development. This is about people and their ideas rather than about their money.

For my materials I am indebted especially to the Bancroft Library, the Henry E. Huntington Library, the Denver Public Library, and the libraries of the University of Oregon and the Colorado State Historical Society, among others, and particularly to Mr. Arthur A. Dailey and others of the Santa Fe Railway, Mr. F. Q. Tredway and others of the Southern Pacific Railroad, John A. Hussey and George L. Collins of the National Park Service, Mrs. Opal Harber of the Denver Public Library, and Thomas A. Vaughan of the Oregon Historical Society. For criticism of my manuscript, I owe much to Martin F. Schmitt and Wendell H. Stephenson of the University of Oregon, Henry Nash Smith of the University of California, and John A. Hussey. The Graduate School of the University of Oregon assisted with funds for checking references.

Eugene, Oregon, 1956   Earl Pomeroy

CONTENTS

ILLUSTRATIONS

[AN ALBUM OF PHOTOGRAPHS PRECEDES THE TEXT]

ILLUSTRATIONS

IN SEARCH OF
THE GOLDEN WEST

HOTEL DEL MONTE

The Del Monte was probably the most famous vacation hotel among Westerners and their visitors alike for fifty years or more. This photograph shows a part of the second structure, built in 1887.

"As some requirement of the public at large has always had a hand either in pointing out almost every well-known spot of picturesque beauty in the world, or at least in developing it," wrote Major Ben C. Truman soon after the original hotel had opened in 1880, "so it was the fact that San Francisco needed a fashionable seashore resort that brought Monterey into celebrity after it had swung around the circle of civilization almost into oblivion." "The Del Monte has been the court in which Dame Fashion holds her levies," boasted its owner, the Southern Pacific Company (1902), "the Mecca toward which Pacific Coast society turns its face on the advent of spring, the sanitarium to which the invalid goes for health, and the pleasure resort to which the weary retreat for rest and recreation."

BOUND FOR PIKES PEAK

Before the Pikes Peak railroad opened in 1890, the pack trip had become conventional. Two Englishmen who were there about 1882 felt out of place in the well-dressed crowd in their worn tweeds and walking-boots, and astonished their guide by going on foot. He said he "wouldn't take twenty dollars to walk it,' and rode."

RAYMOND AND WHITCOMB TOURS

A Winter Trip to California,

WITH A SOJURN OF FIVE MONTHS

*At the Famous Winter Health and Pleasure Resort of
the Pacific Coast, the Elegant*

HOTEL DEL MONTE,
MONTEREY, CALIFORNIA.

185 Days (with all Travelling and Hotel Expenses Included) for only $750.

THE ENTIRE JOURNEY IN PALACE-DRAWING ROOM AND SLEEPING CARS,

And Every Arrangement First-Class.

"Another feature of our excursion system is this: while the traveller secures many little comforts and attentions that could not otherwise be had, he does not subject himself to any special or ostentatious display, which would naturally be obnoxious to persons of quiet tastes. . . . Members of our excursion parties . . . form a select company, and are relieved of the annoyance of being placed in proximity to strangers, and, as it often happens in ordinary travelling, undesirable people."

RAYMOND AND WHITCOMB ADVERTISEMENT IN BANCROFT LIBRARY.

ELEGANT HOTELS

HOTEL RAYMOND, *Pasadena* (*1893*)

Northeast of Los Angeles, where a decade earlier orange groves were succeeding to cattle ranges, Raymond and Whitcomb built the Hotel Raymond, 1883–6. Pasadena became a city at almost one leap when the railroad reached it, wrote one of its promoters (1889), "with all the appliances of eastern cities of a century's growth—a refined and cultured community, without a vestige of the rude elements that have formed an integral part of the typical western towns." "A new order of things had been ushered in," proclaimed another prophet in 1883, "and Anglo-Saxon energy, thrift, and industry were to prevail in place of the indolent, thriftless, easy-going manner of the 'first occupation. . . .' " The Raymond Hotel "will excel in beauty any descriptions yet given of the Garden of Paradise." "There is an utter absence of border life," promised a writer in the *Californian Illustrated Magazine* (1892). "Pasadena might, so far as this is concerned, be on the Hudson or just out of Boston, as all the refinements of the East are here, with but few of the disagreeable features."

This is the original structure, which burned in 1895. Its successor opened in 1901 and closed in 1933. The proprietor of both hotels was Walter Raymond (1851–1934), whose father, a New England railroad magnate, had organized the Raymond and Whitcomb tours in 1879.

HOTEL DEL CORONADO

The work of an Easterner, E. S. Babcock, who went to San Diego for his health in 1884, Hotel del Coronado opened in 1886, a few months before the Raymond, and, indeed, before the town of Coronado was more than a plat. "This gorgeous structure occupies considerably more than seven and a half acres of ground and contains a world of comfort, elegance, and refined enjoyment," boasted the Coronado Beach Company. "Wealth, science and art have here combined to render perfect the enjoyment of life."

BOTH PHOTOGRAPHS IN C. C. PIERCE COLLECTION, TITLE INSURANCE AND TRUST COMPANY (LOS ANGELES) COLLECTION OF HISTORICAL PHOTOGRAPHS.

CLIFF HOUSE, SAN FRANCISCO

Ever since 1863 San Franciscans and travelers have gone to the Cliff House, which overlooks the seal rocks at Point Lobos, just outside the Golden Gate. "Here you can dance or sing, eat, drink and be merry; ogle the seals, or ogle the girls, as you please," wrote a visitor of 1869. "Whatever else you may do, you are not allowed to disturb the seals." This turreted chateau is the second structure of the name, which Adolph Sutro built in 1896 and which burned in 1907. The first Cliff House (1863–94) was much smaller and less pretentious.

THE SPRING AT MANITOU (*about 1910*)

SPIRIT OF THE STREAM:

Sister spirit of the spring,
Fresher, clearer voices sing
Of a white, later race
Taking the swart Indian's place
Art to Nature gives her hand;
Fashion waves her magic wand
And the languorous glamour cast
Veils the glory of the past.

THE SPIRIT OF THE SPRINGS AND STREAM:

White tepees crown our hills,
Sweeter lips now touch our rills;
Under Manitou's bright skies
Fairer faces meet our eyes;
And where crystal waters glide
Happy lovers blush and hide;
Dusky features fade away,
Saxon faces crown To-Day.
—"*Manitou,*" BY EDGAR P. VANGESSEN.

"They call this place the Saratoga of Colorado," reported an early guidebook (1874), "because there are waters here that carry soda and mineral properties, and because Manitou is frequented during the summer season by the *elite* of the territory, eastern *parvenus*, substantial tourists and ailing invalids. It is a desirable sojourning place for one with weak lungs and debilitated constitution, for the air builds up the one and the water regulates the other. There are splendid walks and cozy retreats, and if the lady is only interestingly invalided she can pass the time pleasantly drinking water and waltzing in the pavilion. . . . Life at the springs is divided between flirtations, water-drinking, excursions and mountain climbing."

BALANCED ROCK, GARDEN OF THE GODS

The author of a souvenir pamphlet (1905) called this natural curiosity in
Colorado "the most photographed object in the United States," estimating
that one of the burros had been photographed over 53,000 times. It also has
inspired verse, such as these lines by a Colorado poet, J. L. McDowell:

> *Long, long ere time's relentless task began*
> *Of measuring life by a mortal span,*
> *Ere sun and moon, with radiance bright,*
> *To heavenly hosts revealed the might*
> *Of Eternal Mind in His wise plan*
> *To create a world—and then a man—*
> *Voiceless was the barren earth, and cold*
> *The waters deep which o'er it rolled.*
>
> *Dread glaciers ground their sullen way*
> *And volcanic fires empoisoned day;*
> *Then restless seas affrighted fled,*
> *And mountains grand appeared instead,*
> *While rugged peaks soon towered on high*
> *To appall the sense and please the eye.*
>
> *All this we know, for oft we see*
> *Full many a witness, mute, like thee,*
> *Oh wondrous rock on thy narrow base,*
> *Poised, as it were, for a leap in space,*
> *While far below winds the work of man,*
> *He of creation's inspired plan—*
> *Who in wonder, awe, does gaze on thee,*
> *The work of Nature's God as well as he.*

COMFORT IN THE GREAT OUTDOORS

EL TOVAR, *Grand Canyon (about 1917)*

FURNACE CREEK INN, *Death Valley*

By the time Fred Harvey built El Tovar in conjunction with the Santa Fe Railway (1904), Indian influences had appeared in tourist places, though in this view they seem confined to the vicinity of Hopi House, foreground. The hotel and the spur track that connected it with the main line at Williams made the Grand Canyon accessible as the old stagecoach connections from Peach Springs or Flagstaff had not. Yet, observed John C. Van Dyke (1920), "the hotel is far too beguiling. From that comfortable quarter you look out and perhaps indolently come to the conclusion that you are seeing the whole Canyon. Nine people out of ten rest content with that view and that conclusion. They get no farther than the benches along the Rim. . . . When the evening train goes out they go with it, rather glad that they came, and quite satisfied perhaps that they have 'seen' the Canyon."

Furnace Creek Inn represents still another period, that of the automobile, conventionalized mission themes, and air conditioning.

PHOTOGRAPH OF EL TOVAR FROM ATCHISON, TOPEKA AND SANTA FE RAILROAD COMPANY; PHOTOGRAPH OF FURNACE CREEK INN FROM FRED HARVEY.

EXCURSIONISTS AT MAMMOTH HOT SPRINGS, YELLOWSTONE PARK

Ray Stannard Baker saw some hikers in Yellowstone in 1903, when this picture was taken. "But most of the tourists remain pretty snuggly in their coach-seats or near the hotels. One meets them in great loads, some wrapped in long linen coats, some wearing black glasses, some broad, green-brimmed hats. . . . Occasionally one sees them devouring their guidebooks and checking off the sights as they whirl by, so that they will be sure not to miss anything or see anything twice. . . . One old gentleman, accompanied by his stenographer, after each excursion sat on the piazza, guidebook in hand, and dictated an account of what he had seen."

PHOTOGRAPH BY HAYNES STUDIOS, INC., BOZEMAN, MONTANA; COURTESY NORTHERN PACIFIC RAILWAY.

CALIFORNIA BIG TREES

FALLEN MONARCH   WAWONA BIG TREE   GENERAL JOHNSON

"*Certainly*," wrote Samuel Bowles (1869), "they are chief among the natural curiosities and marvels of Western America, of the known world. . . ." Everyone had read about the "vegetable monsters" to be seen on the way to the Yosemite, and those who went were likely to be in better condition to look and admire when they stopped in the groves than when they arrived in the valley. There was no escaping the sanction that authority conferred on the trip. "Travellers had visited it," said Bret Harte of a famous valley in "The Fool of Five Forks" (1874), "and declared that there were more cubic yards of rough stone cliff and a waterfall of greater height than any they had visited. Correspondents had written it up with extravagant rhetoric and inordinate poetical quotation; men and women who had never enjoyed a sunset, a tree, or a flower . . . came from thousands of miles away to calculate the height of this rock, to observe the depth of this chasm, to remark upon the enormous size of this unsightly tree, and to believe with ineffable self-complacency that they really admired nature." One of the great merits of the trees was that one could have his picture taken with one of them, preferably one made more interesting by death, fire, or piercing.

PHOTOGRAPHS FROM TITLE INSURANCE AND TRUST COMPANY (LOS ANGELES)

ROUGHING IT

ALPINISTS ON MOUNT HOOD, BELOW CLOUD CAP (*about 1890*)

When mountain climbers of Oregon organized as the Mazamas in 1894, their object was "to stimulate in people a love of the mountains, and to awaken an interest in the study of them; and yearly to accomplish something which, besides reflecting credit upon the members, should benefit the world. I would emphasize this idea even more firmly," wrote the official historian, "and have this society follow those of Europe in its motives."

"Skirts should be short," advised the Mazamas a few years later, "at least eight inches from the ground."

PHOTOGRAPH IN THE OREGON HISTORICAL SOCIETY COLLECTION.

CAMPERS IN YOSEMITE VALLEY

By 1875 three roads reached the valley floor and opened it, in theory, to vehicular traffic. The first public campground dates from 1878. A Santa Barbaran made a carriage trip to the valley in 1880, camping each night along the way; the next year he planned to stay two months. Yet in the early 1890's, said a writer in *Out West* (1904), the habit was "confined almost entirely to the bohemian element and the devotees of science." The policy of the state park commissioners, as stated in 1894, was to reduce "the number of campers in the Valley to a minimum, by as far as possible removing economy from amongst the motives of campers." This family, who enjoyed both their own wagons and a Chinese cook (right), seem to anticipate the advice of Mrs. Ernest Thompson Seton (1905): "Dear woman who goes hunting with her husband, be sure that you have it understood that you do no cooking or dishwashing. . . . See that for your camping trip is provided a man cook."

PHOTOGRAPH BY GEORGE FISKE, FROM YOSEMITE NATIONAL PARK.

YOSEMITE STAGES ON BIG OAK FLAT ROAD

Even before the Pacific Railroad eliminated the overland stage in 1869, and even after the first road entered the valley in 1874, the Yosemite trip was famous for its perils and tortures. Frederick Law Olmsted reported in 1865 that tourists arrived "in the majority of cases quite overcome with the fatigue and unaccustomed hardship of the journey. Few persons, especially few women, are able to enjoy or profit by the scenery and air for days afterward. Meanwhile they remain at an expense of from $3 to $12 per day . . ., and many leave before they have recovered from their first exhaustion and return home jaded and ill." It was, declared C. A. Stoddard (1894), the "most exhausting, expensive, and impressive excursion which the tourist can make. . . ." Each morning at dawn, "there stood the red instrument of torture at the door, with its huge wheels, and awful through-braces, well-named 'rack,' and falsely named cushions. . . ."

PHOTOGRAPH BY BOYSEN, FROM YOSEMITE NATIONAL PARK.

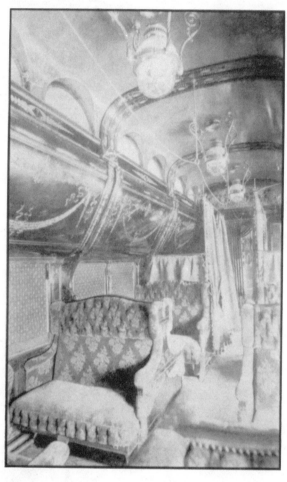

A NEW ERA IN TRAVEL

Nineteenth-century standard sleeping cars were Victorian parlors on wheels, short on ventilation but long on gilt, plush, draperies, and carvings, in a style, complained Edward Bok in *The Ladies' Home Journal* (1904) "that even the most inartistic decorator has discarded years ago. . . ." When he set about to beautify the American home, Bok felt that the Pullman car had profoundly influenced popular taste in interior decoration: "it was this standard that those women of the new-money class were accepting and introducing into their homes!" The early Western railroad traveler had no alternative to such first-class or palace-car accommodations except coaches "without carpets, the seats often without cushions, and not a place for a sick man or child to lie down, day or night, and no room for change of position."

The early immigrant or third-class sleeping cars, which the Central Pacific began fitting up in 1879, had upper and lower berths, "somewhat after the manner of caboose cars," according to the *Sacramento Bee,* but with wooden slats in lieu of upholstery; the passengers furnished their own blankets and straw mattresses. The tourist Pullmans, which appeared in the nineties, served a different clientele, and opened the West to a new democracy of travel. "Whole families bound for Rocky Mountain resorts loll about on the wicker or leather seats," reported a writer in *World's Work* (1902); "one or two people are heating coffee on the range at the end of the car; . . . heads project from the open windows: everybody is happy. In porter service and plush these people are not so well provided as the parlor-car passengers, but to discomfort they will not own. They contend that their berths are as snug as those in the first-class car behind." By 1898 tourist cars were running through as far as from Washington via New Orleans to San Francisco, and continued on that run into the 1930's. In the later forties they began to disappear along with the crowds that had ridden the trains in wartime, the railroads substituting austerely streamlined stainless steel all-room equipment.

PHOTOGRAPH OF STANDARD PULLMAN CAR FROM THE PULLMAN COMPANY; PHOTOGRAPH OF TOURIST PULLMAN CAR (ABOUT 1905) FROM ATCHISON, TOPEKA AND SANTA FE RAILROAD COMPANY.

MOUNT SHASTA SPRINGS (*about 1890?*)

The hotel at Mount Shasta Springs, near Dunsmuir, was actually on a terrace three hundred feet above, served by an incline railway, but the scene resembles that at many other resorts where the hotel was virtually an annex to the station, or vice versa. The large building is the bottling plant of the Mount Shasta Mineral Springs Company. "Possibly a branch railroad may some time be built to the summit of Mount Shasta like the road on Mount Washington," observed John Muir, who tramped the vicinity in 1888. "In the mean time tourists are dropped at Sisson's [later renamed Mount Shasta], . . . whence as headquarters they radiate in every direction to the so-called points of interest. . . . Some demand bears, and make excited inquiries concerning their haunts, how many there might be altogether on the mountain. . . . Others shout, 'Excelsior,' and make off at once for the upper snow-fields. Most, however, are content with comparatively level ground and moderate distances, gathering at the hotel every evening laden with trophies. . . ."

PHOTOGRAPH IN THE OREGON HISTORICAL SOCIETY COLLECTION.

BY THE SEA

SANTA MONICA BEACH (*about 1889*)

BATHING BEAUTIES AT LONG BEACH (*about 1910*)

Backed by the Southern Pacific Company and the electric railways, Santa Monica in the nineties achieved fast connections with Los Angeles and Pasadena and prospect of importance as both a port and a resort; yet none of the California beaches, as such, had social standing or glamor. This stretch of the waterfront along the North Beach Bath House seems hardly distinguishable from the boardwalks of San Francisco (which had never been fashionable south of the Cliff House and Sutro's Baths) or Coney Island. Some travelers felt that there was less swimming than at the Eastern beaches despite the warmth of the water, and blamed feminine influence, which seems limited enough in this photograph. A visitor to Santa Monica about 1890 noted that most of the bathers remained in the surf, close to shore. "Perhaps," he said, "this may be due to the practice of bathing in a sort of full dress, which admits of the ladies being together, and makes it hard for the gentlemen to break away to where few ladies could follow them."

PHOTOGRAPHS FROM TITLE INSURANCE AND TRUST COMPANY (LOS ANGELES).

THE AUTOMOTIVE INVASION OF THE WEST

LOCOMOBILE ON BIG OAK FLAT ROAD (*1901*)

OVERLAND PARK, DENVER (*about 1920*)

When tourists driving two Locomobiles tried to enter Yosemite Park by the Big Oak Flat Road in 1901, the military authorities at Crane Flat Station interned both vehicles, though not this lady driver, who may have been a party to a dealer's advertising scheme.

Shortly after it opened in 1915, Overland became the best known of Western automobile camps, and reached the peak of its popularity in the 1920's. "Automobile camping is vastly different from any other type of outing," said a contributor to *Outing* in 1922, "and is *never* 'roughing it.' You take home and loved ones with you when you autocamp the highway and you make your roadside home as cozy and homelike as the domicile that you left behind."

PHOTOGRAPH OF YOSEMITE SCENE FROM NATIONAL PARK SERVICE; PHOTO-GRAPH OF OVERLAND FROM DENVER PUBLIC LIBRARY WESTERN COLLECTION.

A DENVER–MESA VERDE RUN

Appreciation of the national parks entered a new phase when automobiles first entered them legally, 1908–15, though for several years they were confined strictly to parking areas and prescribed entrance roads. "Remember," Lord Bryce had warned, "that one cannot really enjoy fine scenery when travelling at a rate of fifteen to twenty or twenty-five miles an hour." These Colorado motorists apparently expected a dusty life during the eight days of their trip from Denver to Mesa Verde in September 1917.

PHOTOGRAPH BY GEORGE L. BEAM IN DENVER PUBLIC LIBRARY WESTERN COLLECTION.

1. PALACE CARS
AND PLEASURE DOMES

ENTERING Yellowstone Park in 1889 on his first trip to the United States, Rudyard Kipling confronted a strange apparition of "ghastly vulgarity . . . oozing, rampant Bessemer-steel self-sufficiency and ignorance." It was, they told him, a party of tourists from the East, including very many prominent and representative citizens, most of them wealthy. "Yes, *sir*. Representative and prominent." [1]

Kipling had encountered the tourists' frontier in the Far West, a bridgehead of civilization as striking and as insistent as the frontiers of the trappers, hunters, and miners that preceded it. It was not new when he saw it—

---

[1] "I saw a new type in the coach and all my dreams of a better and more perfect East died away." Rudyard Kipling: *American Notes* (New York: Manhattan Press; n.d. [*c.* 1890]), p. 130.

[3]

around twenty years old as a major feature of the Western landscape—and, like some other frontiers, it was not even so Western as it seemed to be. In a sense it was part of the brew that had spilled over and out of the Eastern cities when the new rich of the 1860's overflowed the pleasure haunts of their predecessors in prosperous society at Saratoga Springs, could not at once get into Newport, and had already seen Europe. Henry James had seen it at Saratoga in 1870. "At the present day," wrote James, "I hear it constantly affirmed, the company is dreadfully mixed." Saratoga had become "dense, democratic, vulgar" as each year returned a larger harvest of visitors to the approved hotels to "lead the simple life amid the blare of trumpets." Even a generation before, in the 1840's, the cry had arisen that Saratoga was no longer fashionable, since one could go there by railroad car from Manhattan in a day and for five dollars;[2] Southern planters shortly had begun to turn in increasing numbers to the Virginia springs, where a man could take his slaves freely and where traditionally aristocratic discomforts and proper inconvenience of access tended to shut out Northerners interested in purchasing exclusiveness for a season at the rate of two or three dollars a day.

The end of the Civil War found the Southern gentry with more pressing business than mineral-water purges and summer flirtation, and the Northern bourgeoisie in-

[2] Henry James: *Portraits of Places* (2d ed.; Boston: Lear Publishers; 1885), p. 327; William F. Dix: "American Summer Resorts in the Seventies," *Independent,* Vol. LXX (June 1, 1911), pp. 1211–15; Harrison Rhodes: "American Holidays; Springs and Mountains," *Harper's Monthly Magazine,* Vol. CXXIX (September 1914), p. 543.

creasingly occupied with diversions that in earlier years had been as much beyond its interests as its means. Its Southern planter visitors largely gone, Newport began to develop that awesomely ritualistic pattern of summer relaxation for New York millionaires that was to reach its climax in the marble-halled cottages built around the turn of the century, and whose charm was in large part that not everyone could enjoy it who wished to; a succession of lesser communities rose and fell in fashionable favor, and found their social levels. President Grant gave Long Branch sovereignty over the Jersey shore and a crushing victory over the Rockaways when he accepted a cottage that became the summer White House; in turn Long Branch shortly saw favor turn to the new "restricted" resorts, such as Ocean Grove and Asbury Park, which by compact and ordinance sought "that note of 'refinement' which is . . . our chief vulgarity." The masses, sorting themselves out according to their incomes, appeared rather at Coney Island and at Atlantic City, though before the subways reached that far the cost of transportation insured that the crowds at Coney were still "clean and neatly dressed, of very respectable social grade. . . ." [3]

The shift and flux in the habits of Americans at leisure seemed to represent a minor social revolution. The American family had not always taken its pleasures away from home. Richard Cobden had been struck on his first trip to the United States in 1835 by the small numbers of women

[3] Harrison Rhodes: "American Holidays: The Sea Shore," *Harper's Monthly Magazine*, Vol. CXXIX (June 1914), p. 9; William H. Bishop: "To Coney Island," *Scribner's Monthly*, Vol. XX (July 1880), p. 365.

in steamers, coaches, and hotels, remarking that "there must be a large proportion of the men who do not marry or otherwise they do not give much of their company to their wives"; [4] even shortly before the Civil War pleasure travelers were few enough to arouse curiosity and questioning among their fellow passengers.

By the early 1880's family groups of tourists (with women uniformly exceeding men) were dominating whole trains to Florida and California, and whole steamers to Europe. "As they have acquired wealth with the increase of years," explained a writer in *Outing and The Wheelman,* which celebrated the new interests, "the American people have become nomadic in their habits." They went south and east before they went west in large numbers. At Jacksonville, said Sidney Lanier, "one will find so many New York faces and Boston faces and Chicago faces that one does not feel so very far from home after all"; Henry Adams, who remembered the Europe of the fifties, lamented the hordes of tourists in Paris "who stare and gawk and smell, and crowd every shop and street." "Of course," he wrote some years later, "all America is here. I pass my life in avoiding it, but to meet one man or woman whom I want to meet, I must face a score whom I wish dead, or

[4] Richard Cobden: *American Diaries* (Princeton: Princeton University Press; 1952), p. 121; Isabella Bird Bishop: *The Englishwoman in America* (London: J. Murray; 1856), pp. 136–7. "The passengers seemed all to be on business," reported another English visitor. "I have met no American travelling for pleasure." John MacGregor: *Our Brothers and Cousins . . .* (London: Seeley, Jackson, and Halliday; 1859), p. 106. But cf. Thomas L. Nichols: *Forty Years of American Life* (London: J. Maxwell and Company; 1864), Vol. II, pp. 1–2.

[6]

who wish me dead." [5] But nowhere was this influx of travelers more striking than in the American Far West, where each newly completed transcontinental railway shortly bore a trainload of Eastern excursionists peering through Pullman palace-car windows at the remnants of the frontier.

Nowhere, moreover, was it more assured than in the Far West of the seventies and early eighties that the tourist was a gentleman, at least to his banker. In a generation when six-room houses rented for eight dollars a month and schoolteachers taught for two hundred dollars a year, a railroad trip from coast to coast and return cost around three hundred dollars—more, that is, than in the twentieth century—with meals additional; one might expect to spend a total of about eight hundred dollars to take in northern California, leaving out Salt Lake City and the Colorado Rockies. Side trips to points beyond San Francisco to north or south meant extra fares, and usually at higher rates per mile, especially in stagecoach or narrow-gauge country: stagecoach fare for a trip from San Francisco to the Yosemite came to around eighty dollars in gold, and one paid nearly as much more for board—"the sorriest lodging and the simplest fare"—guides, and

[5] John Ransom: "The St. John's Region in Florida," *Outing and The Wheelman*, Vol. III (February 1884), pp. 321–7, Sidney Lanier: *Florida: Its Scenery, Climate, and History* . . . (Philadelphia: J. B. Lippincott & Co.; 1876), p. 69; Adams to C. M. Gaskell, August 25, 1867, in *Letters* . . . ed. Worthington C. Ford (Boston: Houghton Mifflin Company; 1930), Vol. I, p. 130; Adams to M. H. La Farge, May 29, 1900, in *Henry Adams and his Friends* . . . , ed. Harold D. Cater (Boston: Houghton Mifflin Company; 1947), p. 491.

horses. Before "the cars" began running in 1869, the cost of stagecoach travel all the way from the Mississippi River had been much higher, by perhaps three times, though society had not been proportionately better: no one had traveled by stage unless he had to, and the trip was a nightmare of bruises and bad company. "Even now," said a British naval officer who had made the trip the year before, I cannot think of my companions in some parts of the overland journey without a shudder." "Everybody's back hair comes down," wrote Samuel Bowles, of the Springfield *Republican*, "and what is nature and what is art in costume and character is revealed—and then, hardest trial of all, morning breaks upon the scene and the feelings—everybody dirty, grimy, faint, 'all to pieces,' cross. . . ." An Englishman figured the cost per day after the railroads came as about two and a half times the cost of travel in Europe.[6] The advantage of a Western over a European trip therefore was in avoiding seasickness and foreign languages rather than expense.

It was possible, it is true, to cut the cost in half by traveling second class (later third) in cars attached to freight trains at unpredictable schedules and a fortnight's journey from coast to coast in the early years—"as near an approach to . . . purgatory as is possible," said one traveler. Such carriages exist, admitted Baedeker, "but

[6] Harry Jones: *To San Francisco and Back* . . . (London: Strahan and Co.; 1878), pp. 110–12; E. H. Verney: "An Overland Journey from San Francisco to New York . . . ," *Good Words*, Vol. VII (June 1, 1866), p. 383; Samuel Bowles: *Our New West* . . . (Hartford: Hartford Publishing Co.; 1869), p. 87; J. F. Campbell: *My Circular Notes* . . . (London: Macmillan and Co.; 1876), Vol. I, p. 130.

scarcely concern the tourist." For a few years it seemed that the horrors of the emigrant cars and the high cost of the first-class cars served to sift the choicest of Eastern grain on the Far West, insuring the predominance of "a superior class of people": "It costs too much to get here for 'the scum of the earth' to be among them," as a southern Californian put it. Cheap fares to the Atlantic resorts, advertised a Western railroad, meant that they no longer had a homogeneous society of well-bred and cultured people, whereas expense, among other factors, insured the company of wealthy and cultured Englishmen and Easterners in Colorado.[7]

The Western lines prided themselves on running the most luxurious of sleeping-cars into the wilderness, fit settings for their expensive patrons, and as different from the emigrant cars as the best river-steamboats of the sixties were different from the canal boats of the thirties. Even foreigners, who were likely to rebel at the twin deprivations of privacy and fresh air in American trains (one called his Pullman the Black Hole of Calcutta), usually conceded that little expense had been spared. "I advise none but the rich to visit America with travel in view," wrote an Englishman. "But those to whom 'money is no object' . . . can wander in the States with more comfort and luxury than anywhere in the world." The cars that even some of the first excursionists took in 1869, boasted one of them,

[7] I. W. Boddam-Whetham: *Western Wanderings* . . . (London: R. Bentley and Son; 1874), p. 101; Karl Baedeker: *The United States* . . . (New York: Charles Scribner's Sons; 1893), p. xx; *Land of Sunshine*, Vol. I (October 1894), p. 99; *A Bouquet from the Garden of the Gods,* Chicago, Burlington, and Quincy Railroad (n.p.; 1884), pp. 2–4.

"would make the eyes of an Englishman pop painfully on beholding the triumph of American railroading genius":

The sleeping cars are fitted up with oiled walnut, carved, and gilded, etched, and stained plate glass, metal trappings heavily silver-plated, seats cushioned with thick plushes, washstands of marble and walnut, damask curtains, and massive mirrors in frames of gilded walnut. The floors are carpeted with the most costly Brussels, and the roof beautifully frescoed in mosaics of gold, of emerald-green, crimson, sky-blue, violet, drab and black.[8]

Until the late eighties most Pullman passengers had to leave their sanctuaries to mingle with the masses at wayside eating-stations offering "square dinners" and "elegant lunches" unless they carried lunch baskets or had taken one of the weekly extra-fare "gilt-edged" trains, which carried "restaurant cars" as well; they returned with renewed appreciation for the corridor of civilization in which they lived.

One of the strongest attractions of the Pullman in the land of equality being "that it enabled the rich to create the clearest possible inequality in the conditions of even ordinary travel," as an English visitor put it, an added refinement, much recommended by those who had been able to afford it, was a private car, or even a special train. Thus one could command the best personal service and cuisine and be free of worry over meal stops and connections, especially the horror of not being able to get a berth

[8] Boddam-Whetham: *Western Wanderings*, pp. 29–30; Edward Money: *The Truth about America* (London: Sampson Low, Marston, Searle & Rivington; 1886), pp. 63–4; *The Cincinnati Excursion to California* . . . (Cincinnati: 1870), pp. 24–5.

beyond Ogden. The William Seward Webb family went from New York to California in 1889 in a four-car train for a party of twelve, served by a maid, two cooks, two nurses for the children, and eight porters; one car had been remodeled into a nursery for Mrs. Webb and the children. Mr. Webb also hired a Pinkerton detective to safeguard the family at night west of Kansas City, and arranged gongs that could be used to call the servants and in case of attack by highwaymen. It was with a group of wealthy friends in a private car that Ralph Waldo Emerson went to California in 1871, and glimpsed the Yosemite. Ernest Ingersoll, who had been a member of a geological survey party in 1874, took his wife and three friends on a "summer's ramble in the Rocky Mountains" ten years later, in three narrow-gauge cars that they rented from the Denver and Rio Grande Railroad. "Roughing it, within reasonable grounds," he remarked afterward, "is the marrow of this sort of recreation." The railroads advertised such service at charges only slightly higher than the cost of first-class tickets (for extended tours, as little as twenty-five dollars a day) ; some gentlemen maintained their own cars and amused themselves by cutting into transcontinental trains and dropping off at sidings as they fancied. The first individually owned private car, the City of Worcester, was built in 1876 for a Worcester businessman, Jerome Marble, who the next year took a party of eighteen on a three-month hunting-trip as far as Bismarck, terminus of the Northern Pacific Railroad. An inveterate traveler who had witnessed the meeting of the rails at Promontory in 1869, Marble was so well pleased with his car that he formed the Worcester Excursion Car Company in 1878 to rent similar cars to private parties, and the enterprise throve until the Pullman Company put it out of business in 1894.[9]

Actually by the late eighties the special train had less advantage to offer than before, except in prestige and in freedom of movement on stopovers and side trips, which most travelers did not take. Through Pullmans were running daily to the coast, and the first of the named trains began to offer added comforts and exclusiveness at extra fare (always featured in the advertising and sometimes even in the name of the train itself), plus the company of other well-to-do passengers. As far as speed was concerned, the Far West had no "limited" trains in the Eastern sense of the term until the 1930's, but the Sunset Limited, the Overland Limited, and the California Limited (the "train of luxury," "exclusively for first-class travel"—"the only train to Southern California . . . that does *not* carry *second*-class sleepers and second-class passengers") in the nineties, later the Golden State Limited and the Extra Fare Santa Fe de-Luxe, all offered special comforts and exclusiveness, as well as faster schedules. Diners were as lavishly appointed as Pullmans, and the stewards prided themselves on offering fresh oysters, pheasant, imported wines, and other delicacies, not the antelope or bear steak of some of the early station eating-houses before the era of Fred Harvey. It was a rare occasion when there was

[9] Lord Charles Russell: *Diary of a Visit to the United States in the Year 1883* . . . (New York: United States Catholic Historical Society; 1910), p. 46; William Seward Webb: *California and Alaska* . . . (2d ed.; New York: G. P. Putnam's Sons; 1891), pp. vi–vii, 2–4, 14; Albert G. Waite to Martin F. Schmitt, January 5, 1954 (University of Oregon).

any threat to the advertised amenities. (When passengers on the Northern Pacific saw a party of delegates to a political convention boarding their train, they asked the cook in some alarm if there would be enough food; he inquired: "Were they Republicans or Democrats, for . . . the Republicans eat most, but the Democrats drink most.")[1] Library and lounge cars (and special lounge cars for ladies, with smoking forbidden) further distinguished first-class from second-class accommodations.

Meanwhile the improvements in public train accommodations made possible the added refinement of the conducted tour, an arrangement that rivaled the private car in satisfaction to self-conscious gentility and reassurance of safety from discomfort, at considerably lower cost. Thomas Cook, inventor of the public excursion train and the package tour, who more than anyone else introduced travel to the British middle class, had arranged to chaperon tourists through the eastern United States in 1865–6; by 1872, after handling a European tour of the American Knights Templar, he had established American agency offices, and himself undertook an exploratory trip around the world by way of Salt Lake City and San Francisco, reporting to the public through letters in *The Times*. Hotels and eating houses were satisfactory, but sleeping-car arrangements emphatically were not: "the admixture of strangers and sexes is very repulsive to English travellers." Messrs. Raymond and Whitcomb, of Boston, met some of this objection on the score of privacy when they ar-

[1] Mrs. E. H. Carbutt: *Five Months' Fine Weather* . . . (London: Sampson Low, Marston, Searle & Rivington; 1889), p. 59.

ranged their first excursion party to the Pacific Coast in 1881, contracting for through service in entire cars for their patrons. Operating chiefly from the Boston area, later from New York and Philadelphia as well, Raymond stressed the advantages of association with "tourists of a refined and cultivated class," particularly family parties, and featured previous passenger lists in his advertising; it was Raymond also who first assured each patron of exclusive claim to one berth (two to a section) and first guaranteed regular dining-car service. The idea of the transcontinental conducted tour soon caught on. Cook and other agents established similar arrangements, as some of the railroads did also, and within several years Americans were being " 'Cooked' about their vast continent," said one traveler, "on a scale becoming their eminence in all that is big." [2]

The Raymond and other tours, like the gargantuan balconied hotels Congress and United States at Saratoga Springs, presented a characteristically anomalous picture of exclusiveness on a large scale, open to those who could pay the tariff and pass the most elementary tests of social acceptability; like the more favored tourist hostelries of the day, they discouraged "certain races." "During the holiday season," said an English visitor, "the hotels are full of these huge travelling parties, and in their presence the individual traveller is sometimes a little lost sight of unless he takes care to assert himself." Yet the typical

[2] *The Times* (London), January 23, 1873, p. 4:5–6; *Three Months in the United States and Canada* . . . (Yeovil: Office of The Western Gazette and Pulman's Weekly News; [1886?]), p. 30.

Raymond party seldom much exceeded fifty or sixty; if it loomed large, it was because of its size relative to the whole touring public, which was still so small in the early eighties that passenger lists were telegraphed from way stations to appear in the San Francisco newspapers, and perhaps because of the impression it made on a public that respected wealth and display in East or West. "To go from New York to San Francisco," noted the historian E. A. Freeman, who visited the United States in 1881–2, "is talked of as if it were no greater matter than to go from London to Inverness." [3] Yet the experience was still unusual enough to warrant a book or letters to the home newspaper.

Preponderantly past middle age, and like summer society at Newport before the Navy corrected the ratio by establishing the War College, preponderantly female, a Raymond party tended to develop a sense of mutual dependence and social solidarity that sometime took the shape of arrangements for reunions when the trip was over; it cherished its prearranged comforts, and returned to the train after each brief sortie into the unprotected world beyond with a sense of home-coming and gratitude. "Jay Gould," rejoiced one Raymond excursionist, a New York clergyman, as he noted the crudities of Arizona passing by, "can have no more or better attention than we. This is the Perfection of Travel. It is the heaven of rest." [4] It was also effective insulation from the world outside. Even if the attraction of the group lay in a sense of high adven-

[3] Ibid., p. 31; Edward A. Freeman: *Some Impressions of the United States* (New York: Henry Holt & Company; 1883), p. 231.
  [4] Stephen Merritt: "From Ocean to Ocean! . . ." (typed manuscript, Huntington Library; [1892?]), p. 15.

ture and large undertaking, rather than in a desire to
cling to some of the physical niceties of Eastern life, it
kept the tourist from seeing the West as it was, and for
that matter the Westerner from seeing the tourist as he
was; it maintained a gulf and a contrast between tourist
and resident in the eyes of each, while bringing them closer
in a physical sense than most Easterners would have come
without the assurances that the agencies offered.

Arriving in the West, the typical gentleman or gentle-
woman tourist moved his bags into a hotel that offered, on
a more expansive scale, comforts similar to those promised
on the trip. In San Francisco it was likely to be the Palace,
the largest and costliest of American hotels when it opened
in 1875, a young city in itself, as self-contained under its
glass roof as a luxury train, with shops and tropical gardens arranged around its central courtyard and marble
driveway in the Viennese style; in Denver it was for a time
the Windsor, advertised on its opening in 1880 as the
largest and most elegant between San Francisco and Chicago. In the Western resort towns, as in Florida, it was
likely to be large and pretentious enough to grace a large
city, and built by Eastern capital, especially railroad capital; in fact, the resort hotels of the elite, more often than
not, belonged to the railroads, and the resort towns were
the hotels. The pattern closely paralleled that of Florida
when Henry M. Flagler built a series of great winter hostelries along with the Florida East Coast Railroad; but by
the time Flagler opened the Ponce de Leon at St. Augus-
tine (1888) and the Royal Poinciana at Palm Beach
(1894), the greatest of the Far Western resort hotels were
already famous. "In Europe," said a French traveler who

visited the United States in 1887, "the hotel is a means to
an end. In America it is the end. . . . Hotels are for [the
Americans] what cathedrals, monuments and the beauties
of nature are for us." [5] Nowhere was this truer than in the
West.

The first Western tourists had found little that was attractive in public accommodations outside of San Francisco and Denver. Henry M. Stanley described the early
hotels along the Pacific railroad as "whitewashed Mugby
Junctions": "The proprietors of these establishments vie
with each other for exorbitant charges and poor fare."
Travelers learned by bitter experience that "every tumble-
down shebeen with a keg of chain-lightning whiskey in it
is an 'hotel'. . . ." When they were few and had provided
themselves with letters of introduction, they found it safe
and prudent to trust to private hospitality in the more
settled areas. William Chapman Ralston, who built the
Palace Hotel in San Francisco at the end of his spectacular career as California's leading financier and promoter,
entertained a steady stream of Eastern and European
guests at his Menlo Park estate in the early seventies.
"The country settler takes you out of town and keeps you
there," recounted an English traveler, "afterward passing
you on to his neighbours, who entertain you, and again
pass you on to their neighbours, so that you soon get introduced and entertained by the whole country-side." [6]

[5] Max O'Rell [Paul Blouet]: *Jonathan and His Continent.
Rambles through American Society* (Bristol: Cassell & Company;
1889), p. 295.
[6] Henry M. Stanley: *My Early Travels* . . . (New York:
Charles Scribner's Sons; 1895), Vol. I, p. 146; Oliver North
[W. Mullen]: *Rambles after Sport* . . . (London: The Field

Some tourists realized the advantage of avoiding large groups so that they might enjoy such courtesies and be less conspicuous as outsiders.

But private hospitality could not serve for long. "Now the throng of visitors throws every resident back on the instinct of self-preservation," observed one who came (1880) when the tourist had lost scarcity value as an envoy from the outer world. As the railroads and the tourists penetrated new parts of the West, businessmen extolled the possibilities of Eastern-style tourist hotels as good investments in themselves and as means to attract investors in other and larger enterprises. "Monterey *will* become one of the most fashionable summer resorts for the wealthy," insisted some local promoters in 1875, deploring the sloth of the Spanish element and calling for "men of energy and capital." [7] As in Florida, the answer came in large part from the railroads, which could look forward not only to the profits of carrying tourists to the hotels they built, but to the general development of the country that the tourist trade would advance. The Western railroads were peculiarly alert to such possibilities because the competition of the Suez Canal, completed in the same year as the Union Pacific-Central Pacific overland line, and the decline of silver mining a few years later cut into the returns they had expected on transcontinental freight traffic.

Office; 1874), p. 37; *From Ocean to Ocean* . . . ([London]; 1871), p. 46.

[7] Caroline H. Dall: *My First Holiday* . . . (Boston: Roberts Brothers; 1881), p. 423; *Hand Book to Monterey* . . . (Monterey: Walton & Curtis; 1875), pp. 22, 24.

The Southern Pacific Railroad, through its construction subsidiary, the Pacific Improvement Company, built the first of the great Western tourist resorts, the Hotel del Monte, at the southern end of Monterey Bay. An invalid Bostonian, Caroline Dall, who visited Del Monte several months after it opened in June 1880, felt that it was "furnished and finished in a manner that would not suit the Pacific shore for half a century. . . ." It was "intended for a public that does not yet exist." Yet the public came, and the hotel prospered; Mrs. Dall, who found little else to suit her (even the Pacific Ocean itself, nearby, was "deficient in salt"), was of a small minority of doubters and dissenters, along with Robert Louis Stevenson, who lamented the exchange of the Monterey he had known for the new "resort for wealth and fashion." San Francisco society descended on Monterey for the opening, the ladies in toilets "exceedingly rich, costly and elegant," and society of San Francisco and other cities, Eastern and Western, has remained in the environs of the Monterey peninsula, if not at the hotel, ever since. The ground floor of the hotel reminded visitors of the Grand Union at Saratoga; the presence of Navy and Army officers, who shortly found it convenient to hold summer maneuvers nearby, recalled Newport; the landscape was chiefly English in inspiration, eventually with a cypress hedge labyrinth modeled after that at Hampton Court. Del Monte was a regular stop on the Raymond tours and a favorite among prosperous travelers and Californians alike for its urban comforts and graces against a carefully refined and refashioned rural background, its warmed salt-water baths and carriage drives on private roads along a wild surf; the hotel itself close enough to the beach "so that those who prefer to bathe in the ocean need not tire themselves by walking to reach it." The first Raymond tourists, not knowing what to expect, had offended "the dressy San Francisco women" by appearing in their traveling clothes, leaving most of their trunks for San Francisco,[8] but soon their successors knew that a sojourn at Del Monte was no mere seaside interlude.

Meanwhile Colorado had made more gradual beginnings, though the territory had started out with a governor, the irrepressible Gilpin, who conceived of his job as an adventure in press agentry. "What will I do for you if you stop here among us?" he once appealed to an English tourist. "I'll name that peak after you in the next survey." There was no first-class hotel in Colorado before The Antlers, which General W. A. J. Palmer of the Denver and Rio Grande Railroad opened at Colorado Springs in 1883. Palmer had laid out Manitou, near the Springs, in 1871 in the hope that it would become "a first class Colorado Watering place & spa," and society's invalids and dilettantes flocked in even before hotels were ready to receive all of them; tent colonies contrasted strangely with the handsome residences that sprang up in Colorado Springs. The walls of a temporary hotel at Manitou in 1871 had large spaces between the boards. But fashion so embraced

[8] Dall: *My First Holiday*, pp. 333–4, 196; Robert Louis Stevenson: *Across the Plains* . . . (Leipzig: B. Tauchnitz; 1892), p. 104; *San Francisco Daily Alta California*, June 7, 1880, p. 1:2; John S. Hittell: *Bancroft's Pacific Coast Guide Book* (San Francisco: A. L. Bancroft & Co.; 1882), p. 117; "East and West," *Overland Magazine*, 2d series, Vol. I (February 1883), p. 208.

Manitou that the social ritual developed apparently with relatively little reference either to hotel facilities or to the natural environment, or, for that matter, to the physical ills that originally had justified the resort. Illness, in fact, tended to become a conversation piece; sometimes it seemed that dyspepsia exceeded consumption, which young ladies were said to counterfeit or induce for its cosmetic effects. Fashionable life at Manitou, observed an English visitor in 1880, seemed "more frivolous, not to say faster, than at similar places in the Old World." The ladies' "breakfast toilets are good enough for the dinner-table, while for dinner they dress as we do for the opera. . . . American ladies never walk, but they go out 'buggy-riding' in dancing shoes and ball dresses, or amble about on ponies in highly ornamental riding habits. All this seems very odd among the mountains. . . ." Intent on transplanting the pleasures of the Eastern States, social leaders of Colorado Springs built the Cheyenne Mountain Country Club at Broadmoor, three miles away, "so as to have some place to drive to"; here they lounged at a casino "modeled after the most famous of the German and Italian casinos," or indulged in pigeon-shooting and polo, much as the gentry of Long Island, or rode out to hounds, with coyotes substituting for foxes.[9]

[9] Herbert O. Brayer: *William Blackmore, A Case Study in the Economic Development of the West* (Denver: Bradford-Robinson; 1949), Vol. II, p. 85; [Rose G. Kingsley]: *South by West, or Winter in the Rocky Mountains and Spring in Mexico* (London: W. Isbister & Co.; 1874), pp. 55–6; Daniel Pidgeon: *An Engineer's Holiday* . . . (2d ed.; London: K. Paul, Trench & Co.; 1883), p. 140; S. Nugent Townshend: *Colorado* . . . (London: The Field Office; 1879), p. 110; Lewis M. Iddings: "Life in the Altitudes, the Colorado Health Plateau," *Scribner's*

Elsewhere in Colorado, farther into the mountains, scores of Western would-be Saratogas set their caps for the Eastern tourist, without matching the successes of Denver, Colorado Springs, and Manitou. At Georgetown, northwest of Denver on Clear Creek, a Bostonian was planning in 1867 "the greatest hotel in the world," with full confidence in the future: "Soon every young couple that marries in the East will come right out here to the West, honeymooning." But though Georgetown eventually boasted one of the most curious and luxurious of the smaller Western hotels, the Hotel de Paris, tourists knew it as a stop on a spectacular stretch of mountain railroad rather than as a fashionable resort. The tourists of the eighties liked to wind along the narrow-gauge lines through the Rockies, stopping for a few hours en route, but they seemed to prefer the outer slopes to the wild interior of the mountains for prolonged visits. When the great attraction of Colorado Springs was, as one visitor said, "Eastern life in a Western environment," there was no point in overdoing environment. It was not until 1893 that first-class resort accommodations appeared in western Colorado, and then at Glenwood Springs, which was far enough west to command considerable stopover traffic among transcontinental travelers. When the railroad came to Glenwood in 1887, the bathhouses were crude sheds, the tubs no more than holes excavated with a shovel and rented for fifteen cents a customer (Indians bathing free of charge, and grumbling at the refinement); but the

Magazine, Vol. XIX (February 1896), p. 143; *Panoramic Views Along the Line of the Denver and Rio Grande Railroad*, Denver and Rio Grande Railroad ([Chicago: Poole Bros.; 1898]).

Hotel Colorado reached five stories high, "in the Italian style, the Villa Medicis in Rome having given inspiration for its central motive. . . ." Its proprietor was Walter Raymond;[1] its principal patrons were of the type of the Raymond excursionists, who passed a few days there rather than a season. There was no sizable settlement of recurrent visitors as in the neighborhoods of Manitou and Monterey.

On the Pacific Coast the Hotel del Monte retained a unique advantage by virtue of its proximity to San Francisco: one could "run down to the city" in three hours by the Del Monte Limited, "The Fastest Train in the United States West of the Missouri River," and guests from "the city" constituted a steady substratum of the elite. Del Monte was to San Francisco what Manitou was to Denver, and no other Western city stirred the tourists as San Francisco, so Western and still shining with the luster that Joaquin Miller and Bret Harte had applied and recorded as the Mecca of the forty-niners, and yet so unlike the wild West of the plains and mountains. "You can still enjoy a certain amount of the old wildness in the interior," said an English visitor, "and when you are tired of it you can run to San Francisco and sit down to an eight-o'clock dinner that even Paris could not beat."[2]

Southern California, when the tourists first came there,

[1] John White: *Sketches from America* (London: Sampson Low, Son, and Marston; 1870), pp. 326–7; Iddings, "Life in the Altitudes," p. 143; George Kendrick: *The Cottage Camps of Early Days* (MS. dictation, 1934; Colorado Historical Society); Walter Raymond: *The Colorado, Glenwood Springs, Colorado* . . . (n. p.; [1893?]).

[2] Frank W. Green: *Notes on New York, San Francisco, and Old Mexico* (Wakefield, England: E. Carr; 1886), p. 56.

seemed to offer little more than an alternative route to San
Francisco and Monterey, and the contrast of desert and
orange grove. As late as the early eighties, in fact, the
term "southern California" (then usually without the capital "S") sometimes meant all of California south of San
Francisco, and to the Easterner chiefly the two peninsulas
of San Francisco and Monterey and the fashionable areas
of Menlo Park and the Hotel del Monte. Santa Barbara
had the first tourist hotel in the southern half of the state,
the Arlington (1874), but visitors were relatively few
until 1903, when the Southern Pacific completed its coast
line between Los Angeles and San Francisco, providing
the direct railroad service that tourists seemed to demand.
In the early seventies it was receiving a regular but small
and unpretentious infiltration of Easterners in search of
health and a quiet and bucolic rather than fashionable
atmosphere; Kate Douglas Wiggin, who went to Santa
Barbara from Maine at seventeen, later remembered attentions from the Eastern college men who had come nomi-
nally to buy farm lands or to rest weak lungs. There were
few dances, "because there was so much bathing and horseback riding, so many picnics in the Cathedral Oaks and
along the many trails through the canons, so many suppers
on the beach—in short, such a habit of living out of doors
morning, noon, and evening, that there was little time for
indoor gayeties." It was still "but a little country town,"
reported an English visitor in 1893, though he complained
of overdressing, even at breakfast: "the women wore their
imported gowns, and tried to out-dress each other, as they
might do in a big city or at a fashionable 'Eastern States'
watering place." While it was nearer to Los Angeles,

Santa Monica, the Long Branch of the Pacific Coast, lacked both a residential district of its own [3] and a metropolitan population nearby to sustain its hotels. Relatively few railroad passengers went to any part of the entire southern half of the state before 1883, when the Santa Fe broke into the Southern Pacific monopoly and the Southern Pacific itself began through service to California by the "Sunset Route," which it boosted both to meet its competitor and because the company's profits were greater on the long haul by way of New Orleans than on the shorter "Overland Route" haul by way of Ogden. Then the tide turned. Los Angeles became the center of real-estate speculation without parallel until the Florida boom of the middle 1920's. Promoters, "ranchers," and tourists attracted each other and fed each others' hopes; and Pasadena became rival to Del Monte.

During its first decade Pasadena was a Western lotus-land inhabited by Middle Westerners of temperance principles. Its founders, a group of would-be orange growers in Indiana, dispatched a committee to California in 1873, and shortly began to stake out orchards and homes at the foot of the San Gabriel Mountains. By 1875 there was enough of a town to call itself Pasadena, and shortly enough sense of exclusiveness to prompt a ban on liquor

[3] William H. Bishop: "Southern California," *Harper's New Monthly Magazine,* Vol. LXV (October 1882), pp. 713–28; Kate Douglas Wiggin: *My Garden of Memory* . . . (Boston: Houghton Mifflin Company; 1923), p. 58; Charles G. Nottage: *In Search of a Climate* (London: Sampson Low, Marston & Company; 1894), p. 281; Mrs. Frank Leslie: *California. A Pleasure Trip from Gotham to the Golden Gate* . . . (New York: G. W. Carleton & Co.; 1877), p. 270; *Boston Evening Transcript,* April 15, 1882, p. 8:2.

dealers. Then the tourists came in force, and Pasadena came into its glory.

Los Angeles itself was at first of little interest to Easterners, who wanted above all else to see orange groves as proofs of the New Jerusalem, and moreover it lacked hotel space and good company. "It has been the Botany Bay of both California and Mexico," said a visitor of 1867–8, who found its architecture as tiresome as its society. Raymond and Whitcomb elected to honor instead Pasadena, which was conveniently located on what became the main line of the Santa Fe Railway. The railway donated the site for the new hotel; the town donated the water; New England contributed not only the services of Mr. Walter Raymond, who became the proprietor, but the hotel staff, which, after working the summer season in the White Mountains from June to October, moved to Pasadena to work the winter season from November to May. When it opened in 1886, the Raymond was "literally a Boston or New York hotel built among the orange groves of the San Gabriel, even its waiters being New England girls brought out every season for the purpose." It was, emphasized the management, "a hotel for particular people with means." It retained a special prestige in Pasadena even after newer Pasadena hotels of similar style had appeared, as, for instance, the Hotel Green, whose headwaiter brought his entire crew from the Raymond and Whitcomb Grand Hotel, of Chicago, and which promised "the conveniences of New York hotel life" along with "the semi-tropical beauties of Italy, and the fruits and flowers of Southern California." San Diego likewise was slow to rival Pasadena as a winter refuge for wealth, though it

offered the attractions of a seaside resort and by 1888
boasted of the largest of the West Coast resort hotels, del
Coronado, which could house more than one thousand
guests and air them around two thousand feet of porches.
Its architecture was of "a mixed character, partaking
largely of the Queen Anne style, and having also much
that is characteristic of the Elizabethan era," as well as
"many of the excellences of other schools, both ancient and
modern." [4]
Elsewhere in the West there was hardly a mountain, a
seaside cove, or an eruption of foul-tasting water that did
not nourish ambitions for another Manitou or Pasadena,
and that did not wait for a fairy godmother railroad president to conjure up another New England hotel for elderly
Cinderellas in flight from Eastern winters. Oregonians
hoped that railroad connections would make their state
"the summer place of the wealthy who live below us and
of many Eastern people. Our lovely bays will become more
famous than the Italian and our beautiful seabeaches will
furnish watering places more sought after than Long Island and Saratoga." But perhaps the Northwest developed too late. A generation later it still had "no Del
Montes, no Del Coronados to draw those who want modern

[4] Charles L. Brace: *The New West: or, California in 1867–
1868* (New York: G. P. Putnam & Son; 1869), p. 279; Charles F.
Holder: *Southern California: . . . A Guide-Book* (Los Angeles:
Times-Mirror Co.; 1888), p. 23; *The Raymond . . . A Place
for Particular People* ([San Francisco: Norman Pierce Co.;
1904]), p. 5; *Traveler*, Vol. II (December 1893), p. 90:1; *Hotel
Green, Pasadena* (leaflet) (n. p.; [1898?]), 3; T. S. Van Dyke:
"Around San Diego Bay," *Overland*, 2d series, Vol. XI (Feb-
ruary 1888), pp. 117–19; *Coronado Beach* (Chicago: Rand,
McNally & Co.; 1888), p. 10.

comforts—no special attractions for those who do not care to 'rough' it. . . ." [5] The nearest equivalents appeared north of the international border, where the Canadian Pacific Railway built the Banff Springs Hotel in 1888.

The gentleman tourist continued to go west, and he continues still. The luxury trains still carry their heaviest loads into Los Angeles in January and February, in contrast to the humbler accommodations that run fullest in the summer. The Hotel Green and the Huntington, heirs to the traditions of the Raymond, still expose expensive Eastern senility to the winter sunshine on their ample porches.

Yet much of the old glamor has departed. The gentleman tourist remains, but he and his hotels no longer dominate as they once did. If Pasadena still wears an air of transience, as if the whole city might be a mirage or an enormous stage-set, it now owes it less to the hotels than to the private residences. Over the years substantial numbers of the guests at the Raymond and the Hotel Green have moved into their own houses, stucco mansions on wide lawns that have swallowed up the orange groves, and that to the passer-by usually seem as impersonal and uninhabited as new and well-groomed. The Hotel del Monte spawned more secluded but no less sumptuous residences along the Seventeen Mile Drive in the 1920's and afterward; and finally, though twice rebuilt after fires, in 1887 and 1924, it closed its doors permanently to civilian trade in 1942, joining the United States Navy. In a sense this drift of wealth at leisure from hotels to private homes may

[5] *West Shore*, Vol. III (December 1877), p. 64; *Pacific Monthly*, Vol. XVII (October 1907), p. 392.

seem to represent a departure from the pattern of the Eastern States, whose wealthy families overbuilt so fantastically during the twenty years or so before the First World War while the younger generations moved their pleasures into the hotels; yet it parallels a general decentralization in American society over the last half century, dictated or facilitated in large part by the automobile. At Colorado Springs the twentieth-century hotels not only prospered, but multiplied enormously; their guests, however, were less often millionaires from Boston and New York than delegates to conventions of commercial and fraternal organizations; and there was little hope that even an Air Force academy would make it into a mountain Newport. The conducted railroad tour persists and prospers, averaging recently around ten million dollars a year in railroad fares, though the old luxurious Raymond and Whitcomb tour, which continued to serve the quality trade, was a fatality of the depression of the 1930's. The same years saw the rise of the bus line tour: the Greyhound Company began its personally conducted "Western Wonder Tours" in 1935 inauspiciously enough, with all of six passengers. Twenty years later it was escorting 4,656 over assorted routes in a season.[6] Today Thomas Cook and others have come to feature coach-class transportation in their pre-packaged tours, and sometimes even to sell it on the installment plan.

The Pullman tourist, in fact, had his heyday in the eighties, when the West seemed almost his exclusive prov-

[6] *The New York Times,* February 9, 1936, XI, p. 9:5; ibid., June 28, 1936, X, pp. 12:6–7, 13:2; C. D. Kirkpatrick to author, July 3, 1956.

ince. Then a larger tourist public began to move in. The West was never the same thereafter, and not merely because of the changes in the make-up of trains and in the accommodations at resorts. The more significant change seemed to be in what tourists and others thought of the West, and this change may have followed on the number and kind of tourists only in the sense that the impact of a dramatic performance may change when an intimate audience in a small theater gives way to a city seated in a stadium. At any rate, the West of Raymond and Whitcomb began to dissolve into the Wests of the American Automobile Association and the All-Year Club of Southern California.

2. EUROPE
IN THE WILDERNESS

But for the testimony of photographs and rocks and trees, it would be easy in a fanciful mood to suppose that the West had gone through a series of remarkable physical changes during the last century and a half, comparable to the ice ages of prehistory. The Wests that successive travelers and tourists saw and thought they saw since the 1870's are not much less different, on another plane, than the Garden of the World that Senator Benton and General Frémont reported in the 1850's is different from the Great American Desert that Major Long reported in the 1820's.[1]

[1] *The Garden of the World; or, The Great West* . . . (Boston: Wentworth and Company; 1856); Henry Nash Smith: *Virgin Land: The American West as Symbol and Myth* (Cambridge: Harvard University Press; 1950), pp. 174–83.

Witnesses tended to describe themselves, their aspirations, fears, and intellectual backgrounds as much as the new lands they visited.

It was, in fact, not the West—the newer part of the New World—that many of the gentlemen tourists sought beyond the Missouri River, but rather Italy, and the older part of the Old World. Californians hoped that the building of the Pacific railroad in 1869 would bring them traffic that had moved from the East Coast resorts to Europe, and for thirty or forty years or so after 1869 the transatlantic standard obsessed tourists and still more those who invited tourists. The railroad journey itself conventionally prompted comparison with an overseas voyage: the station at Chicago or Omaha was the quay, a vast confusion of crowds scrambling for berths, baggage, pickles, and lunch baskets; the plains and the desert were the sea; the train, in gently rolling motion, was the ship, bearing its passengers from one civilized port to another while they explored its secrets and each others'. And then the shores of the Mediterranean. To those whose faith sustained them, California was the Italy of America, the Riviera, or perhaps the Palestine. Monterey Bay was the "Naples of the New World," though Santa Cruz, "the Newport of the Pacific Coast," which it encloses, boasted the climate of "the Isles of Greece, in which ardent Sappho 'loved and sung,' " and the sunshine through the trees at Cypress Point was "a pleasant, subdued light, such as is met with in the ancient minsters and Moorish alcazars of Europe"; the Monterey cypresses reminded a Raymond tourist of the cedars of the Roman Campagna. Southern

California was "an Italy . . . without the trying features of that exquisite land"; it had no beggars or unpleasant odors. Occasionally such comparisons badly disappointed more critical visitors, as Horace Greeley, who asked, on first seeing the brown hillsides and alkali plains of central California in the summer heat of 1859: "Is this the American Italy? It looks more like a Sahara or Gobi." A visitor to San Francisco who had been told that some buildings were "of the Italian order" commented that "the greater number were of the Ramshackle order." [2]

Nor did similarities to the Old World stop at the coast line. Western hot springs resembled the most celebrated spas of Karlsbad, Ems, and Baden-Baden, or perhaps the "Pools of Siloam." Senator Benton had compared the Colorado Rockies to the Swiss Alps, without their "drawback of avalanches and glaciers," Pikes Peak to Mont Blanc; and thereafter Alpine similes intruded into the figure of the ocean crossing, and helped the traveler to transport himself in fancy to more famous scenes. "So surrounded are you by snowy summits that you can easily

[2] *San Francisco Daily Morning Call*, May 14, 1869, p. 1:3; *The Yosemite Book . . .* , California Geological Survey (New York: J. Bien; 1868), p. 27; A. J. Wells: "California Summer Resorts," *Out West* (Los Angeles), Vol. XIX (July 1903), p. 119; *Monterey California; The Most Charming Winter Resort in the World . . .* (n. p.; [1881?]), p. 13; Mary E. Blake: *On the Wing; Rambling Notes of a Trip to the Pacific* (Boston: Lee and Shepard; 1883), p. 146; Elizabeth B. Custer: "Memories of 'Our Italy,'" *Land of Sunshine,* Vol. III (July 1895), pp. 51–2; Horace Greeley: *An Overland Journey, from New York to San Francisco . . .* (New York: C. M. Saiton, Barker & Co.; 1860), p. 325; Samuel Smiles, ed.: *A Boy's Voyage around the World . . .* (London: J. Murray; 1871), p. 245.

forget you are in Colorado." [3] Colorado was the Switzerland of America, or, in a more daring mood, Switzerland the Colorado of Europe, though along the "Switzerland Trail of America" one found Eldorado Springs and Boulder, respectively the "Coney Island of Colorado" and "the Athens of Colorado"; and the less pretentious coastal resorts, while neighbors to France and Italy, aspired only to be Atlantic City or Long Branch.

The random incidence of such associations satisfied neither Westerners nor tourists, but before the early 1900's there seemed to be no satisfying alternative. Classical literature and art, all the aura of history and respectability, enshrined the Old World rather than the New; short of taking them on clearly imaginary travels, one could not much more satisfactorily invoke the great authorities of the genteel tradition than by suggesting that they would have liked what they saw if they had seen it, and by comparing what they had seen in Europe to what they had not seen in America. "Dante would have reveled here; Rembrandt would have gloried in the mystic shades." "All lovers of forest scenery are familiar with Chateaubriand's magnificent descriptions of the primeval woods in *Atala* and among the pineries of the Sierra Nevada, many of his pictures can be fully realized." Even the Grand Canyon of the Colorado recalled the approved criteria of European culture: "It is the soul of Michael An-

[3] Benton also compared Utah to "central Persia, and . . . that valley of Shiraz, celebrated as incomparable by the poets, but matched and surpassed in the recesses of the Wahsatch and the · Anterria. . . ." January 16, 1855, in *The Garden of the World*, pp. 364, 370, 375; Edwards Roberts: *Shoshone, and other Western Wonders* (New York: Harper & Brothers; 1888), p. 65.

gelo and of Beethoven. It flashes instant communication of all that architecture and painting and music for a thousand years have gropingly striven to express." [4]

The real actors of the past, the Spaniards and the Indians, were slow to win acceptance into polite tradition, or to qualify as eyewitnesses. "The effacement of the Spanish element in New Orleans is enough," wrote the English journalist George A. Sala after crossing America in 1877; "but its disappearance in California is even more complete. The *nombres de Espana* only remain; the *cosas* thereof have entirely vanished." As the venerable capital of New Mexico, and one of the few excuses for a stop on the southern excursion-route to the Pacific, Santa Fe drew some visitors, but relatively few of them found or expected to find the glamor of the era of the pack train and wagon traders. "I had always heard of people going to Florida or California, and more occasionally to the West, but no one ever went to the Southwest," recalled Mabel Dodge Luhan, who went there from New York in 1916, when artists had been congregating in New Mexico for a generation. "Hardly anyone had ever even heard of Santa Fe." "It is said to be rich," reported a visitor of the eighties; "if so, it is exceedingly modest in its display." The Governor's Palace, said another, was "an oblong adobe, completely uninteresting and unimaginably ugly. In fact, the people of Santa Fe seem utterly destitute of taste. . . ." An English visitor found Monterey "a poor, dirty little place;

[4] Alfred Lambourne: *Pine Branches and Sea Weeds* (Salt Lake City: Donohue & Henneberry; 1889), p. 27; C. A. Higgins: *Grand Cañon of the Colorado River* . . . (Chicago: Passenger Department Santa Fe Route; 1900), p. 10.

it was founded by the Spaniards in 1602, and I should say it had not made much progress since that time." The tourist might take note of such Spanish remnants in passing and even find them quaint and picturesque, but at most they were incidental to the main attractions, said a member of a Raymond party. "He comes chiefly and solely to visit the Hotel del Monte, in comparison with which everything else sinks into significance." In the seventies the conventional reply to the objection that California lacked historical scenery was not that it had missions but that it had natural scenery, sea resorts, "bands of music, and English faces by the score," and furthermore that Englishmen often failed to see their own historical places. It is not surprising, then, that the founders of the early tourist resorts, like the early home-builders, overlooked local architectural tradition to build Swiss chalets and English manors. At Del Monte, "Swiss cottages" bordered a "modern hotel of Swiss Gothic architecture" that reminded one, boasted the management, "infinitely more of a modern English country mansion than of an American watering-place hotel." "Alas for the little town!" Robert Louis Stevenson had written, "it is not strong enough to resist the influence of the flaunting caravanserai, and the poor, quaint, penniless native gentlemen of Monterey must perish, like a lower race, before the millionaire vulgarians of the Big Bonanza." [5]

[5] George A. Sala: *America Revisited* . . . (London: Vizetelly & Co.; 1882), Vol. II, p. 205; Mabel D. Luhan: *Intimate Memories*, Vol. IV, *Edge of Taos Desert* . . . (New York: Harcourt, Brace and Company; 1937), p. 3; Almon Gunnison: *Rambles Overland; A Trip Across the Continent* (Boston: Universal-

An American or Western antiquity began to command attention and approval in the 1880's, most impressively in some parts of the West that were most heavily settled and where the dangers of the frontier were most surely past. "The customs and costumes of the Indian tribes grow more interesting as our acquaintance with them becomes less familiar," observed a Coloradan. "In a word, what ceases to be common begins to be valued." It was the Spaniard who was still less familiar and who first came into fashion. When Helen Hunt Jackson published *Ramona* (1884), setting a pattern for glucoside sentimentalizing over the years of Spanish and Mexican control in the Southwest, the Hispanophiles were already stirring. A Los Angeles editor and promoter, Charles F. Lummis, became typical of the new enthusiasm and one of its dynamos. A New Englander who had known Theodore Roosevelt at Harvard and never ceased to boast of his Eastern antecedents and those of southern California, Lummis became in effect press agent for the Spanish-American and Indian Southwest, a one-man tourist agency, and infected a section with his mania, defending Spain during the Cuban troubles, raising funds to restore the remains of missions, writing verse and love letters in Spanish and living

---

ist Publishing House; 1884), p. 186; William H. Rideing: *A-saddle in the Wild West* . . . (New York: D. Appleton and Company; 1879), p. 142; Rose Pender: *A Lady's Experience in the Wild West in 1883* (London: G. Tucker; 1888), p. 24; Susie C. Clark: *The Round Trip from the Hub to the Golden Gate* (Boston: Lee and Shepard; 1890), pp. 114–15; Frederick A. Binney: *California Homes for Educated Englishmen* . . . (London: Simpkin, Marshall; 1875), pp. 25–6; Robert Louis Stevenson: *American Notes*, p. 104.

on concoctions of olives and red peppers.[6] The older European motif did not surrender at once; in fact, the most spectacular seashore resort development on the southern California coast in the first years of the twentieth century was Venice, built 1904–05, in its heyday boasting canals, renaissance palaces, and gondolas. But thereafter tourism in the Southwest was coming to speak with a pseudo-Spanish accent. Pasadena, ultimate stronghold of respectability, eventually built its palatial Moorish city hall at the intersection of streets called Euclid and Ramona.

The Indian came into style somewhat more slowly than the Spaniard. Most Americans could feel akin to Thoreau at least in his unwillingness to imitate the aborigine: "What a coarse and imperfect use Indians and hunters make of Nature! No wonder that their race is so soon exterminated." Their dilemma, as Westerners, was that the Indian was a barrier to their plans to take his land, a barrier that they could demolish in better conscience if they considered him a beast or savage whose person and culture had no strong claim to survival at the expense of superior beings; yet on the frontier they shared some of his environment, which obviously affected them also, and which as Americans, exponents of the democratic environmental principle in contrast to the aristocratic principle of heredity, they could not easily ignore. The easiest course was to ignore the Indian himself. While as early as the 1870's the promotors of the Colorado railroads had adorned their lines

[6] *The Great Divide,* Vol. III (June 1890), p. 53:1; see Edwin R. Bingham: *Charles F. Lummis, Editor of the Southwest* (San Marino: Huntington Library; 1955), and files of *Land of Sunshine* (Los Angeles: 1893–1901) and *Out West* (Los Angeles: 1902–23).

with conventional lovers' leaps (Dolores Canyon, for instance, commemorating the remarkable daughter of the
high priest of Montezuma, who had fled from Mexico after
the conquest, and died to escape from Coronado), there
was relatively little interest in living Indians, or even in
relics of dead Indians except as they resembled the antiquities of the other hemisphere. Even *Ramona* aroused
some skepticism about the California Indians ("they were,
with few exceptions . . . a most inferior people"), and
in general its readers accepted it as glorification of the
Spanish-speaking rancheros rather than as an appeal for
the Indians that the rancheros had exploited. Thus Mrs.
Jackson, like Upton Sinclair when he published *The
Jungle*, had the unhappy experience of seeing the public
applaud her novel but ignore the message that she had
intended in favor of a minor theme that happened to have
more current appeal. Travelers passing the Pueblo villages
of the Southwest in the eighties were invited to recall the
villages of ancient Egypt and Nubia, Nineveh and Babylon, rather than to study the remnants of American aboriginal life; the people were "like the descendants of Re-
becca of Bible fame." "It is not often that one would want
to call a tourist's attention to an Indian village," remarked
a traveler of the Western tribes. The Crows who danced
to celebrate the completion of the Northern Pacific in
1883 sold their brass ornaments at high prices to Henry
Villard's foreign guests, at a handsome advance over the
original cost to Villard, who had given them to the Indians a few hours earlier; [7] Americans ordinarily were no

[7] Henry D. Thoreau: "Chesuncook," *Atlantic Monthly*, Vol.
II (July 1858), p. 229; E. McD. Johnstone: *"By Semi-Tropic*

more than mildly curious about the aboriginals who watched at desert railroad stations.

William H. Jackson, the photographer, and a party of government geologists attached to the Hayden expedition had discovered the cliff dwellings of the Mesa Verde area in southwestern Colorado as early as 1874, but they were so little known before the nineties that it was popularly supposed that their builders were refugees from the Spaniards who "preferred imprisonment within these gloomy canon walls, to either baptism or hanging." It was not until about the end of the century that the Santa Fe Railway began to feature Indians in its magazine advertising, as it has featured them during most of the time since. The Indian may be said to have arrived as a tourist attraction when a group of Colorado businessmen found it profitable in 1905 to build reproductions of parts of the Mesa Verde cliff dwellings near Manitou, having quarried the materials from ruins in a less accessible region. In a pueblo that the proprietors built nearby, Indian families lived during the summer to dance and make pottery and beadwork for travelers; for a fee one could be photographed with them before the ruins. Tourists were not quite ready to leave the main lines of travel to go to the Indian, but he had achieved a negotiable value as decoration. "Good Indian legends

---

Seas." Santa Barbara and Surroundings (Buffalo: Matthews, Northrup & Co.; 1888), p. 5; *Las Vegas Hot Springs* (Chicago: 1882), pp. 7–8; *Conklin's Modern Nineveh and Babylon* . . . (n. p.; 1883), p. 4; Theodore Gerrish: *Life in the World's Wonderland* . . . *A Graphic Description of the Great Northwest* . . . (n. p.; [1887]), pp. 306, 338; "Dance of the Crow Indians," *Harper's Weekly,* Vol. XXVII (December 15, 1883), pp. 798–9, 800.

can be grown in almost any locality with a little care and
attention," remarked the *Independent*, "and it adds an
interest to a very ordinary cliff to know that a persecuted
and necessarily beautiful Indian maiden leaped thence to
her death. . . . All that we need is great events and great
authors." [8]

It is not altogether paradoxical that southern California, where the new enthusiasm for Spanish and Indian
culture seemed to focus, had drawn especially heavily on
immigration from the older states in the last years of the
century, and liked to boast of the fact, setting itself apart
from the pioneer West. "Nowhere else in the world had
such a class of settlers been seen," observed a witness of
the boom of the eighties. "Emigrants coming in palace-
cars instead of 'prairie schooners' and building fine houses
instead of log shanties, and planting flowers and lawngrass
before they planted potatoes and seed corn. . . ." It was
this message that Lummis and his fellow promoters held
out to the prospective tourist. People with money, Lummis
said, "naturally fear and shun the raw, unfinished civilization of most Western cities. But Los Angeles is . . . no
frontier town." Most of the early "boosters" reserved
things Hispanic for a colorful but well-laundered and conventionalized backdrop, which substituted for the vener-
ability of the East Coast but without significantly adul-
terating Eastern culture. An agent of the Los Angeles
Chamber of Commerce went as far as to contend (1902)

[8] James P. Boyd: *Wonders of the Heavens, Earth and
Ocean* . . . (n. p.; 1888), p. 645; *The Manitou Cliff Dwellings,
"The Mystery of America"* (n. p.; n. d.); *Snyder's Guide to the
Pike's Peak Region*, Vol. IX (August 1911); "The Tourism In-
dustry," *Independent*, Vol. LV (August 20, 1903), p. 2005.

that "Southern California has less of the old California character than any other part of the State. The old-time Spanish settlements found here and there appear like islands in the sea of modern American progress." Even Lummis, who was perfectly capable of glorifying at once the pre-Columbian tribes of Mexico and the current regime of Porfirio Díaz, which ground down their descendants, managed somehow to remain a New Englander inside his serape, ridiculing the idea that one must learn Spanish and assuring Easterners who hesitated to come west that they would find "The Right Kind of People." There was "no distinctly foreign element, except the Chinese, and only a few of them." He boasted of a state conquered by Pullman; of how distance and railroad rates constituted "a remarkably effective Restriction of Immigration—of the sort we are now nationally trying to restrict." [9]

If Americans seemed inconsistent in their attitudes toward the living remains of other American cultures, which often bored them as tourists and embarrassed them as Westerners, and their attitudes toward dead and dying

[9] Theodore S. Van Dyke: *Millionaires of a Day: an Inside Story of the Great Southern California "Boom"* (New York: Fords, Howard & Hulbert; 1890), p. 45; "Los Angeles, The Metropolis of the Southwest," *Land of Sunshine*, Vol. III (June 1895), p. 45; Harry E. Brook: *The City and County of Los Angeles* . . . (Los Angeles: Kingsley-Barnes & Neuner Co.; 1902), p. 43; "The Right Kind of People," *Land of Sunshine*, Vol. II (December 1894), p. 10; Charles F. Lummis: "The Right Hand of the Continent," *Out West*, Vol. XVIII (March 1903), pp. 307–8. "We are Easterners—just lucky ones who got away. Our schools are such schools as Eastern people always make. Only, a little ahead; for . . . we could not help but learn something by the way." "Tenderfoot College," *Land of Sunshine*, Vol. II (March 1895), p. 70.

cultural remains, in which both tourists and Westerners began by the eighties and nineties to discover a sentimental interest, it was because American standards of taste were insecure and much in flux. Nature in the nineteenth century had to meet the test of approved criteria, and primarily the criteria of romantic and sentimental European art and literature. "Travels, to be good for anything, must be literary," pronounced the editors of the new *Magazine of Travel* in 1857. In effect, this meant that they must be European, even at a time when Europe itself had long been outgrowing the cult of the picturesque and was looking to new and freer interests. By the 1790's Jane Austen was poking fun at the dicta of the high priest of taste in landscape, William Gilpin, the vicar of Boldre, and only the vulgar still demanded Italian ruins in English gardens. America followed by perhaps seventy-five years, its new rich being about that much newer. Thoreau and Emerson themselves respected Gilpin's authority, and the generation following readily conceded the superiority of the European scenery that Gilpin described, and that appeared enshrined in the engraved picture-books on American parlor tables. "The partially cultivated country it is," said Thoreau, "which chiefly has inspired, and will continue to inspire, the strains of poets, such as compose the mass of any literature." Americans in general were more disposed than Englishmen had been to look for moral and spiritual qualities in scenery—perhaps the Puritan tradition required that travel be the means of self-improvement—but they departed from the rigidities of eighteenth-century English taste chiefly by sometimes substituting the English standard for the Italian, and then the Eastern

for the English. They still demanded the sanction of literature (or at least of the printed word) and of an older culture at a time when, as Frank Norris was to complain, "no
contemporaneous poet or chronicler thought it worth his
while to sing the story or tell the tale of the West because
literature . . . was a cult indulged in by certain well-bred
gentlemen in New England who looked eastward to the
Old World . . . for their inspiration," leaving the frontier largely to the "yellowback" libraries. In an age when
General Lew Wallace sat at his desk in the governor's palace at Santa Fe to write not of the West that surrounded
him but of the early Christian era,[1] the most approved
themes trespassed only rarely on reality.

Eventually the new Spanish interest merged into an
American reply to European standards, so that the Spaniard, the American pioneer, and the Indian joined hands
posthumously, but in its early stages the American response was less revolt than acceptance. By the middle of
the nineteenth century Spain had entered the genteel tradition through the writings of Washington Irving and
Henry Wadsworth Longfellow; the literary vogue of
Spanish California ranch life developed after George

[1] *Magazine of Travel; a Work devoted to Original Travels,
in Various Centuries* . . . , Vol. I (January 1857), p. iii; Elizabeth W. Manwaring: *Italian Landscape in Eighteenth Century
England* (New York: Oxford University Press; 1925); William D. Templeman: *The Life and Work of William Gilpin
(1724–1804), Master of the Picturesque and Vicar of Boldre*
(Urbana: University of Illinois Press; 1939); Thoreau: "Chesuncook," p. 316; Frank Norris: *The Responsibilities of the Novelist* . . . (New York: Doubleday Page & Company; 1903), pp.
62–3; Lew. Wallace: *Ben Hur, A Tale of the Christ* (New York:
Harper & Brothers; 1880).

Washington Cable and Grace Elizabeth King published their romantic stories of Spanish and French Louisiana. New Orleans achieved a startling reincarnation of Gallic themes that seemed to suggest that during the brief years of French control, between 1800 and 1804, the Mississippi had been a tributary of the Seine, New Orleans itself a suburb of imperial Paris. In the stories of Bret Harte and, in later years, of Gertrude Atherton, and Stewart Edward White, Spanish and Mexican California seemed a romantic refuge for Old World chivalry; while the Argonauts were heroes and the authors of progress, they also had destroyed paradise, which had been something finer. The golden age of Spanish California extended to the gold rush of American California, and back before the American Revolution—perhaps in some senses back to the Middle Ages, before the Protestant revolt, since there was no sense of religious alienation among the pious sons and daughters of the Middle West who venerated Fathers Serra and Lasuén. The Westerner who enshrined the Spanish past of his new home was not rebelling against the East fundamentally; rather he was trying to mold the history of the West into the nearest representation or equivalent of the East and of Europe that seemed possible with the materials at hand. He might have moved to the Far West to escape not merely Eastern winters but the rigidities of Eastern society, to which his new wealth did not automatically admit him; yet he did not aspire to be an innovator, a democrat, a leveler. It was only natural that he should recreate early Westerners who were as old as the Puritans and as courtly as the planters of the old South.

If Westerners tried to fit their seaside resorts into a European Baedeker, and tried to put Mexican California posthumously through the stylized paces of a minuet, the Western landscape according to contemporary description in general takes on the mournful aspect of a steel engraving from a volume of views of the sublime and the picturesque. "My own impression," said a visitor asked for his sensations on first beholding the Yosemite, "so skillfully is the view arranged for pictorial effect, was that of looking upon some perfect picture." The noblest aspect of scenery was the sublime; the corresponding emotion was awe, which, if we may believe the evidence of memoirs and guidebooks, the tourist registered, after a conventional interval of silence, by praising what he had seen as "most pictorial," "charmingly artistic," "peculiarly opulent in special picturesque points," "full of picturesqueness," or "the very sublimity of moral and material grandeur." The Pacific was "not only the greatest and the noblest, but the most romantic and amiable ocean"; one saw it, if possible, from an "Inspiration Point." Some of the favorite views were those that evoked thoughts of the dreadful majesty of divine power. The "stupendous and gloomy grandeur" of the Royal Gorge of the Arkansas River suggested an elaborate fancy: that "the Almighty in His wrath had driven the mountain asunder to make a sepulcher for the sun. And the ancient sun . . . comes, every day a little while, and shines into the great abyss, calmly and pensively, like a passing martyr smiling into his own grave." [2]

[2] Lambourne: *Pine Branches,* p. 45; *A Souvenir of the Beautiful Rio Grande* . . . , Denver and Rio Grande Railroad ([Denver: c. 1893]), p. 6.

Some descriptions of Western scenes took shapes that in context suggest limitations in vocabulary rather than in idea, but the places that inspired tourists were no less standard and mandatory than their adjectives. Some travelers spoke of turning, "palled with the fashionable frivolities . . . of the shoddy centers of the east; with the beaten paths of summer travel," to "new scenes" and "new people" in the West, the "awful and impressive handiwork of nature," looking for "new and grand scenes that have not been visited or pictured, and which constantly have a charm of freshness about them which it is impossible to find about those places of which much has been said or written." Yet in the main theirs was a modest revolt against æsthetic conventions. The typical tourist sought out only what the guidebook recommended, and according to schedule he felt the prescribed emotions—of satisfaction of having seen what "everyone" saw, of wonder and awe at God's work and at dreadful reminders of the turmoil of the creation. He was still intimidated by the prejudices of an earlier generation, which required that scenery be sanctioned by history, that is, that it be European. "The moment you travel in America the victory of Europe is sure," G. W. Curtis had said (1852). "We have none of the charms that follow long history. We have only vast and unimproved extent. . . . The idea of the great western rivers . . . or of a magnificent monotony of grass or forest, is as impressive and much less wearisome than the actual sight of them." "The Rocky Mountains," according to James Fenimore Cooper, "must possess many noble views . . . but the accessories are necessarily wanting; for a union of art and nature can alone render scenery perfect." In practice art meant not merely the cultivating hand of civilized man on the ruder part of the landscape, and history not merely association with great events in the mind of the beholder, but assurance to the beholder that competent and fashionable critics of scenery had had time to enshrine nature in words or paint, and were available to point out and interpret to him what he ought to see. Master scenes, said the critic E. L. Magoon, "unveil them-selves most fully to the enraptured, and pour the effulgence of their splendid mysteries into the fixed eye of him only who gazes on the charms he has studiously sought. . . ." [3]

It was only consistent with the age's preoccupation with the picturesque—a grim calcification of the lively response to nature in a Byron or a Wordsworth—and with conventional reactions to famous scenes, the more memorable insofar as they approximated the irreproachably famous and picturesque scenes in the European Baedeker, that tourists should have beaten a path to a series of Western oddities and curiosities. In a sometimes almost literal sense these seemed to substitute for the ruins of Rome and Pompeii, the catacombs, cathedrals, and museums that American tourists venerated in Britain and on the Continent. Their interest is distinct from a general liking for the out-

[3] [Charles E. Harrington:] *Summering in Colorado* (Denver: Richards & Co.; 1874), p. 15; *Popular Science Monthly*, Vol. XXV (July 1884), pp. 313–15; Samuel A. Fisk: "Colorado for Invalids," *A Guide to the Grand and Sublime Scenery* . . . (n. p.; 1883), p. 2; *The Home Book of the Picturesque* . . . (New York: G. P. Putnam; 1852), pp. 6, 56; James Fenimore Cooper: "American and European Scenery Compared," George W. Curtis, ed.: *Lotus-Eating: A Summer Book* (New York: Harper & Brothers; c. 1852), pp. 138–9.

doors: it demanded specific and identifiable points whose impact was immediate and that could be represented in a paragraph or a picture frame. In 1853 some enterprising Californians had destroyed a giant sequoia at the Calaveras grove by removing the bark, which went on display in New York City; by 1857 the bark from another tree was at the Crystal Palace at Sydenham. Although eventually there was criticism of such wanton "gratification of curiosity-lovers," several generations marveled at how five men had had to work for twenty-five days to fell one tree, and at how many people had been able to dance on the stump. An Ohio clergyman rebuked those Americans who thought that only Europe was worth seeing: "Do they know that there is in California a house standing on the stump of a tree that has been felled, having room enough in it for a parlor twelve by sixteen feet, and a dining room ten by fifteen feet . . . ? Do they know that squashes grow weighing over one hundred pounds, and beets weighing over one hundred pounds . . . ? Then let them give up their European trips and come and see." By 1876 a fine of fifty dollars was imposed for felling a big tree in order to take a section to the centennial exposition at Philadelphia, but it was still acceptable in the eighties to add interest to trees by cutting holes for men and carriages to pass through them; a section of still another tree went to the world's fair at Chicago in 1893.[4]

[4] *Ballou's Pictorial Drawing Room Companion*, Vol. XVII (October 22, 1859), pp. 264–5; Bishop Calvin Kingsley: *Round the World: A Series of Letters* (Cincinnati: Hitchcock and Walden; 1870), Vol. I, p. 293; "Californian Giants," *Living Age*, Vol. LII (February 14, 1857), pp. 438–9; *Blackwood's Magazine*, Vol. XCIX (February 1866), pp. 196–9; *Guide to the*

In the ten years following the Civil War, probably more tourists visited "the Geysers" than the Big Trees and the Yosemite Valley, nearby. They were a volcanic area north of San Francisco, beyond Sonoma, where fumaroles, rather than geysers in the usual sense, released vapors that the generous-minded were willing to call infernal. The same trip could include the petrified trees, which one visitor called "the most impressive things in California," and a spectacular stagecoach ride in custody of a jehu who promised all assurance of safety and all appearance of danger. "When the Pacific road is finished," wrote another traveler of the Geysers, "it will be the summer trip for our New York friends, and second only to Niagara." For a time the springs at Calistoga, where most tourists stopped on the way, were known as the "Saratoga of the West," though a fire (1868) destroyed the main buildings, and thereafter guests were quartered in tiny cottages (each with a classical or historical name, a lattice summer-house, a balcony, and a date palm and cypress in front) more reminiscent of the Virginia Springs before the Civil War than of the great hostelries at Saratoga. "It is worth while to visit the place," reported Grace Greenwood, "for the sake of the excellent society you are very sure to meet there. . . ." But aside from a few invalids, most visitors came and went within a day or two, shuddering successively at the stagecoach ride, the waters, and the geysers themselves. "The Geysers are ex-

Grand and Sublime Scenery, 20; Frederick Simpich: "Northern California at Work," *National Geographic Magazine,* Vol. LXIX (March 1936), p. 328; Francis P. Farquhar, *Yosemite, the Big Trees, and the High Sierra, A Selective Bibliography* (Berkeley: University of California Press; 1948), pp. 5–13, 39–40.

hausted in a couple of hours," reported the Springfield editor, Samuel Bowles. "They are certainly a curiosity, a marvel; but . . . like a three-legged calf, or the Siamese twins, or P. T. Barnum, or James Gordon Bennett, once [sic] seeing is satisfactory for a lifetime." [5] By the eighties the much larger geysers and springs of the Yellowstone were becoming generally accessible, and Niagara was safe from its Western rival.

Yosemite likewise was primarily a curiosity that the tourist surveyed as quickly as possible, chiefly from the valley floor, without attempting to absorb the atmosphere of the larger Yosemite beyond. As one traveler put it, "all the celebrated features of Yosemite can be enjoyed from a carriage." Even the California Geological Survey, comparing the Sierra with the Alps, found "sublimity and grandeur, rather than beauty and variety. The scenery perhaps will produce as much impression, at first, as that of the Alps; but will not invite as frequent visits, or as long a delay among its hidden recesses." Most visitors stayed only two or three days (Horace Greeley's party only one), though half to two thirds had come from out of the state, and transportation to and from San Francisco in the seventies cost about eighty dollars and about four

[5] Benjamin F. Taylor: *Between the Gates* (Chicago: S. C. Griggs and Company; 1878), pp. 164–5; Demas Barnes: *From the Atlantic to the Pacific* . . . (New York: D. Van Nostrand; 1866), p. 110; Francis C. S. Sanders: *California as a Health Resort* (San Francisco: Bolte & Braden Co.; 1916), p. 255; J. G. Player-Frowd: *Six Months in California* (London: Longmans, Green & Co.; 1872), pp. 60–1; Grace Greenwood: *New Life in New Lands* . . . (New York: J. P. Ford and Company; 1873), p. 265; Samuel Bowles: *Across the Continent* . . . (Springfield, Mass.: S. Bowles & Company; 1865), p. 280.

days of ordeal by stagecoach and dust, at hours fixed to suit the stagecoach company rather than the tourists. Somehow the trials of the trip failed to screen out those who cared less for nature than for fashion; well-dressed lady tourists, complained a New Englander, disdained to associate with educated men in plain clothes. John Muir scorned their "blank, fleshly apathy" in the face of nature: "They climb sprawlingly to their saddles like overgrown frogs pulling themselves up a streambank through the bent sedges, ride up the valley with about as much emotion as the horses they ride upon, and comfortable when they have 'done it all,' and long for the safety and flatness of their proper homes." The trip having become fashionable, those who made it were grimly reluctant to admit that they had been "taken in" but little interested in seeing more than the points that fashion prescribed. "I wouldn't have missed the trip for anything," tourists often commented after visiting the Valley or some other celebrated spectacle, "and I wouldn't make it again for a good deal more." Muir rejoiced on his part that most of them floated "slowly about the *bottom* of the valley as a harmless scum, collecting in hotel and saloon eddies, leaving the rocks and falls eloquent as ever and instinct with imperishable beauty and greatness." [6]

[6] Charles A. Bailey: "Unfrequented Paths of Yosemite," *Overland*, 2d series, Vol. VIII (July 1886), p. 88; *The Yosemite Book*, California Geological Survey, p. 82; Horace Greeley: *An Overland Journey from New York to San Francisco in the Summer of 1859* (New York: C. M. Saxton, Barker & Co.; 1860), pp. 303–8; John E. Lester: *The Atlantic to the Pacific . . .* (Boston: Shepard and Gill; 1873), p. 177; Olive Logan: "Does it Pay to Visit Yo Semite?" *Galaxy*, Vol. X (October 1870), pp. 498–509; *Traveler*, Vol. I (January 1893), p. 3; John Muir:

The other great park of the century, Yellowstone, represented to an even greater degree natural curiosity or eccentricity. There was a brief period, shortly after Easterners first heard of the region and before they knew it through Thomas Moran's paintings and William H. Jackson's photographs, when they were hard put to appreciate the geysers themselves. "There was something so revolting in the general appearance of the springs and their surroundings," wrote an early visitor, "the foulness of the vapors . . . the noisy ebullition, the general appearance of desolation, and the seclusion and wildness of the location—that, though awe-struck, we were not unreluctant to continue our journey without making them a second visit." Then the geysers became familiar to the public at large, and the chief attraction of the park. While some resort operators advertised luxurious accommodations of "a sort of Saratoga in the wilds of Montana" long before there were even habitable tents, still for many years the basic attractions were these "wondrous and curious freaks of Nature. . . ." "This realm of mighty marvels, within whose boundaries Nature, in frenzied mood, has wreaked her most appalling freaks and wildest fantasies," boasted a promoter, "will never cease to attract thousands of yearly tourists and wonder-seekers from all parts of the world." Such ecstasies left many tourists unprepared for the "dreary and disappointing character" of most of the scenery of the park, that is, for its representative wildness. "It is a mistaken idea that the Yellowstone abounds in grand scenery," wrote a professional advocate of West-

Letters to a Friend . . . 1866–1879 (Boston: Houghton Mifflin Company; 1915), pp. 80–1.

[53]

ern travel. "All its central area consists of forest-ground table-lands that are exceedingly monotonous. . . ." Yet perhaps only geysers and stalactites could break through the indifference of Americans like an old couple from Chicago that Kipling saw and who, perhaps in a kind of Puritanical antagonism to natural beauties, disapproved scenery as "ongodly." Most visitors followed a conventional route along the springs, canyon, and falls, lakes, and geysers. Those who appeared in hiking clothes to venture into the wilderness away from the standard sights drew—or thought that they drew—disapproving glances from the finely dressed ladies at the hotels. President Arthur evoked much comment when he returned shabby and dirty after roughing it: "Besides, the skin hung in strips from his nose, which did not improve his appearance." [7]

The rock formations rather significantly known as the Garden of the Gods, near Colorado Springs, had a typical and dependable appeal, despite the misgivings of some

[7] N. P. Langford: "The Wonders of the Yellowstone," *Scribner's Monthly*, Vol. II (May 1871), p. 11; Herman Haupt: *The Yellowstone Park* . . . (New York: J. M. Stoddart; 1883), p. 5; Roberts: *Shoshone, and other Western Wonders*, p. 206; Kipling: *American Notes*, p. 136; J. J. Aubertin: *A Flight with Distances* . . . (London: K. Paul, Trench & Co.; 1888), pp. 85, 88–97; Earley V. Wilcox: "Trip around Yellowstone Park," *Rocky Mountain Magazine*, Vol. III (January–February 1902), p. 263; Gerrish: *Life in the World's Wonderland*, pp. 182–3; Georgina M. Synge: *A Ride through Wonderland* (London: Sampson Low, Marston & Company; 1892), p. 59; William Hardman: *A Trip to America* (London: T. V. Wood; 1884), p. 175. Finding a rude shanty, deserted except for two skunks, Lord Dunraven asked: "Is this abomination of desolation the luxurious summer resort mentioned by those unprincipled prophets in Helena?" *The Great Divide*, pp. 343–4.

old-fashioned spirits who felt that "something less heathen-
ish (for a name) would better have befitted these Christian
days." In some respects they represented the extrem-
ity of interest in the grotesque. "No other point of interest," boasted the Denver and Rio Grande Railroad, "is
more unique or more to be admired than this curious freak
of nature." Its admirers thought that they saw (or at
least said that they saw) a stag's head, "curious birds and
crawling serpents," "an eagle with pinions spread," a seal
making love to a nun, and an elephant attacking a lion,
among other "grotesque and picturesque sights." "There
is little doubt," complained one visitor, "that the average
tourist is so intent on finding these monstrosities, that he
misses the grandeur and glory of the place." More significantly, perhaps, the tourist saw the Old World as well.
He might "pass under the shadow of China's great wall,
muse among Palmyra's shattered and fallen columns,
stand face to face with the mysterious Sphinx of Egypt,
gaze upon the Temples of Greece, or the Castles of England and Germany, or the old Abbeys which pious monks
upreared." [8] The exchange of Western curiosity for European antiquity had become almost literal.

By the eighties a standard assortment of curious and
grotesque sights awaited tourists on the Western circuit,
corresponding to the offerings of the lithographed books

[8] *Out West* (Colorado Springs), Vol. I (June 20, 1872),
p. 3; *"Around the Circle"* . . . , Denver and Rio Grande Railroad (n. p.; 1889), p. 32; William D. Bickham: *From Ohio to
the Rocky Mountains* . . . (Dayton: Journal Book and Job
Printing House; 1879), pp. 95–6; Gunnison: *Rambles Overland*,
p. 214; *Among the Mountains: A Guide Book to Colorado
Springs* . . . (Colorado Springs: 1873), p. 109.

and illustrated lectures. Before leaving Chicago for San Francisco they inspected the stockyards, as "no one regards a visit to Chicago as completed till he has seen a pig killed and cut up." "One day I went to the pig-slaughtering house," recalled Sarah Bernhardt, who was there in 1881. "Ah, what a dreadful and magnificent sight!" (Pig-sticking and packing, noted an English visitor, were "regarded as a fine art, to be visited by the stranger as rare pictures and stately cathedrals are elsewhere sought out. . . .") In Colorado they dipped south from Denver to Colorado Springs, Manitou, and the Garden of the Gods, perhaps also climbing to Helen Hunt Jackson's grave in Cheyenne Canyon, to leave inscribed calling cards among the stones and cut flowers that other pilgrims had carried there in her memory. A Colorado trip was incomplete without a ride on the narrow-gauges, whose engineering seemed as spectacular as the scenery ("Everybody who is anybody, and who comes to Denver takes the trip around the [Georgetown] 'Loop' "). Farther west, Utah was unthinkable without an attempt to penetrate the mysteries of polygamy at Salt Lake City between trains. "I have an uncontrollable desire," wrote an English visitor, "to ask every man I meet how many wives he has and how things work with his mothers-in-law." [9] Then the Sierra,

[9] Henry W. Lucy: *East by West, A Journey in the Recess* (London: R. Bentley and Son; 1885), Vol. I, pp. 38–9; Sarah Bernhardt: *Memories of My Life* . . . (New York: D. Appleton and Company; 1907), p. 418; Hattie Horner: *"Not at Home"* (New York: J. B. Alden; 1889), pp. 139–40; Emma A. Gage: *Western Wanderings and Summer Saunterings* . . . (Baltimore: The Lord Baltimore Press, the Friedenwald Company; 1900), p. 76; Molyneux St. John: *The Sea of Mountains, an Ac-*

seen from the tracks along the precipice at "Cape Horn";
Yosemite and the Big Trees; and finally San Francisco,
where one plumbed the Chinese opium dens on Washington
Street and surveyed the Pacific from the Cliff House before departing for the Geysers, the petrified trees, and the
Hotel del Monte. It was a routine for a cast-iron constitution, even though the visitor who hastened around the circuit with grace and compulsive intensity often absorbed
little more of Western life than those who spent their entire Western sojourns in the rocking chairs of the Raymond and the Del Monte.

As Raymond and other managers added new options—
notably the Yellowstone, Alaska, Canada, and Mexico—
the standard tour changed in extent rather than in spirit.
When John Muir first visited Alaska in 1879, the tourists
had not yet discovered it. The railroads to Portland and
Seattle (1883–7), connecting with steamers on the inland
passage route, shortly made the trip one of the easiest and
most popular in the Western repertory; by 1888 over two
thousand excursionists went from Puget Sound to Sitka in
a season. Alaska became "the American Switzerland"—or
Switzerland "the European Alaska"—and vastly superior
to the European version because it offered "full benefit of
a sea water voyage without the accompanying nausea," the
sight of glaciers without "miles of railroad travel" and
"weary hours of climbing," indeed "A Voyage that Should
Satisfy the Most Romantic." The Pacific Coast Steamship
Company advised against stopovers, and few were rash
enough to undertake them: "There are no 'Palace' Hotels

count of *Lord Dufferin's Tour through British Columbia in 1876*
(London: Hurst and Blackett; 1877), Vol. I, p. 61.

in Alaska. Unless you have business to attend to you will
not desire to remain over there a trip, but you will go
when and where the steamer goes, and you will have an opportunity of seeing the principal objects of interest. . . ."
And then on the return "you will have lots of stories" and
be "the lion of your social gathering and the envy of
those who stayed at home or went to the springs." While
the cost of the trip was trivial, at $350—"hardly the price
of a French costume, a ring, or a bracelet"—the majority
of the passengers were ladies and gentlemen "of refinement
and taste, since the only magnet that can draw them is the
hope of enjoying fine scenery . . . devoting their time to
travel . . . full of fact and anecdote. . . ." [1]

Standardization of interests and spectacles called forth
American efficiency to enable travelers to see the most in
the least time, if possible from their Pullman cars. Resort
hotels strove for direct railroad service: a Pasadena hotelman donated a station building for the Santa Fe Railway
in 1887 in order to have the main Pasadena stop on his
property, later the Hotel Green; the Hotel Colorado at
Glenwood Springs attracted guests by the spectacle of its
outdoor swimming pool along the tracks, where lady trav-

[1] John Muir: *Travels in Alaska* (Boston: Houghton Mifflin
Company; 1915), p. 19; Maturin M. Ballou: *The New Eldorado:
a Summer Journey to Alaska* (Boston: Houghton Mifflin Company; 1889), p. 97; Henry T. Finck: *The Pacific Coast Scenic
Tour* . . . (New York: Charles Scribner's Sons; 1890), pp.
233–5; Bushrod W. James: *Alaska. Its Neglected Past and Its
Brilliant Future* (Philadelphia: The Sunshine Publishing Company; 1897), pp. 20, 67; *Four Thousand Miles North and South
from San Francisco*, Pacific Coast Steamship Co. (San Francisco:
[1896]), p. 15; Septima M. Collis: *A Woman's Trip to Alaska*
(New York: Cassell Publishing Company; 1890), pp. 193–4.

elers could look through their Pullman car windows at daring gentlemen bathing in warm spring water during a snowstorm; the Santa Fe Railway itself built a series of luxurious tourist hotels at main station stops. It was said that many visitors glimpsed the Garden of the Gods from the hotel steps and drank the mineral waters from bottles at the railroad station. The railroads advertised daily excursion train service for sight-seers, ranging all the way from the kite-shaped track excursion of the Santa Fe system in California, which was a one-day trip, to the Denver and Rio Grande's celebrated five-day trip, "Around the Circle," of a thousand miles. Stagecoaches met the trains to carry tourists to points of special interest and back with no more than necessary loss of time: the drive through the Mariposa Grove was so arranged that the "tourist can 'do' the greater number of the trees without the trouble of leaving the coach. . . ." [2]

By the nineties short line and branch railroads were running sight-seeing trips to some of the more spectacular Western mountain peaks, following the examples of New England and Switzerland, where Henry James had dourly expected "to see the summit of Monte Rosa heated by steam-tubes and adorned with a hotel setting three tables d'hote a day." Mount Washington had a railway in 1869, Pikes Peak (after attempts as early as 1880) in 1890, Mount Lowe, near Pasadena, in 1893, and Mount Tamalpais in 1896. By 1900 there was rail service to the edge

[2] L. F. Chapin: *Thirty Years in Pasadena* . . . (n. p.; 1929), Vol. I, pp. 269–70; [Charles E. Harrington:] *Summering in Colorado* (Denver: Richards & Co.; 1874), p. 99; Lambourne: *Pine Branches and Sea Weeds*, p. 33.

of the Grand Canyon, by 1907 to El Portal, a short ride from the Yosemite Valley. Arrived among the clouds, the traveler found a restaurant or hostelry, as "Ye Alpine Tavern" on Mount Lowe; at Pikes Peak he could send telegrams to friends and, descending, buy a newspaper listing his name among the day's visitors. "Americans often seem to travel for the mere satisfaction of going through a new country, and staying the night in a new hotel," observed an Englishman. "They add them to their collection, so to say, as an entomologist adds a beetle." Sometimes they seemed under a kind of joyless compulsion to follow the routine that the guidebook prescribed in the time allotted between trains. (Visitors to Santa Fe "read every inscription, because it is their duty to. They are here but two days, and must see everything.")[3] It had become possible, by the nineties, to tally up visits to some of the hitherto most inaccessible of places by the simple process of buying additional railroad coupons, and with little more physical effort than it took to collect the silver souvenir spoons that remain in Victorian sideboard drawers as testimonials of such adventures.

Penetrating to mountaintops and valleys that had withstood the efforts of the pioneers, and finding in some of them the familiar comforts of the East, the typical tourist of the generation after the Civil War nevertheless found the impact of the wild West profoundly disturbing. When the Far West was only Iowa, many travelers had rejoiced

[3] Henry James: *Transatlantic Sketches* (4th ed.; Boston: J. R. Osgood and Company, 1888), p. 231; G. W. Steevens: *The Land of the Dollar* (2d ed.; Edinburgh: W. Blackwood and Sons; 1897), p. 253; Clarence A. Miller: "A City in the Old West," *Overland*, Vol. IV, 2d series (October 1884), p. 339.

ORDEAL BY WILDERNESS

to discover that prairie country was not necessarily flat and swampy, as the wet prairie lands of Indiana. Accustomed to associate wilderness with dense forest growth, they amused and reassured themselves by the fancy that they were "travelling through scenes embellished by the hand of art." The rolling meadows were lawns or parks, broken by "groves and clumps of trees . . . scattered . . . to beautify the landscape. . . ." "It seemed," wrote a French hunter, "as if we had been introduced, by some sudden enchantment, into the fair image of an English garden, designed by one of the most skilful horticulturists of Great Britain. . . . It would have been easy for us to fancy ourselves in front of a paddock belonging to an opulent Lancashire farmer." In anticipation they could see the towns and mills along the river banks, oxen displacing the buffalo.[4] But even Iowa lost some of its charms as the rawness of the first occupation replaced the promise of primeval nature; the wildflowers vanished long before thrifty beds of sage, mint, asters, and primroses blended the farmhouse into the landscape. And the high plains and the mountains lay beyond.

Awakening as his Pullman car crossed the plains of the Platte, west of Fort Kearney, the tourist found himself on a desert that was almost continuous, in one form or another, until he reached the promised land of California.

[4] J. B. Newhall: *Sketches of Iowa, or, The Emigrant's Guide* . . . (New York: J. H. Colton; 1841), pp. 15, 19–21; Benedict Revoil: *The Hunter and Trapper in North America* . . . , trans. by W. H. D. Adams (London: T. Nelson and Sons; 1875), p. 31; Dorothy A. Dondore: *The Prairie and the Making of Middle America* . . . (Cedar Rapids: The Torch Press; 1926), pp. 157–8, 178–9.

[61]

"There will our fight with savage nature cease," wrote a New Englander traveling by private car in 1886, "and . . . we shall, like the Athenians of old, 'delicately march in pellucid air.' We must cross deserts and scale mountains till we reach the Eden of the West and tread the Hall of Montezuma." It was impossible meanwhile for the æsthetic imagination to take roots in rocks and sand. Oases like the parks of Colorado were for the most part off the main track; one had to put into port, so to speak, for such relief from fifteen hundred miles or more of stark and unfriendly wilderness. "The only good thing yet discovered in the Rocky Mountains," remarked an early excursionist, "was a government subsidy. . . ." "They are as far from beauty as haggardness is remote from health." "What a tremendous old stoneyard." "The general appearance of the country was more repulsive to the eye than I thought to find it," said a visitor to Colorado in 1876. "If her wealth consisted in the beauty of her external appearances, then she truly would be one of the poorest countries on the face of nature." Even Pikes Peak, for all its fame and historic associations, oppressed the senses: "the dreariness of the desolate peak itself scarcely dissipates the dismal spell, for you stand in a hopeless confusion of dull stones piled upon each other in odious ugliness, without one softening influence, as if nature, irritated with her labor, had flung her confusion here in utter desperation." The common reaction was not unlike that of the seventeenth-century Englishman, James Howell, who had complained of the "high and hideous" Alps, which bore nothing useful as the mountains in Wales did: "these uncouth huge monstrous excrescences of nature, bear nothing (most of them) but craggy stones." [5]

West of the continental divide one crossed wastes that not even the early railroad-promoters had ventured to boost.

> We strike the Great Desert
> With its wilderness howl,
> With its cactus and sage,
> With its serpent and owl,
> And its pools of dead water,
> Its torpid old streams,
> The corpse of an earth
> And the nightmare of dreams. . . .

The Santa Fe Railway (1886) promised of Arizona and California east of Mojave little more than that they were no worse than Nevada, which was inflicted on those who chose to go farther north: its desert was "the narrowest and cleanest of all those howling wildernesses which, by a peculiar dispensation of Providence, every transcontinental line must cross." In later years, when the reputation of Southwestern scenery was changing, an English traveler found a wholly unexpected delight in western Colorado and Utah: "this desert . . . was the one thing that nobody seems to have thought it worth while to advertise,

[5] Mrs. J. Gregory Smith: *Notes of Travel in Mexico and California* (St. Albans, Vt.: Printed at the Messenger and Advertiser Office; 1886), p. 6; *Cincinnati Excursion* (1870), p. 28; J. T. Reister: *Sketches of Colorado. Valuable Information . . .* (Macon, Mo.: Examiner Printing Company; 1876), pp. 51–2; Bickham: *From Ohio to the Rocky Mountains,* p. 118; James Howell: *Epistolae Ho-Elianae . . .* (Boston: Houghton Mifflin Company; 1907), Vol. I, pp. 112–13.

and the one thing that no words can overpraise or equal."
The Mesa Verde area, said an early visitor, was one "of
the very worst portions of the United States": "repulsive
plains of dry and thirsty sand, whose dreary waste is di-
versified only by jagged buttes and the splintered remains
of volcanic dikes." The Arizona mountains were "only
giant dust heaps, tumbled in inextricable confusion"; the
desert cactus "the most unlovely vegetable creation on
earth," "the reptile of the vegetable world." And the central route offered chiefly the distraction of a side trip to
Salt Lake City, with the æsthetic relief of fertile fields as
well as the spectacle of interesting marital associations
("One feels like taking off his hat to Brigham Young; and
but for his fearful social faults, one might do so"); Nevada was no better than Arizona. "Nature has denied to
this wretched region any compensation of flower, stream,
bird, or even curiosity," wrote the author of a volume on
Our Country's Scenic Marvels (1893). "It is the very
nakedness of bleak desolation, and stretches its cursed
length through a distance of 600 miles." A Raymond and
Whitcomb tourist expressed surprise when a cowboy told
her that he had lived in Nevada for twenty-five years.
"Whatever did you find to do here that long?" she asked.
And the exile valiantly sustained her impressions: "Oh!
I drink whisky mostly. I don't drink it like you drink, I
just swalleys it right down." [6]

[6] Benjamin F. Taylor: *Between the Gates* (10th ed.; Chicago: S. C. Griggs and Company; 1883), p. 12; Santa Fe time-
table, February 1886; Steevens: *Land of the Dollar*, p. 227; Ernest Ingersoll: *Knocking round the Rockies* (New York: Harper
& Brothers; 1883); pp. 163–4; Blake: *On the Wing*, pp. 82–3;
D. N. Richardson: *A Girdle Round the Earth* (Chicago: A. C.

The impact of the West must have been all the greater because of the contrast between the stark reaches of the desert and the ornately carved and upholstered Pullman car from which the tourist looked out on them, a little piece of the East both to its passengers and to the Westerners who came to the station to inspect the day's arrivals. On the tracks "the magnificent palace-cars shone forth in all their pristine grandeur of plate glass, polished metal, highly varnished wood . . . luxurious velvet, mahogany, and silver-mounted interior;" alongside, "the flimsy mushroom 'city' of matchboard houses, uncouthly new, grotesquely tasteless. . . ." G. A. Sala, the British journalist, was surprised to find the Pullman restaurant cars similar to those in England, although the American bill of fare carried more dainties; but outside the Pullman lay the world of the pioneer. Lord Dunraven tells of how he and his wife, arriving at Fort McPherson, Nebraska, in 1871, "found ourselves, when we stepped on to the platform, plunged suddenly into the wild and woolly West." The train was "like a slice out of one of the Eastern cities set down bodily in the midst of a perfect wilderness." As a triumph of modern engineering and industrial enterprise it sometimes stirred the imagination more than the backbone of a continent over which it strode, so that the adventurous could find excitement in it, as the quintessence of physical energy, while the timid clung to the reassurance of familiar comforts. "What a fierce wild pleasure," wrote

McClurg and Company; 1888), p. 2; J. W. Buel: *America's Wonderlands. A Pictorial and Descriptive History of our Country's Scenic Marvels* . . . (Boston: J. S. Round; 1893), p. 182; William H. Wiley and Sara K. Wiley: *The Yosemite, Alaska, and the Yellowstone* (London: J. Wiley & Sons; [1893]), p. 82.

Walt Whitman on a trip to the Rockies in 1879, "to lie in my berth at night in the luxurious palace-car, drawn by the mighty Baldwin—embodying, and filling me, too, full of the swiftest motion, and most resistless strength! . . . The element of danger adds zest to it all. On we go, rumbling and flashing, with our loud whinnies thrown out from time to time, or trumpet-blasts, into the darkness." The railroad, he thought as his enthusiasm mounted, was perhaps the most signal illustration of growth beyond primitive barbarism. In an age when the very sound of a train's whistle seemed like a magic incantation, calling into life the commerce, wealth, and civilization that Westerners dreamed of, there was no greater drama in a barren landscape.[7]

Yet it was more than boredom that repelled the traveler in the desert, more than the counterattraction of the locomotive, though boredom came easily to a generation of Americans that liked to take its pleasure on the run, intensely, gregariously, and according to schedule. It was likewise more than physical discomfort, though alkali dust regularly filtered in through the cracks to coat faces and clothing and plush upholstery in Nevada, and slow schedules made it impossible to avoid the burning desert heat during the summer months. Discomfort and even pain regularly attended visits to many of the wonders manda-

[7] William A. Baillie-Grohman: *Camps in the Rockies* . . . (New York: Charles Scribner's Sons; 1882), p. 292; Sala: *America Revisited*, Vol. II, p. 139; Dunraven: *Past Times and Pastimes* (London: Hodder and Stoughton Limited; 1922), Vol. I, pp. 72–3; Walt Whitman: *Complete Prose Works* (New York: D. McKay; 1914), pp. 132–3; *West Shore*, Vol. XVI (May 3, 1890), p. 546.

tory on the grand tour: a whole generation of early tourists to the Yosemite could share affectionate memories with Mrs. Cady Stanton, who had alternately walked and slid into the valley because she was too broad to ride, and arrived "perfectly exhausted, having sent the guide . . . [for] a wheelbarrow or four men with a blanket to transport me to the hotel." [8]

Eventually a carriage road went into the Yosemite, and eventually the railroads learned to settle the dust along their roadbeds with oil, but there was still a vast gulf between the nature that the English romantic poets admired and nature west of the Missouri River. It consisted partly in the difference between places that the poet had already seen and praised and those that, by accident, he had not; partly in the difference between the American West and Eastern and English landscapes that were more civilized than their literary admirers realized or admitted. When the lake poets sought the refining and purifying influences of nature, they looked to pastures, plowed fields, and village skylines that had known the hand of man longer than some of the new factory towns that they scorned. It is true that Wordsworth and Shelley and Byron lived in a revolutionary age and felt a revolutionary or democratic passion as foreign to the middle-class tourists of the eighties as the passion of Walt Whitman; that the tourist who knew some of their verses was likely to be ignorant of their philosophy; and yet one may wonder whether Southey and Coleridge would have enjoyed the solitudes

[8] Elizabeth Cady Stanton: *Eighty Years and More (1815–1897)* . . . (New York: European Publishing Company; 1898), pp. 292–3.

of Utah, whether Byron would have found wild nature as appealing among the insect-eating aboriginals of the Pacific Coast as among the descendants of the Hellenes, whether even Wordsworth would have found the fundamental virtues as easily in a half-breed trapper a thousand miles west of Omaha as in the simple cotter he saw from the window of his study, content in his orderly simplicity as his ancestors since the Norman conquest.

But the West, lacking the pleasant pastoral landscapes of rural England, offered not only the untamed desert but the setting of a national history far too recent and too threatening to incorporate into a philosopher's picture of nature expressing the moral purpose of the universe. In contrast to the ordeals by saddle and stagecoach that were invariably good material for caricature, the real dangers and hardships of the West were far too close to incorporate entirely into the realms of the humorous, the romantic, and the picturesque. "There is perhaps a sort of shamefulness in sitting in a dining-car," wrote Christopher Morley, riding through Iowa in 1933, "looking out on the Overland Trail which was beaten through in furious toil and danger." Such thoughts were less likely to occur to the traveler while others were still walking. As late as 1881 the threat of raids in the Southwest led the Santa Fe Railway to provide trains with Winchester rifles, and passengers to feel that they were re-enacting and equaling the perils of the pioneer wagon-crossings. (Recalling the trials of a woman who had crossed the desert in 1853, a tourist supposed that "the inconveniences she experienced were not really much greater to her than ours were to us.") Although Indians were doing war dances and otherwise

exhibiting themselves for the entertainment of excursionists as early as 1866, when the first railroad tourist parties
went west of the Missouri, the Indian as a major tourist
attraction, as featured advertising copy, as a human
equivalent to the geographical curiosities of earlier generations, belongs to the twentieth century. While the war
whoop still echoed over the plains he might seem more con-
temptible than dangerous; he was considerably less than
attractive, even to those who took proud pleasure in the
contrast between "uncouth savages . . . low and brutal
in their habits," and the "beauty, intelligence, and refinements" of the excursionists.[9] There was an uncomfortable
aspect of proximity in the Indian, the emigrant train, and
the homesteader's cabin, which represented the experience
and the peril of the race if not of the individual; the tourist who found such scenes repugnant or uninteresting was
likely, on the other hand, to enjoy quite unreservedly the
Chinese opium dens in San Francisco through which his
guide led him on a pre-arranged schedule without a hint
that the danger and the degradation were less than they
seemed to be.

The nature that the tourist professed to admire, in ef-

[9] Christopher Morley: *Internal Revenue* (Garden City:
Doubleday, Doran & Company; 1933), p. 95; Loring Converse:
Notes of What I Saw . . . (Bucyrus, Ohio: Forum Steam Printing House: 1882), pp. 19–22, 27; [Silas Seymour:] *Incidents of
a Trip through the Great Platte Valley, to the Rocky Mountains
and Laramie Plains* . . . (2d ed.; New York: D. Van Nostrand;
1867), pp. 86, 89–90; Baron de Hübner: *A Ramble Round the
World, 1871*, trans. by Lady Herbert (New York: Macmillan
and Co.; 1874), p. 68; Grace Greenwood: *My Life in New Lands*,
p. 349; "Dance of the Crow Indians," *Harper's Weekly*, Vol.
XXVII (December 15, 1883), pp. 798–9.

fect, must not be too natural, or too close to the history of
the long struggle of Americans across a continent. Looking down from a mountaintop, he found himself searching
hungrily for signs of human occupation, and fixing with
a sense of relief on tent or cabin. Such, said one critic of
American scenery, was the superiority of Mount Washington, overlooking a New England landscape of "brightness
and life, smooth pastures and pretty houses," to Long's
Peak. A group of travelers in western Wyoming gratefully
took refuge in a "little glade," "weary with incessant far-
seeing" and "thankful that we could not see even the
loftiest summits. . . ." [1]

It is not altogether accidental that the places where
tourists stayed longest, in Colorado and California, were
those where art had repaired the omissions of nature, or
nature seemed to counterfeit art, as in the parks of Colorado. Visitors to the Ralston estate south of San Francisco, near what is now Stanford University, wondered
"why the forest trees are not cut down and fruit trees
planted in their stead." ("They were answered that the
forest trees were preferable, being much cleaner and nicer
for the shade of a park.") The great winter nature festival
of southern California was the Pasadena Tournament of
Roses, somewhat belligerently staged on New Year's Day,
when even Pasadena's roses sometimes were not at their
best, rather than a pilgrimage to the uncultivated displays
of cactus blossoms on the desert. When the winter visitors

[1] W. H. Rideing in William C. Bryant, eds.: *Picturesque
America* . . . (New York: D. Appleton and Company; 1872–4),
Vol. II, p. 488; Ernest Ingersoll: *Knocking round in the Rockies*
(New York: Harper & Brothers; 1883), p. 206.

at southern California hotels were in the mood for "more active contact with Nature," they turned to "orange groves and . . . grassy lawns, where breezes fan but do not ruffle," instead of to the mountains nearby. Hikers found few trails, though many carriage roads and eventually a multiplicity of electric railroad routes; the sightseer on foot was as much out of place as in twentieth-century metropolitan Los Angeles. As a writer in *Overland* remarked (1897), people went to the fashionable resorts "not to worship nature, but to see and be seen by their kind. They play tennis and golf, swim in warmed tanks, drive behind fine horses, dress for dinner, and do all these things in the conventional and polite way." [2]

In later years historians of the American West had to penetrate a maze of mythology that made the frontier seem wilder than it was when it was wildest. The legend of nineteenth-century Western barbarism and violence may have been in large part the work of twentieth-century promoters and escapists. Yet there were those who fled then from what attracts us now. The Western resident himself smarted under the stigma of backwardness, and striving to hide the raw edges of what he built, hoped for the compliments and the assistance that visitors and investors might give. He showed the Easterner what he wanted the Easterner to see as well as what the Easterner himself wanted

[2] Mrs. Caroline M. Churchill: *Over the Purple Hills: Or, Sketches of Travel in California of Important Points Usually Visited by Tourists* (Chicago: Hazlitt & Reed, Printers, 1877), p. 12; Edward S. Parkinson: *Wonderland* . . . (Trenton: Mac-Crellish & Quigley, Printers; 1894), p. 10; Charles S. Greene: "Where the Gray Squirrel Hides," *Overland*, 2d series, Vol. XXX (July 1897), p. 62.

to see, and often the two images were not much different. Most Middle Westerners and Easterners meanwhile could not dissociate themselves from the roughness of the West, both genuine and synthetic. It was their fathers' past, for the frontier was not far behind in any American state, as historical time runs, and it was their own or their children's future, for Americans felt themselves a part of the tide that was sweeping over the continent. It was their boast and their shame. It was a part of the present, too, on which their fortunes rested and for which others might praise or reproach them. Sometimes it may have been most in mind when it was least on lips. It fascinated those who were not pioneers as war sometimes fascinates and misleads those who are not soldiers; sometimes in fascinating it attracted, and sometimes it repelled.

3. DISCOVERERS
OF THE WILD WEST

THE TOURIST of the post-Civil War generation seemed in
the main to demand of the American West that it corres-
pond closely to standards that were Eastern rather than
Western, and generally feminine rather than masculine.
Yet there were other tourists, few but early on the scene,
and conspicuous beyond their numbers, who represented a
kind of outpost of masculinity in a feminine jurisdiction,
and tried to meet the West on its own terms. European
travel surpassed anything in America for women, wrote
an English visitor. "But for men, or rather for sportsmen,
America offers an unrivalled field." Hunters and sportsmen had gone west long before the railroad, though Pullman cars carried them on a vaster scale. Wild nature, said

a writer in *Chambers's Miscellany* (1845), would be "altogether unendurable by persons accustomed to the quiet and orderly life of cities. Strange as it seems, however, there are highly cultivated individuals who, inspired by a love of science, or for the mere sake of sport, voluntarily make part of the fur-trading bands, and consent to remain for years from home, friends, and the world of refinement." [1] In the second half of the nineteenth century they turned increasingly to North America.

The hunter-tourist seems to appear on every hand in the trans-Mississippi West. He is almost a regular fixture of the Western Army post, where the officers and their wives are glad for a change of society; occasionally by special permission he follows a military expedition in the field. He likewise follows the fur traders and railroad surveyors and builders, and when the railroad is built he shortly rides it with his trophies. He is guest at farmhouse and cattle ranch; often he becomes a rancher and is host to his friends. The Scottish sportsman, Sir William Drummond Stewart, joined Nathaniel Wyeth's party of missionaries en route to Oregon in 1834; Sir George Gore hobnobbed in the 1850's with Jim Bridger, who addressed him as "Mister Gore" while they discussed Shakespeare over the campfire. While most of the early hunters who penetrated well beyond the Mississippi attached themselves to parties of traders, as early as 1843 about eighty hunters—"the first pleasure party that ever went up," according to one of

[1] Boddam-Whetham: *Western Wanderings*, p. 363; "Excursion to the Oregon," *Chambers's Miscellany*, Vol. III, No. 138 (Edinburgh [1845?]), p. 2 (introduction to selections from John K. Townsend: *Sporting Excursions in the Rocky Mountains* [London: H. Colburn; 1840]).

them—spent five months on a trip that extended from St. Louis sixty or seventy miles across the continental divide.[2]

The typical hunter-tourist was an Easterner or Englishman of independent income; sometimes he brought substantial amounts of it to the field, in the shape of his outfit. Stewart traveled in 1843 with Conestoga wagons bearing provisions and servants to tend him. A group of three young Englishmen, inspired by stories of self-reliance and independence in books by James Fenimore Cooper and George Frederick Ruxton, started out from St. Louis with only seven attendants, but one of the party lamented before the trip was over: "If I ever get out of this d——d mess, I'll never go anywhere without my own French cook." Some took their English dogs, planning to hunt in style; Sir George Gore probably established a record with a retinue of forty men, one hundred twelve horses, twelve yoke of oxen, fourteen dogs, six wagons, and twenty-one carts. On the other hand, a few took as little as a "knife, flint of steel, and pipe, an iron ladle for melting lead, a tin mug, and two iron kettles," coffee, sugar, and salt.[3]

After the Civil War the hunters increased, as the rail-

[2] R. Rowland to Mrs. M. A. Rowland, St. Louis, January 9, 1844 (Iowa State Historical Society).

[3] George F. Ruxton: *Life in the Far West*, LeRoy R. Hafen, ed. (Norman: University of Oklahoma Press; [1951]), pp. 133–7; Henry J. Coke: *A Ride over the Rocky Mountains to Oregon and California* (London: R. Bentley; 1852), reviewed in *Blackwood's*, Vol. LXXI (February 1852), pp. 187–96; Grantley F. Berkeley: *The English Sportsman in the Western Prairies* (London: Hurst & Blackett; 1861), pp. 5–6, 116; *Contributions*, Vol. I, Montana Historical Society (Helena: 1876), pp. 144–8; John Palliser: *Solitary Rambles and Adventures of a Hunter in the Prairies* (London: J. Murray; 1853), pp. ix–x.

heads pushed westward into the mountains and as more Americans acquired the vacation habit. Even in the early 1870's, before the dandies of Long Island had begun fox hunting with Irish hounds, hunters and Army officers in the Far West, who usually followed game more than Indians, were already affecting the British breechloader and dogs of English breed, and beginning to turn from prairie chickens and buffalo to the so-called nobler game, such as the wapiti, which called for the skill of the stalker and marksman rather than the appetite of the harvester. In the eighties the Northern clubhouses were multiplying along the south Atlantic coast, as on Pamlico Sound, but chiefly for the benefit of those interested in short trips and small game or, as the lodges became more elaborate, the sport—for wives and daughters—of hunting unmarried millionaires. Other alternatives, almost as easy, had come to hand. The railroad meant that suddenly one could ride in luxury from New York in four days, from Liverpool in ten, to ranges that recently had been at least as many weeks away from civilization. As a writer in *Tinsley's Magazine* put it: "Now that locomotion is so rapid that a man can have a picnic over the bones of Ptolemy, a flirtation with the fair maids of Cashmere, or a few days' shooting with the last of the Mohicans, as easily as his great-grandfather could get from end to end of his own tight little island, few of nature's most secluded spots will long remain unpolluted by the irrepressible American's tobacco-juice, or unprofaned by the ubiquitous Britain's empty pale-ale bottles and greasy sandwich papers." "We stepped," wrote two hunters along the Little Bighorn in the nineties, "as it were, from a teepee into a Pullman car. . . ." The Far

West was no longer really far to a man with the right kind
of bank account, and for the time, at least, it offered the
abundant game of virgin wilderness within easy reach of
traveling bedrooms and restaurants and of trained guides
who could point it out, and bring it down if necessary, all
at a cost that, though still high, had greatly diminished.
Moreton Frewen, later brother-in-law to Mrs. Randolph
Churchill, went by rail to Rawlins, Wyoming, at General
Phil Sheridan's suggestion in 1878, to take "the old
'Bridger Trail'—a trail as well known to touring sports-
folk as is the Engadine to Cook's tourists." [4] And although
the hunters were numerous enough, by the seventies, to
justify special railroad excursions and special advertising,
yet in the high Rockies, beyond the main buffalo pastures,
they were few enough still to command hearty welcomes
from ranchers and Army officers.

Socially and economically the Far Western hunter-
tourist of the generation after the Civil War was at least
an equal, on the average, of the winter guests at the Raymond and the Del Monte. He probably surpassed them.
Some Englishmen talked of economy, as of how they could
hunt in Colorado at less than the cost of maintaining a

---

[4] Dixon Wecter: *The Saga of American Society* (New York:
Charles Scribner's Sons; 1937), pp. 446–7; Theodore Roosevelt:
The Wilderness Hunter (New York: G. P. Putnam's Sons;
1900), p. 153; Dunraven; *Great Divide*, p. 11; [George A.
Lawrence:] *Silverland* (London: Chapman and Hull; 1873), p.
135; Hamil Grant: *Two Sides of the Atlantic* . . . (London:
Richards; 1917), pp. 214–16; "Sport in the West," *Tinsley's
Magazine*, Vol. XII (July 1873), p. 621; "With Gun and Palette
among the Redskins," *Outing*, Vol. XXV (February 1895), p.
363; Moreton Frewen: *Melton Mowbray and other Memories*
(London: H. Jenkins Limited; 1924), p. 156.

private preserve in Scotland or a house in London, but a Victoria editor contended that hunters from overseas left at least a hundred pounds for each beast that they took out. The amateur naturalist, Paul Fountain, estimated that six months in Arizona in 1871 had cost him nearly eight thousand dollars, not reckoning the neglect of his business. The railroads made it possible to dispense with some costs but also to add others. Some hunters hired private cars, as a party who stopped here and there for six weeks along the Northern Pacific in the eighties with their own cook and porter; some built their own, expressly for hunting. An added refinement was a refrigerator car for the game. In 1871 a party of wealthy friends of Lieutenant General Sheridan traveled by private Pullman palace car, dining in their own hotel car en route, from New York City to Nebraska, where they met Buffalo Bill Cody.[5]

Perhaps the most expensive and aristocratic hunters were those who were also ranchers and thus had their permanent hunting lodges. The two occupations were almost inextricably mixed. Some sportsmen invested in ranches with their former guides or independently became

[5] F. Barham Zincke: *Last Winter in the United States* . . . (London: J. Murray; 1868), pp. 252–3; William A. Baillie-Grohman: *Fifteen Years' Sport and Life in the Hunting Grounds of Western America and British Columbia* (London: H. Cox; 1900), p. 40; Paul Fountain: *The Great Deserts and Forests of North America* (London: Longmans, Green, and Co.; 1901), pp. 132, 163; A. B. Guptill: "Sport along the Northwestern Border," *Outing*, Vol. XVI (August 1890), pp. 372–3; J. Parker Whitney: *Reminiscences of a Sportsman* (New York: Forest and Stream Publishing Co.; 1906) p. 8; William B. Mershon: *Recollections of My Fifty Years Hunting and Fishing* (Boston: The Stratford Company; 1923), pp. 112–15; [Henry E. Davies:] *Ten Days on the Plains* (New York: Crocker & Co.; [1871]).

stock raisers, liking the life both for the sport in it and because it seemed "more befitting a gentleman than commerce or agriculture." "If the stockman has the faculty to select good men," said a writer in the *Fortnightly Review,* "he need not make himself a prisoner in his ranch, but may treat himself to a month's hunting in the mountains, or even to a trip to England, without imperilling his interests." There were hunters who thus persuaded themselves that their pleasure was by-product of a sound business investment; on the other hand, an experienced sportsman, William Baillie-Grohman, advised prospective ranchers to hunt while looking for range land or learning the details of the business, thus improving their bargaining position and saving themselves annoyance from land agents. Before the collapse of the cattle boom in the eighties there were ranches clearly proportioned to the sporting tastes of Easterners and Englishmen rather than to the demands of the cattle business. The aristocracy of two continents were guests of Moreton Frewen, who entered their trophies in his visitors' book with their names. Frewen had built his ranch house in 1879 on the Powder River near the Big Horns ("at such a distance we would be let alone"), spending about forty thousand dollars, which covered shingles and furniture from Chicago and hardwood from England. His neighbors accepted Frewen, whose enthusiasm for the cattle business was as unrestrained as any Westerner's— or any Englishman's—but his interest in adding a vast game-sanctuary to Yellowstone Park seems to mark him as the hunter-gentleman as well as the rancher. Considerably more in the genteel tradition were the Potter Palmers of Chicago, who owned a ranch north of Laramie between

1886 and 1894. By the time Theodore Roosevelt bought his first ranch on the Little Missouri in 1883, ultimately at a cost of over seventy thousand dollars for about ten years of use, the aristocratic invasion had gone so far that it was said that nine tenths of those in the stock business were gentlemen. "The new West," said a writer in *Lippincott's,* "is largely peopled today with the sons of families in which learning and culture have long been hereditary." Most were less spectacularly aristocratic than Roosevelt's colorful neighbor and antagonist on the Little Missouri, the young Marquis de Mores, who rode out to the chase in style from his chateau with servants and hounds, but few were unresponsive to the lure of sport. Though many had to sell out after the bad years of the later eighties, the tradition changed rather than disappeared. Before the end of the century Eastern sporting clubs, which had begun to establish enclosures in the Adirondacks in the eighties, were planning vast game parks in Wyoming and beyond.[6]

[6] W. Baillie-Grohman: "Cattle Ranches in the Far West," *Fortnightly Review,* new series, Vol. XXVIII (September 1880), p. 450; J. W. Barclay: "Colorado," *Fortnightly Review,* new series, Vol. XXVII (January 1880), p. 126; Pidgeon: *An Engineer's Holiday,* p. 126; William A. Baillie-Grohman: *Camps in the Rockies* . . . (New York: Charles Scribner's Sons; 1882), p. 429; Frewen: *Melton Mowbray,* pp. 168, 172–85, 204; Major Lewis L. A. Wise: "Diary . . . ," Howard B. Lott, ed., *Annals of Wyoming,* Vol. XII (April 1940), pp. 87–92; Forbes Parkhill: *The Wildest of the West* (New York: Henry Holt & Co.; 1951), pp. 257–9; George R. Buckman: "Ranches and Ranchers of the Far West," *Lippincott's Magazine,* new series, Vol. XXIX (May 1882), p. 435; Usher L. Burdick: *Marquis de Mores at War in the Bad Lands* (Fargo: privately printed; 1929); "Sporting Clubs in the Adirondacks," *Outing,* Vol. XVI (April 1890), pp. 74–5; Braillie-Grohman: *Fifteen Years' Sport,* p. 28.

The gentleman clearly had penetrated not only along the Western railroads but deep into the interior. In some of the wildest parts of the continent, the count of millionaires, sportsmen, and acceptable dinner partners ran higher than in the great Eastern cities. Inevitably some failed to fit the West, or the West them. It was not necessarily easy for a wealthy English nobleman, as an extreme case, without any pioneer ancestors later than the Norse voyagers of the early Middle Ages, to appreciate Western scenery and Western society. The barriers of international prejudice shut out the foreigner, and while the crags and moors of Scotland may have resembled some Western landscape, there was a vast change, as one rancher complained, from "Britain's green hills and mossy woods to the dull yellow browns of the 'Rockies'. . . ." Mingling on equal terms with the "lower classes" was a traumatic experience for some who were accustomed to the deference of the European servant or small farmer, and even for some Easterners. Some hunters were, as an English traveler complained (1869) of his own countrymen, "most offensive in their snobbishness." And the great Western hotels drew many who cared little for the outdoors. The guests at the Raymond who rode out to the hunt at the sound of a horn probably had moved West only geographically.[7]

Yet few appreciated nature and Western life more than the sportsman in the West beyond the plains where hunting consisted of dropping quantities of buffalo without

[7] "Some Realities of Ranching," *Chambers's Journal*, Vol. LXI (October 11, 1884), p. 653; M. Philips Price: *America After Sixty Years* (London: G. Allen & Unwin; 1936), p. 29; Charles F. Holder: *All About Pasadena and its Vicinity* (Boston: Lee and Shepard; 1889), pp. 89–96.

regard for skill or trophy. It is true that often the hunter did not know enough to discriminate, and fell victim to the pseudo-Buffalo Bills in embroidered buckskin suits who infested hotel bars and railroad stations at Cheyenne and Denver; yet often his error sprang in large part from a zeal for the Western atmosphere that repelled most tourists. Often he frankly was not interested primarily in the climactic thrill of bagging the game but in the life outdoors. There were far better places than California for sport and large game, said a contributor to *Field* in the sixties: "No, it's the camp out, the glorious climate, the sense of freedom and health." "What we shall do for relief and recuperation I know not," exclaimed a veteran of many trips in the Middle West (1869), "when every Umbagog has a steamer on it, and every White Mountain has a railroad to its top, and every charming nook of wilderness has a first-class hotel and dress dinners. For the joys and profits of the camp lie in its difficulties, physical exertions, denials, and glorious distances from anybody." [8] Artificiality and arrogance could not easily last long in the true wilds, especially as guides met superior airs with tactics that not only fatigued the hunter but defeated the very purpose of his visit; usually the successful sportsman learned to leave his rank at his Pullman car.

The English hunter stood in a special relationship to the

[8] Oliver North: *Rambles after Sport* . . . (London: Field Office; 1874), p. 268; Thomas Carson: *Ranching, Sport and Travel* (London: T. F. Unwin; 1912), pp. 42–3; John M. Murphy: *Rambles in Northwestern America* . . . (London: Chapman and Hall; 1879), pp. 3–5; William Barrows: *The General; or, Twelve Nights in the Hunters' Camp.* . . . (Boston: Lee and Shepard; 1869), p. 225.

West, among other hunters. As a foreigner the Englishman was free of the burden of governing and assimilating
the new country; he had no responsibility for it. A contrast
between the West and the East, or between the West and
Europe, amounted to an interesting novelty rather than
to a reproach against one's own national culture. Although
Englishmen invested liberally in the Far West, their investments in the range cattle industry gave them no direct
stake in seeing the West fill up with farms and cities on
the Eastern model, but rather more in seeing it remain as
wilderness; and this was true especially when their investments had followed on their hunting. Sometimes they may
have admired the American prairies the more for showing
the potentialities of Canada, but the problems of forestall-
ing Indian attacks and meeting the complaints of American miners and farmers fell on other shoulders. They were
neither the Englishman's heritage nor his future. Further,
he had a head start even among Europeans in his outdoor
interests as in his factories: English Alpinists preceded
the French, and astonished Théophile Gautier by their
zeal in the 1860's;[9] the English bathing beaches were
crowded before the warmer shores of the Mediterranean.

The detachment and the enthusiasm of the Englishman
—his complete freedom from a sense of responsibility for

[9] Charles D. Warner: "The Winter of our Content," *Harper's Monthly Magazine,* Vol. LXXXII (December 1890), p. 49;
Lester: *Atlantic to the Pacific,* p. 7; Molyneux St. John: *The Sea
of Mountains; an Account of Lord Dufferin's Tour through British Columbia in 1876* (London: Hurst and Blackett; 1877), Vol.
I, pp. 26–8; Claire-Eliane Engel: *La littérature alpestre en
France et en Angleterre aux XVIIIe et XIXe siècles* (Cham-
béry: Dardel; 1931), p. 231.

the American West and at the same time his great interest in it—took vivid shape in the personal and literary vogues of the California poets, Joaquin Miller and Bret Harte, in the seventies and eighties, the first of a series of Far Western successes in Britain that was to include Ambrose Bierce, Mark Twain, and Buffalo Bill himself. Miller, "Poet of the Sierra," caught on socially when he consented to wear a wild West costume devised for him by a British journalist friend, and for two seasons his poses and bad manners amused London society. Harte remained longer in favor and stayed on, apparently feeling that he had more of a public abroad than at home, and living more surely on his British than on his American copyrights. His popularity depended not merely on his literary skill, in which he surpassed Miller as Miller far surpassed him in personal eccentricity and offensiveness, but on his fundamentally Eastern quality, as a person and as a poet and novelist. As an Easterner, he could look with satirical amusement and later with romantic affection on episodes in frontier history and folklore that embarrassed Westerners trying to pretend that the West had grown up; and it was the East and Europe that enjoyed him most during his lifetime. He had met a cool reception in the San Francisco press when he first published "The Luck of Roaring Camp," whereas Britannia took him to her heart. Years later Walt Whitman had not forgiven him for the "miserable business" of having "taken out only a few ruffians and delirium tremens specimens, and made them representatives of California personality"; similarly, San Francisco rebuffed Miller in 1871-2 for misrepresenting the frontier in *Songs of the Sierra*, which he had published in England.

Rudyard Kipling, when he visited California in 1889, was one of a generation of Englishmen who knew the West as Harte had described it and loved it for the local color that still survived, a generation after the forty-niners, although a San Francisco newspaper reporter told him that "Bret Harte claims California but California don't claim Bret Harte." Traveling from San Francisco to Portland by train, Kipling saw the miner and M'liss and Baby Sylvester, and "waited for the flying miles to turn over the pages of the book I knew. They brought me all I desired. . . ." [1] Along with Kipling, the Englishman was likely, on the other hand, to be impatient with the dullness of a Raymond party rather than charmed with its respectability. "Why is it," asked an English visitor to southern California in 1893, who concluded that he preferred a wagon and a tent to a luxury hotel, "that all the pleasantest Americans seem to come abroad or remain in the Eastern States?" Some Englishmen, as William Baillie-Grohman, showed remarkable and sympathetic interest in frontier customs and

[1] M. M. Marberry: *Splendid Poseur: Joaquin Miller— American Poet* (New York: Crowell; 1953), pp. 77–105, 112–19; George R. Stewart: *Bret Harte, Argonaut and Exile* . . . (Boston: Houghton Mifflin Company; 1931); Martin S. Peterson: *Joaquin Miller, Literary Frontiersman* (Stanford University: Stanford University Press; 1937), pp. 63–8; Hamlin Garland: *Roadside Meetings* (New York: The Macmillan Company; 1930), pp. 447–9; "Three Uncollected St. Louis Interviews of Walt Whitman," Robert R. Hubach, ed., *American Literature*, Vol. XIV (May 1942), p. 146; Franklin Walker: *San Francisco's Literary Frontier* (New York: Alfred A. Knopf; 1939), pp. 324–50; Rudyard Kipling: *From Sea to Sea; Letters of Travel* (New York: Doubleday, Page and Company; 1920), pp. 442–3; Kipling: *American Notes*, pp. 72–4. Walker contends that San Francisco did not reject Harte's early Western verse.

dialect; some made good friends and partners of their guides and occasionally even took them on other hunting trips or back to England.[2] Such acquaintances and traveling companions could be no more embarrassing to a foreigner of secure social station than an Indian chief to be presented at court or a stag head for the trophy room.

In the long perspective of world history the New World and the Old moved together into the outdoors in the nineteenth and twentieth centuries. The industrial revolution and the revolutions in science and theology touched all continents; while England had preceded the rest of the European world, during the Victorian age both America and Europe were harvesting the fruits and the tares of an urban society, and turning to the country much as imperial Rome had turned to building villas and summer homes and celebrating in verse the pastoral beauties of rural Italy, when the barbarians were subdued. No one country took up the park movement from another, said Frederick Law Olmsted, the architect of Central Park and advocate of the Yosemite, who had guided it as it rose in the United States: "It would seem rather to have been a common spontaneous movement of that sort which we conveniently refer to the 'Genius of Civilization.' "[3] The very speed with which new styles spread from continent

[2] Charles G. Nottage: *In Search of a Climate* (London: Sampson Low, Marston & Company; 1894), p. 300; Peregrine Herne: *Perils and Pleasures of a Hunter's Life* (New York: Evans & Co.; 1858).

[3] Frederick Law Olmsted, Jr., and Theodore Kimball, eds.: *Frederick Law Olmsted, Landscape Architect, 1822–1903* (New York: G. P. Putnam's Sons; 1922–8), Vol. II, p. 14; Olmsted: "The Justifying Value of a Public Park," *Journal of Social Science* . . . , No. 12 (December 1880), pp. 152–3.

to continent showed how each was preparing to invent them itself.

Yet Americans, who as settlers of a new land had seen most of the wilderness that they were erasing under smoke and plows and railroads, were rather proud of the civilization that they built than nostalgic for what it replaced. The West attracted them, and its attraction is one of the main facts of American history, but it attracted them as something to fight and exploit more than as something to enjoy as it was. European travelers in America did not fairly represent the Old World—if they wanted civilization chiefly, they were mistaken in not staying on their own side of the ocean—but in their presence the most striking indifference to nature and the charms of outdoor life seemed to be among Americans. Perhaps Americans were too busy conquering a wilderness, as Stephen Leacock has said, to take time off for recreation. "Our people were so close in point of time to the pioneers," recalled Daniel Carter Beard, who had tried to sell nature to adults before he turned to the Boy Scouts, "that they did not appreciate the wilderness." Settlers on the frontier often seemed to ignore the scenery at their very doorsteps, like the shepherd who responded, when asked for directions near Mount Whitney, that there was nothing up there but mountains and snow; or Clarence King's Newtys of Pike; or the farmers who exclaimed at the Frémonts' camping in the Sierra Nevada. "The friendly people of the farm were horrified by our sunburned faces," recalled Mrs. Frémont. " 'Well, well,' one said, 'you looked like real ladies, but now you look like mowers,' and they saw no compensation for such roughing it." An English traveler in western

Nebraska in 1874–5 found that a group of emigrants "could not believe that I was journeying simply for pleasure, and to study the ways of birds, beasts, and fishes." One may discount some such anecdotes as overpatronizing, but cold statistics show, for instance, that Easterners and foreigners far outnumbered Californians in the Yosemite Valley in the early years. Those who had fought the elements across the continent for a home were relatively less interested in climbing mountains for amusement. "The love of Nature among Californians is desperately moderate, consuming enthusiasm almost wholly unknown," complained John Muir in 1890, when the fate of the Yosemite seemed to hang in the balance, and he blamed their opposition to retroceding the park to Congress on little more creditable than jealousy. "A man may not appreciate his wife, but let her daddie try to take her back." As late as 1912, the Santa Fe Railway estimated that one third of those who came to the Yosemite and the Grand Canyon were foreigners.[4]

The American who admired Western scenery in more than its curious or picturesque and pseudo-European as-

[4] Daniel C. Beard: *Hardly a Man Is Now Alive* . . . (New York: Doubleday, Doran & Company; 1939), p. 357; Lilias N. R. Robinson: *A Short Account of our Trip to the Sierra Nevada Mountains* (London: [J. Martin & Son; 1884]), p. 27; Jessie B. Frémont: *Far-West Sketches* (Boston: D. Lothrop Company; 1890), p. 147; Fountain: *The Great Deserts and Forests of North America*, p. 169; John Muir to Robert V. Johnson, March 4, 1890, "The Creation of Yosemite National Park . . . ," William E. Colby ed., *Sierra Club Bulletin*, Vol. XXIX (October 1944), p. 52; *Proceedings of the National Park Conference held at the Yosemite National Park*, October 14, 15, and 16, 1912 (Washington: Government Printing Office; 1913), p. 50.

pects was likely to have much in common with the foreigner. Typically he was no settler in the usual sense himself, and he seemed to labor under no personal or vicarious burden of involvement in the great task of civilizing the frontier. Somehow he had achieved a perspective from which he looked backward on the wild West as something to be enjoyed before it disappeared rather than forward on it as something that he must embrace and conquer in order to survive or to serve the national destiny. If the West was a part of his own past, there was nothing in it that shamed or pained him as he recalled it, no meanness of social background to embarrass his wife and daughters. He might have gone west in search of gold: most of the forty-niners and their successors were young and unattached (hence less restrained than their elders by feminine views of nature) and without serious intention of committing their futures to the new country; many of them traveled with the exuberance of college students on vacation, delighting in shocking their mothers and sisters with daguerreotypes of their beards and flannel shirts before they returned to the East. They succeeded to the extent that for sixty or seventy years thereafter tourists had to be reassured, and Westerners felt that they had to assure them, that the West was no longer wild and woolly—until fashions changed and it was time to convince them that it was as wild as it ever had been. That many young miners remained to settle, whether because they changed their minds or could not pay for the trip back; that many of them looked back from middle age on their youthful adventures as solemn ordeals of commonwealth building, is irrelevant in the main to the spirit in which they had gone.

Even more sympathetic, less inhibited, was the naturalist, as Charles Fenno Hoffman, George Catlin, Clarence King, or John Muir. Catlin saw Indian culture disappearing nearly half a century before most Americans considered it other than an active and present danger; when he went west in 1832, it was in hope of "snatching from a hasty oblivion what could be saved for the benefit of posterity, and perpetuating it, as a fair and just monument, to the memory of a truly lofty and noble race" threatened by "the bane of this *blasting* frontier," that is, by civilization. While the wild West was challenge and menace to most of his contemporaries, to Catlin the East menaced the West, and he looked at the wilderness with some of the painful pleasure of nostalgia: "the further we become separated (and the face of the country) from that pristine wildness and beauty, the more pleasure does the mind of enlightened man feel in recurring to those scenes, when he can have them preserved for his eyes and his mind to dwell upon." Anticipating attitudes toward nature not prevalent for several generations to come, and not unchallenged then, he imagined "(by some great protecting policy of government) preserved in their pristine beauty and wildness, in a *magnificent park*, where the world could see for ages to come, the native Indian in his classic attire, galloping his wild horse, with sinewy bow, and shield and lance, amid the fleeting herds of elk and buffaloes. . . . A *nation's Park*, containing man and beast, in all the wild and freshness of their nature's beauty." Catlin thus anticipated Henry David Thoreau, who appealed (1858) for "national preserves . . . in which the bear and panther, and some even of the hunter race, may still exist . . . not for idle sport or food, but for inspiration and our own true re-creation." [5] Both Catlin and Thoreau seemed to approach the point of view of the twentieth-century ecologist, who looks to nature for the wonders and mysteries of all creation rather than for the decorative and economic purposes of civilized man, and yet they were pre-Darwinians; their instincts were those of love and poetry rather than of science.

A generation after Catlin went West, in 1863, Clarence King, a graduate of the Sheffield Scientific School who had developed a taste for outdoor life during rambles in the Green Mountains, went to California with the twin motives of continuing his geological studies and giving a convalescent friend the benefit of open-air life. Before they arrived, the two young men "became so fascinated with the life and so interested in the vast loneliness of those deserts" that they would "gladly have turned around and traveled right back over the same road." "Civilization!" King once exclaimed. "Why, it's a nervous disease!" [6] With some of the enthusiasm of John Muir, who made devotion to the

[5] George Catlin: *Letters and Notes on the Manners, Customs, and Condition of the North American Indians* (4th ed.; London: the author; 1842), Vol. I, pp. 3, 60, 260–3, cited by Hans Huth: "Yosemite: The Story of an Idea," *Sierra Club Bulletin*, Vol. XXXIII (March 1948), pp. 47–78; Henry David Thoreau: "Chesuncook," *Atlantic Monthly*, Vol. II (August 1858), p. 317.

[6] James T. Gardiner to his mother, September 11, 1863, in David H. Dickason: "Clarence King's First Western Journey," *Huntington Library Quarterly*, Vol. VII (November 1943), pp. 72–3, 86; Clarence King: *Mountaineering in the Sierra Nevada* (Boston: J. R. Osgood and Company; 1872); Edgar B. Bronson: *Cowboy Life on the Western Plains* (New York: G. H. Doran [1910]), p. 329.

Yosemite almost a profession, King tramped through the high Sierra country where no one had gone before, and described it in magazine articles that could have the effect either of preserving the wilderness or, by attracting visitors, of hastening its destruction. It was only natural that King shared his enthusiasm through the Eastern press: he and most others of the early Alpinists and naturalists were strangers to the West, and responded to Western scenery with an outsider's sense of discovery. Catlin, Thoreau, and King were all New Englanders, John Muir a Scot, as earlier Latrobe was an Englishman, Audubon a Frenchman.

At first, till perhaps the eighties, a handful of naturalists, Easterners by origin rather than Westerners, were almost alone in their interest in conservation. When Congress turned the Yosemite Valley over to the state of California in 1864 and set aside the Yellowstone National Park in 1872, it was probably to preserve certain striking and curious phenomena rather than representative wilderness areas; characteristically, Congress omitted from the grant of 1864 the high Sierra areas beyond the Yosemite Valley that were among the chief delights of the nature lovers even before the floor of the valley became a kind of Western Coney Island. Yellowstone was far larger and far wilder, and certainly its two million acres comprehended more than natural curiosities, although Moreton Frewen contended, when he lobbied for an addition in the Wind River Basin in 1879 as a sanctuary for wild life, that the Park was worthless for protecting the great mountain fauna. As late as 1886 Senator Henry M. Teller, a former secretary of the Interior, expressed the opinion that Con-

gress should abandon control of the Yellowstone "except
the small points where these large geysers and other things
are." [7]

By the early eighties, as the Northern Pacific Railroad
and competing lines bit into the virgin areas of the Pacific Northwest, game was still plentiful in the high mountains, though the great herds of buffalo were gone; the
charm of the wilderness seemed to be quickened by a sense
that it could not last much longer. The professional hunters had a new convenience of access to market, and as yet
no one seriously restrained them. Men who knew the West
became increasingly aware that "those who would see the
wilderness as it is, must see it soon." "So rapid the advance
of civilization, that he who would seek the 'wilds of America' will only find them in Alaska." It was in 1880 that a
young Yale student, Frederic Remington, talking over a
Montana campfire with an old wagon-freighter who
mourned the coming of the railroad, realized that "the
wild riders and the vacant land were about to vanish forever," and turned to painting what was left while it was
still there. The first issue of *Forest and Stream* (1873),
whose object was "to studiously promote a healthful interest in outdoor recreation, and to cultivate a refined taste
for natural objects," had announced that it would do battle
to preserve the forests; *Outing*, which gave Remington's
drawings their first wide circulation, pictured the Far
West in large part through nostalgic and often semific-

---

[7] Frewen: *Melton Mowbray*, pp. 176–7; *Congressional Rec-
ord*, 49 Cong., 2 Sess., August 2, 1886, p. 7844, cited in Paul H.
Buck: *The Evolution of the National Park System of the United
States* (Washington: Government Printing Office; 1946), p. 15.

[93]

tional reminiscences of old hunters like Captain R. B. Marcy, who recalled days when the bighorn and the wapiti hardly knew what man was, and buffalo still carpeted the plains. Large game, predicted a contributor to *Outing* in 1888, would be practically gone in a year or two, leaving only the mountains of the larger ranges for good hunting. The Boone and Crockett Club, which Theodore Roosevelt and some of his friends founded in 1887, announced objects that included the preservation of game and the study of natural history, and set out to act as watchdog for Yellowstone and other parks; by 1891 the Rocky Mountain Sportsmen's Association had begun its pressure for fish and game legislation.[8]

Theodore Roosevelt, who became probably the best-known exponent of the wild West after Buffalo Bill Cody, left a voluminous written record of his own views of the West that makes him an apt specimen of the hunter type, though he was as unusual in this as in other facets of his character. He was one of those Easterners who operated genuine cattle ranches; he lived the ranching life at Chim-

[8] J. A. Butler: "Some Western Resorts," *Harper's Magazine*, Vol. LXV (August 1882), p. 341; I. Winslow Ayer: *Life in the Wilds of America* . . . (Grand Rapids: Central Publishing Company; 1880), pp. 15, 527; Frederic Remington: "A Few Words from Mr. Remington," *Collier's Weekly*, Vol. XXXIV (March 18, 1905), p. 16; *Forest and Stream*, Vol. I (August 14, 1873), p. 8; S. C. Robertson: "An Army Hunter's Notes on Our North-Western Game," *Outing*, Vol. XI (January 1888), p. 308; Roosevelt and George B. Grinnell: *American Big-game Hunting; the Book of the Boone and Crockett Club* (Edinburgh: D. Douglas; 1893), pp. 337–9; Roosevelt to Hoke Smith, April 7, 1894, in Roosevelt: *Letters*, Vol. I (Cambridge: Harvard University Press; 1951), p. 371; *Constitution and By-laws*, Rocky Mountain Sportsmen's Association (Denver: 1891).

ney Butte and Elkhorn, taking his turn in the saddle and at the watch, and without the minor refinements of domestic service that even so well acclimatized a Westerner as the future Earl of Portsmouth maintained on his ranch in Wyoming. "I didn't play," he protested later, insisting that he knew the West better from the inside than Hamlin Garland; "*I worked*, while on my ranch." He insisted, in the articles that he sent to the Eastern magazines during his first year in the Bad Lands, on the differences between authentic cattlemen and those unburdened by everyday work, who included professional guides and hunters. The cattlemen, he said, were "a class of residents" with a stake in the country; hunting to them was merely an occasional pleasure, or the means of providing fresh meat. "Altogether, though the ranchman will have time enough to take hunting trips, he will be very far from having time to make shooting a business, as a stranger who comes for nothing else can afford to do." [9]

Yet even Roosevelt never quite dropped the Easterner's approach to the West, or the shape of an Easterner. It was probably only accidental that he came literally in the wake of a flood of tourists, arriving at Little Missouri the day after the excursionists, guests of Henry Villard, who were on their way to celebrate the driving of the last spike on the new Northern Pacific Railroad; or that what prompted him to come was a letter from Howard Eaton, who was the first of the dude ranchers; or that his principal associates were from New Brunswick, and that another was Wil-

[9] Roosevelt to J. B. Matthews, December 7, 1894, *Letters,* Vol. I, pp. 410–11; Roosevelt: *Hunting Trips of a Ranchman* . . . (New York: G. P. Putnam's Sons; 1900), pp. 30, 35, 53–5.

liam H. Sewall, who had been his guide in the Maine woods on a vacation trip during his Harvard College days, in 1876. Certainly he cut a different figure from Villard's friends, who "seemed to think they were roughing it," recalled a witness. "They were the most helpless set of men I ever saw: they could not ride, and they were too fat to walk." But a New Yorker of independent wealth, who had become a Dakotan of sorts by writing a check for fourteen thousand dollars on his first visit, and whose national political importance penetrated even into the Bad Lands, could not seem quite like other men, even when his new neighbors had grown accustomed to his thick-lensed spectacles and he had learned to compromise with Western habits of speech. ("Hasten quickly forward there," he had once called to a cowhand in his high-pitched Harvard accent.) He might take his turn at cooking and other chores, doing them willingly though badly, but a telegram could snatch him back into another world in the East within three days. He was always "Mr. Roosevelt" to his associates. Perhaps he unconsciously revealed class-consciousness when he referred, in his magazine articles, to men that he had insisted on making technically his partners as "one of my cowhands" and "one of the foremen." Occasionally he suggests a kind of Tory democracy, as in describing himself reading *Hamlet* to a Texan cowboy, who proved to be greatly interested.[1] One may wonder if he himself

---

[1] Hermann Hagedorn: *Roosevelt in the Bad Lands* (Boston: Houghton Mifflin Company; 1921), pp. 4, 8, 110; Roosevelt: *Hunting Trips*, p. 176; Alex. Staveley Hill: *From Home to Home: Autumn Wanderings in the Northwest* . . . (New York: O. Judd Co.; 1885), p. 376; Roosevelt: *The Wilderness Hunter*

had noted the parallel to Sir George Gore's evening with Jim Bridger.

More significantly representative of his changing time was Roosevelt's attitude toward the wilderness, the attitude of an outsider who responded to it because much of it was strange and new to him and because he brought to it the perspectives of a more civilized world and of history. "I was just in time to see the last of the real wilderness life and real wilderness hunting," he told an English sportsman in 1897, well after his ranching days were over; and in his *Autobiography* (1913) the former President expressed a nostalgia that he had known even in the years of his youth: "It was still the Wild West in those days, the Far West, the West of Owen Wister's stories and Frederic Remington's drawings. . . . That land of the West has gone now, 'gone, gone with lost Atlantis,' gone to the isle of ghosts and of strange, dead memories." "For we ourselves, and the life that we lead," he wrote only a few months after he had first set foot in Dakota Territory, "will shortly pass away from the plains as completely as the red and white hunters who have vanished from before our herds. The free, open air life of the ranchman, the pleasantest and healthiest life in America, is from its very nature ephemeral." At Medora, he could see the railroad bringing in the East each day, the cattle crowding out the game, new enterprises such as the packing house of the Marquis de Mores crowding out the old life of the

. . . (New York: G. P. Putnam's Sons; 1900), pp. 45, 47; Roosevelt: *Ranch Life and the Hunting-Trail* (New York: Century Co.; 1911), p. 75.

cattlemen; [2] and as a historian he could see it in the framework of a nation's advance.

Roosevelt was writing *The Winning of the West* as well as his informal magazine articles and his life of Thomas Hart Benton during the years when he spent the most time along the Little Missouri; and while the historian depended heavily on the rancher, the rancher also depended on the historian. "We guarded our herds of branded cattle and shaggy horses," he wrote in the preface to *The Winning of the West*, "hunted bear, bison, elk, and deer, established civil government, and put down evil-doers, white and red, on the banks of the Little Missouri, and among the wooded, precipitous foothills of the Bighorn, exactly as did the pioneers who a hundred years previously built their log cabins beside the Kentucky or in the valleys of the Great Smokies." He preferred, he told Henry Cabot Lodge during his first year in Dakota, "that description of sport which needs a buckskin shirt to that whose votaries adopt the red coat"; he had himself photographed in his own fringed buckskin, standing with rifle raised to aim, before the painted sylvan backdrop of a New York studio. It is not unfair to suggest that he may have thought of his hunting shirt as a kind of hereditary badge or coat of arms linking him with the contemporaries of Daniel Boone of whom he wrote, and even with his early

[2] Roosevelt to F. C. Selous, November 30, 1897, *Letters,* Vol. I, p. 721; *Theodore Roosevelt, an Autobiography* (New York: Macmillan Company; 1913), p. 103; Roosevelt: *Hunting Trips,* p. 38; Roosevelt to Anna Roosevelt, June 17, 1884, *Letters,* Vol. I, p. 73; Lincoln A. Lang: *Ranching with Roosevelt* . . . (Philadelphia: J. B. Lippincott Company; 1926), pp. 334–49.

European ancestors who had hung their spoils in "smoky wooden palaces." Many hunters still wore buckskin, he wrote in 1888, as Boone and Crockett had; they had been "the forerunners of the white advance throughout all our Western land," "the arch-type of freedom." In time the hunter of history, appearing again and again in his articles, ran the gamut of his own military and political ambitions. He praised the "master hand" of James Fenimore Cooper and plucked Leatherstocking and his associates into a greater destiny than the novelist's imagination had permitted: "stark pioneer settlers and backwoods hunters; uncouth, narrow, hard, suspicious, but with all the virile virtues of a young and masterful race, a race of mighty breeders, mighty fighters, mighty commonwealth builders." In view of Cooper's great burden of consciousness of the limitations of his frontiersmen, who might be virtuous but as he described them hardly were ready for statesmanship, this seems to reflect a powerful will to believe. Again, while Roosevelt accepted a popular picture of Boone and his fellow hunters as stirring uneasily at the approach of settlement, they were also "the heralds of the oncoming civilization," the archetypes of a long line of "hunter-soldiers" who included George Rogers Clark, Sam Houston, and Kit Carson. Moreover, the great political leaders of the nation, with few exceptions, had been hunters: Washington, Israel Putnam, Webster, Jackson, and Lincoln.[3] Probably it was not difficult, even in the 1880's, to

[3] Roosevelt, *Winning of the West*, Vol. I, p. xliv, in *Works* (New York: Charles Scribner's Sons; 1926), Vol. VIII; Roosevelt to Lodge, August 12, 1884, *Letters*, Vol. I, p. 77; Hagedorn: *Roosevelt in the Bad Lands*, pp. 235–56; Roosevelt: "Frontier Types," *Century Magazine*, Vol. XXXVI (September 1888),

imagine whose name one might properly add to such a list.

A member of an old Manhattan family and a Harvard graduate who liked to picture himself as living the authentic Western life, Roosevelt obviously represented an entirely different type of tourist from the Middle Westerners of southern California who liked to stress Eastern and European standards. As an authentic aristocrat he had no need to insist on aristocracy. As an ardent nationalist, steeped in his own country's history and traditions, and educated both at home and abroad, he felt no compulsion to justify himself by deprecating America to Europeans.

The more extreme range is perhaps not between Elkhorn Ranch and the Raymond, but between Roosevelt, the tourist who denied that he was a tourist, and those tourists who refused to go West and all but denied that they were Americans. Theodore Dwight had complained long before the Civil War of Americans of "foolish, degenerate, luxurious habits" who talked of the beauties of nature in Scotland and Italy but never stirred themselves to see those of America. " 'Of all the scenes in the world,' exclaims Americanus Frenchificatus, 'nothing can compare with sunrise on the Alps!' " There were Englishmen who professed to second Ruskin's comment (1871) on invitations to visit America, that he "could not, even for a couple of months, live in a country so miserable as to possess no castles," but frequently Englishmen also noted how Americans complained that their scenery was "wholly wanting in the interest that historic memories bestow." Charles

pp. 831–2; Roosevelt: *Wilderness Hunter*, p. 262; Smith: *Virgin Land*, pp. 59–70; Roosevelt: *Wilderness Hunter*, pp. 18–20, 22, 25–6, 263–73.

Kingsley told the story of an American at York Minster who remarked: "Ah, if we could transport this to America, we should hear no more about the Alabama claims," and how he had asked an American woman to explain her delight and wonder at what she saw in England. "Because everything is so old," she said, "and we have nothing old in America." "Nothing old?" asked Kingsley. "Have you not the rivers and the mountains and the forests, to which all this is but a mushroom crop?" Henry James contrasted the American's infatuation with the picturesque in Europe with the Englishman's complaints of chill and dirt at the arcades in Berne. "If the picturesque were banished from the face of the earth," said James, "I think the idea would survive in some typical American heart. . . ." [4]

In contrast, Roosevelt not only felt none of the nineteenth century's antagonism, shame, and fear in the face of Western nature but anticipated the next century's interest in immersing itself in the West as a great playground. Still in his twenties when he discovered Dakota and first undertook to interpret it to the East, the young man assumed the tones and authority of the Rough Rider President, commending the "rugged and stalwart democracy" of the wilderness and advocating great national forest-reserves for the whole people rather than private

[4] Theodore Dwight: *Travels in America* (Glasgow: R. Griffin & Co.; 1848); John Ruskin: *Arrows of the Chace* (New York: John Wiley & Sons; 1881), p. 151 n.; Charles W. Dilke: *Greater Britain: A Record of Travel in English-Speaking Countries During 1866 and 1867* (London: Macmillan and Co.; 1868), Vol. I, pp. 223–4; Kingsley: "The Americans at Chester," *Out West*, Vol. I, p. 4; Henry James: *Transatlantic Sketches* (Boston: Houghton Mifflin Company; 1888), p. 232.

game-enclosures for the rich.[5] His was a heartily masculine approach to the West, in contrast to the predomi-
nantly feminine approach of the Raymond tourists, who
put selected scenes in rococo picture frames, greeted them
in sentimental verse, and took the air on glazed sun-
porches.

Yet Roosevelt's reactions were much of his own time.
"I know it is often thought that it is nothing but a sickly
affection to appear charmed at the beauty of a landscape,"
wrote a Colorado miner in 1860, just as civilization and
preciosity descended together on that frontier, "and that
all raptures at a view of nature in mountain, foliage, or
stream, should be left for romantic misses or lackadaisical
young masculines, while sober practical men have other
matters far more important to attend to, and should move
straight on, noticing only what brings the almighty dollar." Roosevelt broke with that tradition, and yet in breaking it he recognized it. While he showed no shame at his
own delight in the beauties of the flowers and songbirds
and small mammals that he said the ordinary wilderness
dweller scarcely saw, and was willing (almost suspiciously
so) to admit that he was a poor shot or that he had a "perfect dread" of bucking, still there was an adolescent quality to his maleness, a disposition to take the West not in
stride but with a leap and a whoop. He greeted it with
unbounded enthusiasm, but as a challenge to be met and
overcome. The hardships that his neighbors endured when
they could not avoid them, he sought out and embraced.
He delighted in proving himself by acts of daring, even
foolhardiness, such as knocking down the drunken bully

[5] Roosevelt: *Wilderness Hunter*, p. 256.

who had announced that "Four-eyes is going to treat," or fording a river in flood, when easier and honorable alternatives were possible. There was a quality of insistence in his manner that often went beyond what the mores of the community demanded, and at the least rejoiced in what would impress others and meet the virile standard that he imposed on himself. "It would electrify some of my friends who have accused me of representing the kid-gloved element in politics," he told a New York reporter on returning from his first summer on his ranch in 1884, "if they could see me galloping over the plains, day in and day out, clad in a buckskin shirt and leather *chaparajos*, with a big sombrero on my head." [6] And the prodigious number of articles he almost immediately began to turn out, picturing himself in his new role, reflects a desire not to let others escape the sight. Further, his was a national as well as a personal mission. The theme of the spread of the English-speaking peoples and their civilization that pervades Roosevelt's *Winning of the West*, as also some of his utterances on public questions a few years later, suggests that the West may have fascinated him not only because of its own charms, and not only because of his personal experiences in it, but because it set off so gloriously the struggles, the virility of the Anglo-Saxon race that overcame it. The West was a kind of antagonist still, although an infinitely more welcome and attractive antagonist than most of his contemporaries had seen as tourists. Perhaps he knew too

[6] Letter, unsigned, June 20, 1860, Golden City, in *Golden Western Mountaineer* (clipping in Colorado Historical Society); Roosevelt: *Wilderness Hunter*, p. 85; Roosevelt: *Hunting Trips*, p. 16; Hagedorn: *Roosevelt in the Bad-Lands*, p. 156.

much history to be free from his time and the past, as most of his contemporaries knew too little.

If Roosevelt did seem to accept some slight measure of what one may call the genteel or Raymond-and-Whitcomb view of the harsh physical quality of the West, there was nevertheless a positive and full-blooded quality in his response that makes the range country as he described it much more vivid and memorable than the curious objects and Mediterranean landscapes that some others affected to cherish. The high plains and the mountains were beginning to break through a screen of preciosity and reach more Americans, some directly, some through Roosevelt's virile prose, some through Frederic Remington's paintings. They had reached another nationalist of his time, Walt Whitman, who in a burst of enthusiasm on a trip to Colorado in 1879 felt that in "this plentitude of material, entire absence of art, untrammel'd play of primitive Nature," he had "found the law" of his own poems. Whitman rebelled against artificiality in scenery as he had rebelled against artificiality in literature. "Modern poetry and art run to a sweetness and refinement which are really foreign to us," he told a newspaper reporter at St. Louis. "Everywhere as I went through the Rocky Mountains . . . especially at Platte Canon, I said to myself, 'Here are my poems, not finished temples, not graceful architecture, but great naturalness and rugged power—primitive nature.' " While I know, wrote Whitman, "the standard claim is that Yosemite, Niagara falls, the upper Yellowstone and the like, afford the greatest natural shows, I am not so sure but the Prairies and the Plains, while less stunning at first sight, last longer, fill the esthetic sense fuller, precede all the rest, and make North America's characteristic landscape." [7]

It is no accident that the West of the high plains country, once so uninteresting to tourists, has come to represent Wests that by nearly every test but the dramatic should look at least as large, or larger. The very brevity of its heroic age constitutes a special claim from the romantic point of view. The cowboy of Roosevelt and Remington lasted for no more than twenty or twenty-five years at the outside, between the time when the railroads first tapped the high range country for the Chicago and Kansas City meat packers after the Civil War and the time when the cattle market broke and the industry reorganized. If the cowboy's time had been longer, if it had been part of the experience of Americans on other and earlier frontiers, perhaps it would have seemed less repugnant at one stage, less glamorous at another. Hamlin Garland, who left the high plains wheat country for Boston in 1884, by 1892 and 1893 had begun to fall in love with the totally different, and to him exotic and romantic, environment of Colorado and California. Discovering the mountains and the Southwest even as he found the means of comfortable living within his grasp, he felt the pioneering enthusiasm of his Garland and McClintook ancestors in a setting new and different enough to seem proof against their recurrent disappointments, "the fulfillment of a boyish dream of exploration," combined perhaps with fulfillment of a dream

---

[7] Whitman: *Complete Prose Works* (New York: Mitchell, Kennerley; 1915), p. 143; "Three Uncollected St. Louis Interviews of Walt Whitman," Robert R. Hubach, ed., *American Literature*, Vol. XIV (May 1942), p. 145.

of a West immune from blights of mortgages and prairie blizzards. "I was filled with ecstatic anticipation. In the High Country I would find beauty and romance." "All my emotional relationships with the 'High Country' were pleasant, my sense of responsibility was less keen, hence the notes of resentment, of opposition to unjust social conditions . . . were almost entirely absent in my studies of the mountaineers." His father and his uncle, retired from farming and so "released from the tyranny of the skies," later joined him in his enthusiasm for this new West.[8]

Eventually, even though after fifteen years or so the Rockies and the Southwest had exhausted their attractions for him as literary material, Garland moved to southern California. When he had Rose of Dutcher's Coolly recall in bitterness a quotation from Lowell: "The wilderness is all right for a vacation, but all wrong for a lifetime," he referred to an older West that was both far less wild, and since they knew its hardships and its dullness, less conceivable for most Americans as vacation country than the ranges, deserts, and canyons that had begun to absorb him. This West-that-was pushed toward the mountains and threatened to spoil them for those who wanted to escape it. Even while Garland was discovering the charms of the Rockies, in 1893, he shrank in a Colorado hotel from men such as he had known on the plains: "The common stock from which I sprang. Heavy featured, clumsy fingered without grace or delicacy. . . . The common class of

[8] Hamlin Garland: *Roadside Meetings* (New York: Macmillan Company; 1931), p. 181; Garland: *Daughter of the Middle Border* (New York: Macmillan Company; 1929), pp. 31, 170.

Americans close down to the criminal classes and yet above them. . . . They were not pleasant these rude young fellows. They interfered with the pleasure of my dinner. I had grown to a certain delicacy which made their manner of eating repulsive." [9] Escape lay beyond the settlements.

Because it was strange, both as scenery and as way of life, the cattle country seemed an appropriate backdrop for romantic unreality. "All the stories I had read," recalled Garland of his childhood in Wisconsin, "concerned themselves either with Indians and trappers in the far West, or with dukes and duchesses in Eastern ancestral castles." The trapper shortly gave way to the cowboy in romantic fiction and in boyhood's romantic dreams. The cowboy had hardly appeared in print before he became superhuman. Charlie Siringo, the Texan whose utter lack of indoctrination in what was expected of him seemed to enable him to write with unmatched authenticity of the life of the cowboy on the southern range—*Fifteen Years on the Hurricane Deck of a Spanish Pony*—and Theodore Roosevelt, who accomplished with the art of the well educated what Siringo accomplished with the artlessness of the uneducated, had barely begun to write about the cattle country when Frederic Remington discovered how well its more dramatic moments lent themselves to pictorial idealization. By the early nineties Owen Wister had written his first Western stories and had begun to build up an appealing image of men who excelled in both the chivalric

[9] Hamlin Garland: *The Rose of Dutcher's Coolly* (New York: Macmillan Company; 1899), p. 149; Hamlin Garland, notebook, "Colorado and the West," 1893 (Doheny Library, University of Southern California).

virtues of Arthurian legend and the harum-scarum roughness of a shooting scrape in a desert saloon: "often in their
spirit sat hidden a true nobility, and often beneath its unexpected shining their figures took on heroic stature." Relative to the Westerner of fact, Wister's cowboys were the
new personification of the Western myth; relative to the
Westerners of most contemporary fiction, they were re-
freshingly real. "What pale, anaemic figures they are,
these creations of the emigre novelists," exclaimed Roosevelt, "when put side by side with the men, the grim stalwart
men, who stride through Mr. Wister's pages!" [1]

Through what Wister and his imitators wrote, as more
consciously in what Roosevelt wrote, ran a strong vein of
nostalgia. Wister had "turned a new page in that form of
contemporary historical writing which consists in the vivid
portrayal, once and for all, of types that should be commemorated," wrote Roosevelt in reviewing Wister's *Red
Men and White* (1895).[2] One may suspect that what attracted Roosevelt to Wister's writings was less their fidel-
ity to Western life than their commemorative and nostalgic spirit, which Roosevelt shared even while inscribing
a much truer picture of the West. The cowboy of popular

---

[1] Garland: *Roadside Meetings,* p. 181; Charles A. Siringo:
*A Texas Cowboy, or Fifteen Years on the Hurricane Deck of a
Spanish Pony* . . . (Chicago: M. Umbdenstock & Co.; 1885);
Mody Boatright: "The American Myth Rides the Range: Owen
Wister's Man on Horseback," *Southwest Review,* Vol. XXXVI
(Summer 1951), p. 158; Theodore Roosevelt: "A Teller of Tales
of Strong Men," *Harper's Weekly,* Vol. XXXIX (December
1895), p. 1216.
[2] Roosevelt: *Harper's Weekly,* Vol. XXXIX, p. 1216.

fiction personified not only the vigor and nationalism of the generation of the Spanish-American War, so that there was something peculiarly fitting in the prominence of Rough Riders on San Juan Hill, but also the rising mood of resistance to engulfing civilization.

Americans had never quite defined or bothered to reconcile the different shapes of the West. Sometimes it was danger, sometimes opportunity, always a challenge to those who tried to make it over into the East. But as long as it continued to demand and absorb their energy, they had little time to enjoy it for its own sake: it gave them pleasure for what it was to be rather than for what it was and had been, and a deeply sustaining pleasure it was, that strengthened them for the continuing struggle. Then a succession of economic misfortunes began to bring home a chilling suspicion, and finally the grim truth: the West was filling up; Western opportunity in the old sense was playing out. Some specific economic crises subsided with the Populist movement of the nineties, but the new prosperity seemed to spring more from factory buildings and corporation securities than from farms and mines. Some of the old excitement was gone, some of the old danger and the old shame, and with them a nation's adolescence. A more mature America felt not only less repugnance at the crudity that had reminded it of how much remained to be done, but a sentimental attachment to the remnants of a cruder West that persisted. The nation, and especially those Americans who were coming to have more leisure and larger incomes but less contact with the soil as they worked, groped for links to the past, almost in the spirit of the middle-aged college alumnus who in a later generation sought refuge from the tensions and the frustrations of the business world by living vicariously the life of an undergraduate on Saturday afternoon. Americans who resented or regretted the settlement of the Old West found a new kinship of spirit with the cowboy, who more than anyone else surviving in recognizable form personifies antagonism toward the settler. Thus they stand against the vast majority of Westerners, including miners, who had welcomed the end of the wilderness, even though the cowboy's herds were only relatively less destructive of grass and game than the plow.

The cowboy nevertheless was much more than relic: for a symbol, he was very much alive, even though when the public first heard of him he was on his way out in his old form, and so could claim some of the glamor of nostalgia. He had help in attaining heroic stature—the help of artists who singled out the most colorful moments in an essentially dreary life, the help of writers like Roosevelt, the help of the nationalistic mood that mounted up in the nineties, following the pallid dilettantism of the years following the great orgasm of Civil War, which had sought out cheap effeminized European substitutes for authentic goods in art, literature, and architecture, as well as in vacation travel. And he had the advantage of a backdrop— the vast reaches of the range country—that remains more as it was in pioneer times than most of the land that has known the miner, the farmer, the modern suburbanite. Above all, however, he himself seemed to be real. It was only in later years that he became a stock figure in fiction and tourist promotions, in some respects as standardized an offering as the West that the tourists knew before him. He still seemed real enough in the nineties so that a generation trained to appreciate the unreal was only gingerly beginning to accept him and the West he lived in as more than fixtures in a picaresque literary form.

4. THE GROWING
TOURIST MARKET

T<small>HE IMAGE</small> of the West that the excursionist knew, or
thought he knew, had begun to crumble in the 1880's even
while the great resort hotels that catered to the new rich
of the East and Middle West were still abuilding and the
excursion trains were extending their circuits to take in
new oddities and wonders, natural and man-made. The
old image could not easily have prevailed much longer. Its
weakness was not only that patterns of taste and recreation were changing all over the world but that America
and the West also were growing up. Each decade saw more
families with leisure time and money to spend in it; the
West as well as the East was becoming urbanized, and
even its more modest towns spawned their vacation spots.
Gradually this mass market became more important to the

tourist industry as a whole than the patronage of the elite. The great profits in the Western tourist and vacation industry came not from serving squab to the few but from selling gasoline, hamburger sandwiches, and postcards to the many, who lived in Los Angeles and Seattle as well as in Cincinnati and Boston.

Some of the unfashionable resorts had considerably preceded the extravagances of the eighties. In the early years they were smaller than the Del Montes and the Manitous, but soon they lagged less in size than in the incomes of their visitors and in the respect that they commanded from newspaper society-editors. Nor did most of them strive to become much more distinctively Western than the great tourist-hotels. Some of the first resort towns were conscious transplants from the East Coast. When the California Methodists, deploring the "sinful waste of time" in amusements carried beyond the extent "required to rest and reinvigorate the mind and body," established the Pacific Grove Retreat on the Monterey peninsula in 1875, they modeled it after Ocean Grove, which the New Jersey Methodists had founded in 1869. Each began with heavy emphasis on camp meetings; each was a tent city in its early years, and developed a kind of Methodist Gothic style of architecture in which wood gradually replaced cloth without entirely erasing its temporary and summertime aspect; each contrasted with a more fashionable neighbor, so that Ocean Grove was to Long Branch what Pacific Grove became to Del Monte. "Thither, in the warm season," wrote Robert Louis Stevenson, who knew Pacific Grove when he lived at Monterey, "crowds come to enjoy a life of teetotalism, religion, and flirtation, which I am willing to think blameless and agreeable." Chautauqua meetings began in 1880, and a moral and religious atmosphere persisted long after the Methodists relinquished control. The Pacific Improvement Company, that versatile alter ego of the Southern Pacific Railroad, which operated Pacific Grove as a kind of inexpensive alternative to the Hotel del Monte, assured patrons that "no immorality of any kind is permitted on the grounds." By the nineties the Sabbatarian rigor of the place had noticeably relaxed; cottages, many of them owned by city families, were replacing tents rented by the week; and summer-session classes in botany and zoology for college and preparatory credit were succeeding to the original camp-meeting emphasis on sermons and prayer.[1]

The spirit of moral and intellectual improvement extended meanwhile also to Long Beach, which was host to the first southern California Chautauqua Assembly in 1884 —"a quiet resort, comparatively free from the noise and bustle incidental to large crowds of transient visitors and the saloon element"—and later, in the first years of the new century, to Huntington Beach (1904) and to Mount Hermon, in the Santa Cruz Mountains (1905), "for rest and recreation and summer homes, and for Mid-Summer Assemblies or Bible Camp." In Oregon, Gearhart modeled itself after Pacific Grove in the nineties, laying out lots for cottage homes or camps near a Chautauqua auditorium

[1] *California Christian Advocate*, October 1, 1874, p. 6:1; *Pacific Grove, A Piny Paradise by the Broad Sea* (Pacific Grove: [1893]), pp. 1, 6; *Hand Book of Monterey* . . . (Monterey: Walton & Curtis; 1875), p. 51; Stevenson: *Across the Plains*, p. 83; *The Christian Seaside Resort*, Pacific Improvement Co. (n. p.; 1881).

and a hotel; by 1896 another rural Chautauqua Assembly was scheduled for Shasta Retreat, which the Methodists hoped would "be in the way of a mountain resort what Pacific Grove is to the sea"; and in 1902 the Colorado Chautauqua, which previously had held sessions at Palmer Lake (1900), prepared for the Garden of the Gods Assembly and Summer School.[2]

The bulk of Western vacationers by the nineties were neither rich enough for Del Monte and the Raymond nor good enough for Pacific Grove. The *Nation* called attention in 1891 to a national drift toward the English idea of a longer country-season that took fewer families to the "regular" resorts, more to farmhouses, country villages, and groups of cottages, as well as to Europe: "summer migration is seeking the rural quietudes and moving away from the old centres of mere fashion. . . . The great resorts are becoming the summer homes of the class, while the remote places are sought for by the mass." The West shared in the national tendency to the simple life, perhaps in part out of necessity: though many of the Western lake and beach villages aspired to something grander, there was no escaping the fact that their senior citizens were fishermen and farmers rather than millionaires. While the California and Oregon coasts had their equivalents to Southampton and Nantucket and to the Adirondack resorts, they developed chiefly on a humbler scale; some of them had the unashamedly rural quality of the New Eng-

---

[2] R. N. T.: "By the Seaside," *Land of Sunshine*, Vol. I (September 1894), p. 70; Frances F. Victor: "Northern Seaside Resorts," *Overland*, 2d series, Vol. XXIII (February 1894), p. 144.

land resorts of the twentieth century, but hardly anyone realized that they were quaint, and that their backwardness was a negotiable asset. Near Santa Cruz, Camp Capitola (presumably named after a heroine in sentimental newspaper fiction), whose visitors in the seventies were chiefly campers who brought their own tents, had cottages and a hotel by the middle eighties ("the most English-looking cluster of cottages, on a sea-beach"), as well as the shacks of Chinese and Italian fishermen; a group of expatriate Englishmen built a group of more pretentious cottages on the cliff some distance away. Santa Cruz itself, which laid some claim to fashion, was "like some New England town washed ashore on this distant coast. . . ." [3] While Raymond and Whitcomb sometimes sent their parties to places with society as heterogeneous as at Santa Cruz, these were essentially local resorts, where families from San Francisco and the cities of the interior valleys stayed weeks or months, perhaps as long as the school calendar permitted.

Meanwhile "going out of town" to a "cottage" or tent was becoming the custom at Portland also, although the Northwest, hampered by poor transportation and slight population, was slow to develop resorts of any size. At Newport, Oregon, in the seventies, most of the vacationers

[3] "Changes in Summer Migration," *Nation*, Vol. LIII (September 17, 1891), pp. 210–11; Julian Ralph: "The Spread of Out-door Life," *Harper's Weekly*, Vol. XXXVI (August 27, 1892), pp. 830–1; Ben C. Truman: *Tourists' Illustrated Guide to the Celebrated Summer and Winter Resorts of California* . . . (San Francisco: H. S. Crocker & Co.; 1884), pp. 246–7; Dall: *My First Holiday*, p. 285; Henry Meyrick: *Santa Cruz & Monterey* . . . (San Francisco: San Francisco News Publishing Co.; 1880), p. 5.

lived in tent camps near the beach, coming to the hotel for folk dances two evenings a week and for church services on Sunday; the town's name represented an entirely un-consummated ambition, and no one seriously attempted to transfer the manners of its Eastern prototype. A Portland paper advised visitors to Clatsop Beach in 1863 to expect solitude, and to pack their trunks with "plenty of old clothes—and some old Bourbon"; eighteen years later Tillamook still offered little more than clamming, crab-bing, surf bathing, and the comforts of boarding with an Indian family: "Ladies are at an immense premium." While Astoria and Seaside, which claimed to be the "oldest fashionable summer resort on the Oregon coast," soon had orthodox hotel and boarding-house accommodations, in the main a tradition of informality persisted there as in the lesser California resorts.[4]

Life in a small Western seaside resort around the turn of the century was lazy and relaxed. From September to June most of the vacation cottages stood closed, shutters fastened, porch chairs inside, rank growth of weeds out-side; the proprietors of the tiny grocery stores, boarding houses, and "apartments" marked time and exchanged hopes for the coming season. The beaches reverted to sea birds, save when winter residents came to gather driftwood. Then there was a bustle of arrivals, chiefly women with children fresh from the restraints of schoolroom, woolen underwear, and high-topped shoes, and more eager to as-

[4] "The Cottage by the Sea," *West Shore*, Vol. XII (July 1886), p. 200; Wallis Nash: *Oregon: There and Back in 1877* (London: Macmillan and Co.; 1878), pp. 154–6; Scrapbook No. 112, p. 47 (Oregon Historical Society); "Oregon's Barnegat," *West Shore*, Vol. VIII (March 1882), p. 42.

sure themselves that their old haunts were still there than
to help with trunks and broom; and the normal summer
routine set in, of afternoons on beaches and porches, of
hikes to the wild berry patches, of occasional fishing and
clamming expeditions, of country church-bazaars and
whist-parties, of watching at the nearest dock or railroad
station for week-end visitors and for fathers and grand-
fathers come from the city for a week or two, afterward
of standing in line for the post-office window to slide up with
a creak and a bang when the mail was ready. Old clothes
were customary even at the hotel and at the summer houses
of the well-to-do, built a little apart from the others. "Life
is still very simple at the beaches of the northwest coast,"
said *Sunset* in 1914. "Society comes down from Portland
and Tacoma and Seattle, but it does not bring a lot of
trunks." [5]

When autumn came and the last of the school children
had returned to the city, a few houses remained in use, including perhaps a hut or two on the beach. Some of those
who stayed were invalids, come west for their health. The
health seekers were merging more with the residents and
becoming less conspicuous in the principal vacation resorts. In the seventies and eighties the tubercular, the
dropsical, and the scrofulous had thronged, when they
could afford it, to the resort hotels, and religiously purified
themselves at the fountains and in baths of mud or salt
water. "All the people are sick," reported a visitor to

---

[5] Bertha H. Smith: "Sandyland! They Who Go down to the
Sea in Summer . . . ," *Sunset*, Vol. XXXIII (August 1914),
p. 305.

Manitou; and strangers commonly introduced themselves by asking: "What is your complaint, sir?" Even in the nineties the Hotel del Coronado in San Diego proudly quoted the recommendation of Charles Dudley Warner on its stationery: "for weak hearts, disabled lungs, and worn-out nerves." But already communicable disease had become socially less acceptable; the pallor of the consumptive had gone out of style among young ladies; and chambers of commerce were solicitously seconding the advice of physicians who warned against undertaking the trials of a journey westward when seriously ill. Mineral springs were still well-advertised assets, especially if one could demonstrate that they had as much Epsom salts or arsenic as some European spa; a visitor to the Yellowstone in 1902 reported Thermopolis Hot Springs crowded with patients with "disgusting skin diseases," the sick beds placed even between the dining tables of restaurants and hotels. Arkansas Hot Springs (which claimed Hernando de Soto as its discoverer and first European patron) as late as 1925 had more visitors than any other national park. But Thermopolis obviously was of low caste, and Arkansas no longer was growing rapidly, though it had come to emphasize riding and hiking among its charms as well as sitz baths and purges. Many of the better resort towns, as Pasadena, offered nothing more specific than climate, which was gradually becoming opportunity for activity as well as surcease from rheumatism and the complications of senility. Others, as Del Monte, quietly ceased to emphasize their curative resources. Pacific Congress Springs, whose waters were said to be almost identical to those of Ems (properly celebrated in Owen Meredith's *Lucile*),[6] became better known as an interurban railroad's picnic ground.

Even by the middle eighties the typical invalid who came west could no longer afford to stay at a tourist hotel: his income was too low, and his disease lasted too long. The bargain railroad-rates of 1886–7 attracted thousands of tuberculars who supposed that the price of a ticket to Los Angeles bought recovery, and sometimes arrived as innocent of funds as ignorant that one does not live out of doors in winter even in southern California. If they survived and remained, it was not likely to be at one of the "better" resorts, where prices were relatively high. Many others, more prosperous if not always better advised, came west in hope of regaining their health as gentleman farmers among the citrus groves, where even the frailest females might work usefully and salubriously at picking lemons.[7] As farmers they were residents rather than tourists, and as farmers, like the consumptives who were seeking out dry air and sunshine in the desert (which had not yet, for the most part, learned to be fashionable), they were decidedly less conspicuous than the invalids who had rocked on the porches and sipped the waters at Manitou.

Rich invalids and rich Eastern tourists generally con-

[6] Campbell: *My Circular Notes*, Vol. I, p. 46; Earley V. Wilcox: "Trip Around Yellowstone Park," *Rocky Mountain Magazine*, Vol. III (January–February 1902), pp. 265–6; George W. James: *The H. M. M. B. A. in California* (Pasadena: G. W. James; 1896), pp. 318–21.

[7] John Baur: "The Health Seekers and Early Southern California Agriculture," *Pacific Historical Review*, Vol. XX (November 1951), pp. 347–63.

tinued to go west, but by the nineties others were clearly
eclipsing them on Western beaches and mountains. The
Far West continued to be largely rural in extent, with
greater stretches of uninhabited and even uninhabitable
land than the East and Middle West; therein lay much of
its potential fascination for the tourist, as well as the key
to its economy. But it was and is also one of the most urban
of rural sections: not only has it produced cities at an
early stage, as San Francisco and Denver, that seem to
concentrate the essence and energy of urbanhood beyond
their Eastern cousins of similar size, according to the dull
yardstick of the census taker, but its people have tended
to live in town even while living off the country. Even in
1870 nearly a third of the people of the Pacific Coast
States lived in towns of 2,500 population or more, against
a fourth in the entire nation, and the coast has continued
to be more urban by that test. By 1900 more than half of
Californians lived in town, by 1920 more than two thirds,
by 1930 nearly three fourths. And from long before the
days of rural electrification and radio the Far Western
farmer has been a man of persistently urban habit, which
may follow on the distance from his farmhouse to his neighbor's (either too great for rural visits or so short that he
lives, in effect, in a suburb), or on his prosperity and the
high capitalization and elaborate technique of irrigation
agriculture, or on his close dependence on canneries and
refrigeration plants. Being a city man by residence or
habit and taste, he has taken a city man's pleasures. He
was taking them in such numbers before the end of the
century that no one could ignore him and his wife and chil-

dren, not even the railroads, which had begun by prizing more highly those who paid first-class fare all the way from Chicago or beyond.

Meanwhile the people of the older states also were moving from country to city, and getting enough of the good things of life so that they wanted more. While the riches of new mills and foundries filtered down less evenly than they were to do fifty years or so later, and from the point of view of the second half of the twentieth century this was a time of stringent inequality and narrow comforts, still each decade saw thousands more Americans with vacation time and vacation money, and with a disposition to spend time and money away from home. The old progress of America from one agricultural frontier to another was slowing down, but the new American, who typically had moved from rural to urban frontier, seemed to continue the ancestral tradition of abandoning the hearthside, if only for amusement and for an evening or a season.

The railroads discovered, in effect, the possibilities of selling Western travel on a large scale during the twenty years or so after the rate wars of 1886–7. When the Santa Fe entered Los Angeles in 1887 and the price of a ticket from Missouri River points fell for a year to twenty-five dollars or less, the railroads drew more settlers, speculators, and adventurers than tourists in the ordinary sense; the colonist fares begun in 1900—low one-way rates, good on specified days only—resembled the conditions of the price war, and drew a similar clientele. But no one could escape thereafter the possibilities of a mass market for the West, poorer than the Raymond tourists and richer than the tramps who, in the eighties, were already following the crops and the weather. By the late eighties and early nineties convention and exposition round-trip rates began to draw the crowds; eventually (1906) these special reductions, designed at first for delegates only and later for anyone who chose to travel at the time, merged into regular summer tourist fares. In the later eighties, moreover, the roads introduced an improved tourist Pullman sleeping-car, symbol of a new era in tourism as the carved and painted palace-car had been a generation earlier. The new tourist-car was not luxurious, nor was it exclusive. In later years it evoked memories of "cane seats that put bunyons and a beautiful basket weave impression on the backs of one's legs—the brooding, lingering smells of the stale food, with the lusty odor of garlic predominating. . . ." [8] Some of the passengers prepared their meals in an oven in the heater at the end of the car, and washed their dishes at the sink. But the tourist car made Western pleasure-travel possible and reasonably comfortable for many who could not afford first-class fare and could not stand the bare wooden benches of the earlier second-class sleepers, where the passengers who came prepared arranged their own straw mattresses and bedding. Now a porter made the berths; on some trains a special tour conductor rode the cars from coast to coast, giving a cut-rate approximation of what the first-class excursionists enjoyed, and at no extra cost.

In the same years the electric interurban car wrought a minor but significant change in local tourist-travel. Once the tourist left the main railroad lines in the seventies he

[8] D. M. Spangler to W. W. Fonda, May 21, 1942, Santa Fe Railway advertising files (Chicago).

had had to choose between the discomfort of the public stagecoach and the high cost of the private carriage. In the late eighties the trolley wires began to fan out from Western cities: by 1896, for instance, one could ride from Pasadena to Mount Lowe and to Santa Monica, and the chambers of commerce were publishing photographs of happy Easterners playing in the snow after lunch and in the surf before dinner. "The electric car," said *Out West*, "is the poor man's carriage." [9] The Pacific Electric Company in the Los Angeles area and other electric lines operated special excursions for tourists—as the Wishbone Route of the Denver and Intermountain, or the Orange Blossom Route of the Pacific Electric—in addition to a thriving local business in school and family picnics. The transit companies' parks, beaches, and pavilions became as popular in the Far West as east of the Mississippi, and did much to meet and excite a popular appetite for outdoor recreation.

The steam lines offered similar local holiday and sight-seeing service; some of the narrow-gauge lines in the Colorado Rockies found that tourists paid more than freight; and on the West Coast branch lines sought out the resort towns, where they did not create them. Two lines converged on Santa Cruz in 1876 and 1880, bringing the whole Monterey Bay area within three or four hours of San Francisco, and at a third or a fourth the old charge by stage-coach or steamer, though a third projected line, the Ocean Shore, never reached its goal. Mrs. Frank Leslie rode on a

[9] William E. Smythe: "Social Influence of Electric Lines," *Out West*, Vol. XIX (December 1903), p. 695.

typical "picnic car" on a narrow-gauge line in Marin County, north of San Francisco, in 1877 : "platforms quite close to the ground and furnished with bare benches." [1]

The railroads, both steam and electric, thus figured in shifts in American recreational habits that in a later day seemed products of the automobile alone. Even camping was likely to start with a train trip. Most of the local lines were willing to leave fishermen and campers not only at the main resort destinations but in the midst of the mountains; by the nineties the Southern Pacific was advertising special campers' fares and free checking of tents, stoves, and other camping equipment, and the Denver and Rio Grande followed a few years later.

The automobile eventually moved more tourists still, and carried them further afield, but at first it was a rich tourists' amusement rather than a major means of transportation. Dr. H. Nelson Jackson, the Vermont physician who made the first transcontinental automobile crossing with his chauffeur in 1903, reported that the trip had cost him eight thousand dollars; he lost twenty pounds in weight as well in the nine weeks that it took. Appropriately enough, the Automobile Club of California scheduled its first race-meet (1903) at the Hotel del Monte, the playground of northern California society; the elite from San Francisco spent two days or more on the trip, while the proletariat traveled the same distance by train in three hours. Most tourists kept themselves more within the radii

---

[1] Mrs. Frank Leslie: *California. A Pleasure Trip from Gotham to the Golden Gate* . . . (New York: G. W. Carleton & Co.; 1877), p. 188.

of their runabouts' electric batteries, going perhaps from Colorado Springs to Manitou, or from the Hotel del Monte to Carmel by way of the Seventeen Mile Drive.[2]

If any of the promoters of automobile travel envisioned its ultimate uses by the masses, their first thoughts seemed to center about the rich, and particularly rich Easterners. The railroads, which supported the good-roads movement generously, were indifferent enough to the prospect of automotive competition to encourage Easterners to bring their cars along to California for winter touring—by train, of course; *Sunset,* then the Southern Pacific's promotional magazine, suggested (1904) making four overnight stops on the way from San Francisco to Los Angeles. James J. Hill himself persuaded the American Automobile Association to schedule the Glidden Tour of 1913 along the line of the Great Northern Railroad to Glacier National Park, and provided Pullman cars and diners in lieu of hotel accommodations for the drivers. The leaders of the automobile industry championed the transcontinental routes, which appealed most to the American imagination because they seemed least possible, and which would serve the clientele that seemed most interested in automobile touring. The motorcar tourists in southern California, noted a visitor of 1913, were prosperous Eastern city types, the mainstays of the big hotels—bank directors, corporation presidents, "young bloods, without hats and in white flannels, talking golf, polo, and motor cars . . .

[2] *The New York Times,* January 16, 1955, p. 92:1; ibid., June 28, 1936, X, p. 7:1–4; Arthur Inkersley: "Touring in California," *Sunset,* Vol. XII (December 1903), pp. 125–6; Arthur Inkersley: "Automobiling at Del Monte," ibid., Vol. XIV (January 1905), pp. 285–7.

elderly ladies of comfortable embonpoint, with lorgnettes and lapdogs." The railroad was still "the poor man's automobile"; for that matter, an automobile tourist in Oregon in 1913 met a family moving from Kansas to British Columbia by horse-drawn covered wagon. As late as 1919, well within the era of Henry Ford's Model T, a tourist computed the costs of an automobile trip from New York to California as $677.22 for fifty days, plus $304.19 for railroad transportation across an impassable stretch of desert.[3] Long stretches of the Lincoln Highway were still no more than pious hope and impious propaganda.

The big change came in the 1920's and thirties, as the cheaper automobiles multiplied and the paved highways extended to take the new traffic. The tourist continued to be (as he continued to be still later) of more than average wealth and income: in 1931, for instance, the count of Cadillacs driven by out-of-state tourists in northern California ran over twice the count for the whole United States. But suddenly there were vastly more tourists and vastly more of them in their own cars—in California nearly four times as many in 1923 as there had been in 1920. By 1929

[3] Victor Eubank: "Log of an Auto Prairie Schooner," *Sunset*, Vol. XXVIII (February 1912), p. 188; Wallace W. Everett: "On the King's Highway," ibid., Vol. XIV (December 1904), pp. 125–31; Bellamy Partridge: *Fill 'er Up: the Story of Fifty Years of Motoring* (New York: McGraw-Hill Book Company; 1952), p. 117; Charles F. Saunders: *Under the Sky in California* (New York: McBride, Nast & Company; 1913), pp. 201–2; Rufus Steele: "In a Friendly Outdoors," *Sunset*, Vol. XXXIII (July 1914), p. 59; E. Alexander Powell: "Chopping a Path to Tomorrow," *Sunset*, Vol. XXXI (November 1913), pp. 895–8; Beatrice L. Massey: *It Might Have Been Worse* . . . (San Francisco: Harr Wagner Publishing Co.; 1920), p. 145.

there were more than twice as many again, and the increase continued during the thirties after a brief dip in one year, 1930,[4] and despite the surveillance that state border patrols exercised, to see that those who came to the Golden State had come to spend money rather than to earn or beg it. The Western sight-seeing buses increased sharply during the twenties and then declined as the sight-seers moved to their own cars.

The automobile meanwhile had been edging past the train in volume of tourist traffic. The railroads did not restore full normal service after the First World War until 1921 and 1922 (in some parts of the West, 1925), with their usual excursions, vacation specials, and week-end fares; normal fares and even the special summer excursion rates, which were resumed in 1922, ran higher in the twenties than they have been at any time since. In the depression years fares dropped drastically: the Southern Pacific, for instance, began running a Sunday excursion train from San Francisco to Santa Cruz, on Monterey Bay, the Suntan Special, in 1931 at two dollars a round trip, less than Sunday fares had been even before the war, and cut this to $1.25 in 1934, in contrast with the week-end excursion rate of $4.86 in 1921. By 1936 the coach-class fare, round trip, between Chicago and San Francisco had dropped to $65, and in new, air-conditioned cars running at the same speed as the limited trains; it had been $144.26 in 1921. After 1937 the Western lines established "economy" trains

[4] *Ninth Annual Report*, Californians, Incorporated (San Francisco: 1932), pp. 4–5; *San Francisco Chronicle*, February 24, 1924, p. 4A:1; *California Motor Vehicle Statistics*, California Highway Patrol (Sacramento: State Printing Office; 1932).

offering special inducements such as meals priced at twenty-five to thirty-five cents, free pillows, hostesses or nurse-couriers, and lounge cars for tourist passengers.

Well before that time more than half of the summer traffic went by automobile rather than by train, and it never returned. Over a long period, at least since the nineties, the railroads had been more successful in attracting long-distance than short-distance traffic: revenue from interline passengers increased more rapidly than revenue from local passengers, and then, even before the First World War, local passenger revenue began to fall off, despite cuts in local fares. In the early twenties the tourist traffic to the West by railroad increased enormously: the Santa Fe, for instance, carried thirty-nine per cent more passengers to California in 1923 than in 1922.[5] The Southern Pacific was confident enough to acquire and broad-gauge the Lake Tahoe line, starting through Pullman service in 1926, and celebrating the occasion with a golden spike ceremony at Tahoe Tavern and an "Old Trail Week." But over the decade coach travel fell off sharply, both absolutely and relative to first-class travel. By 1929 revenue from Pullman and parlor passengers on Class I railroads for the first time in railroad history exceeded revenue from day-coach passengers. Especially on short trips, of a day or less, when he did not need a sleeper, the traveling American was becoming his own engineer.

The tourist might still be more prosperous than the American who stayed at home, but the automobile repre-

[5] *The New York Times,* December 9, 1934, IX, p. 14:6; mimeographed memoranda, n.d., Southern Pacific Company (San Francisco); *San Francisco Chronicle,* July 29, 1923, p. C9:5.

sented a new democratization of vacation travel. In the same years when the average American had more time for trips away from home, and more money to spend on them, he could buy gasoline to carry his whole family from his own front door for what he alone would have to pay to ride the train. The growing Western highway systems, growing in response to his demands, represented his expanding opportunity and the opportunity of the sections that they fed. Delays in completing a direct transcontinental route to San Francisco Bay meant that most westbound tourists turned southward, at Salt Lake City, toward Los Angeles, until 1925, and San Franciscans developed neuroses as they watched southern California outstrip them in population and the tourist trade. Traffic regularly exceeded expectations as new routes opened up, and not only diverted travel but created it. An almost revolutionary expansion in week-end and holiday travel took place as auto ferry service developed between 1921 and 1927 on San Francisco Bay itself, long a major bottleneck for automobiles. The railroads suffered and began to cut service on short lines to vacation resorts. Eventually many of them gave up the ghost: the Argentine Central Railroad, to the top of Mt. McClellan, one of the most popular of mountain-climbing roads, was abandoned in 1918, the Mt. Tamalpais and Muir Woods Railway in 1927; the tracks of the Yosemite Valley Railroad were removed in 1945. One of the few survivors on the mountains by mid-century was the Pikes Peak Railroad, which continued carrying passengers after the Second World War—under plexiglass domes— despite automobile competition that included the Broadmoor Hotel's fleet of air-conditioned and pressurized

Cadillacs.[6] The Southern Pacific abandoned its direct line through the mountains to Santa Cruz in 1940 and also cut service to Monterey and Pacific Grove; the old Ocean Shore Railroad had given up its attempt to run a third line to Santa Cruz twenty years earlier. The Pullman passenger had to join the masses on the highway or stay at home.

Meanwhile the airplane, which in 1929 took passengers coast to coast in forty-eight hours in a co-ordinated plane-train service, was eliminating time as a barrier to Western tourist travel, even while most Americans had more time for their vacations than they had had before. It was even crowding out the pack mule in trips to some of the wilder places: in the fall of 1928, for instance, hunters were crossing the Grand Canyon by air to shoot deer in the Kaibab National Forest.

As the tourist and his conveyance changed, his importance to the West changed as well, and ultimately much more. In the early years, from the 1870's into the eighties and nineties, the tourist was above all else a potential investor; and even in later years the wealthy investor was the primary target in much promotional strategy. "Everything which tends to increase the number of our visitors of the more cultured and wealthy class, and to render their visit pleasant and attractive," remarked a Portland editor of the coming of one of the first Raymond parties to the Pacific Northwest, "is beneficial to our growing towns and developing industries." "If we appeal to this class

[6] David Lavender: *The Big Divide* (Garden City: Doubleday; 1948), pp. 279–80; *The New York Times*, July 25, 1955, p. 15:2–3.

successfully," said a speaker at a meeting of the See America League at Salt Lake City in 1906, "the other [laboring] class will come of itself, while the well-to-do will become attached to the Western world and plant enterprises that will win the other class and make them needful, and make their coming practical." The Western railroads, which held heavy stakes in the development of their own territory, aimed at the investor class, in their advertising, in the facilities they offered for tourists both on the limited trains and in railroad-built hotels such as the Del Monte, and in the various and costly courtesies that they offered to wealthy travelers. They shared the attitude of Westerners generally, even before the railroads, in the days when the mining rush had passed and the hard truth had penetrated that a man had to put gold into the ground before he could take gold out, when the most exciting rumor that could spread was that wealth had arrived on the stagecoach, and when those who had funds to invest were well advised to conceal the fact lest they be pestered beyond endurance. "The *gentleman* is out of place on Montgomery street or in the mining camps," warned a writer in *Overland* in 1868, "unless he can be furnishing aid in the shape of money towards the development of resources." [7]

Meanwhile the tourist was assuming other roles. From perhaps roughly the 1890's into the 1920's he was preeminently a potential settler, who after enjoying a sample of the product might place a continuing order. And since

[7] *West Shore*, Vol. X (July 1884), p. 199; *Official Proceedings*, See America League, First Annual Conference: Salt Lake City, January 25–7, 1906 ([Salt Lake City: 1906?]), p. 89; T. H. Rearden: "Over-Crowded Professions on the Pacific Slope," *Overland*, Vol. I (September 1868), p. 251.

then, though a high percentage of settlers continue to be returned tourists, he has been primarily a regular source of revenue as he tours: selling the sample has become an end in itself. The tourist's roles lapped each other and included other roles still: the tourist-investor merged into the tourist-judge, who might confer the approval that the West craved as well as capital; the tourist-as-tourist, who seems to represent the most commercial object, singled out for what he may be induced to spend before he leaves, at the same time may be most difficult to separate from others in the "tourist trade," since increasingly he brings his family along on business trips, and increasingly he comes to visit friends and relatives, or at least stays at their houses rather than at the resorts, and often only his automobile license plates show that he is away from home. According to a survey made in 1950, 42.8 per cent of tourists stayed with friends and relatives at their destinations, only 24 per cent at hotels and resorts.[8]

The lures that the Westerner sets for the tourist tell something about both of them. Before the nineties tourism was, in the main, a custom-made operation; the tourists worth cultivating were wealthy or influential rather than numerous or prospective settlers. The Eastern newspapermen who attended a convention of the International League of Press Clubs at San Francisco in 1892 were few enough to travel in one special train, which dropped them off along the Pacific Coast to be wined and dined and to send back flattering reports for publication. During the

[8] *The Vacation Travel Market of the United States: A Nationwide Survey, #1*, Curtis Publishing Company (Philadelphia: Curtis Publishing Co.; 1950), p. 45.

general economic depression that shortly followed, the Western chambers of commerce realized the possibilities of promoting mass movements to take up the slack in immigration and travel; soon they were concerned not with scores but with thousands. The members of the Christian Endeavor Society, who met at San Francisco in 1897, were not unusually rich, but they were gratifyingly numerous, and their hosts, counting the profits, realized some of the possibilities of attracting crowds. Still this was a time when, despite the implications of lagging farm prices, most Westerners felt that the West needed more immigrants, and while the railroads enjoyed the money that the travelers left behind them, there was a general feeling that the real function of the tourist was to prepare for the settler. The large conventions were successful because they attracted many who might fall in love with the country and come again to stay. "If there is a teacher in the whole East," tartly warned *Sunset* in 1899, "expecting to come to California for the purpose only of attending the meeting of the National Educational Association Meeting, will not that teacher kindly stay away? You can just as well send $2 for a copy of the proceedings and read that work on your back doorstep and save us and yourself much trouble." "These thousands of tourists coming to Colorado," reported the Denver Civic and Commercial Association in 1917, "are spying out the land, and they find our land flowing with milk and honey, and when they go back home they cannot help advertising the desirable features of Colorado for home-making. . . ." [9]

[9] I. F. Coope: "Santa Cruz—the City of Mountain and Stone," *Sunset,* Vol. V (September 1900), pp. 236–8; Thom-

As long as the tourist seemed interesting chiefly as prospective investor or prospective settler, it was natural that in seeking to attract and entertain him those who advertised the West should emphasize the charms, especially the degree of civilization in the Eastern sense, of Western cities and residential areas. Nature was a parade of wonders for brief inspection on side trips from the civilized parts of the West, or a benevolent climate congenial to Eastern aches and social prejudices. "Nice neighbors," advertised the Santa Clara Valley Improvement Club in 1902; "most excellent educational and church privileges—equal to Boston and Philadelphia." It was especially natural to emphasize the Eastern aspects of the West when conventions and expositions accounted for a very large part of Western tourist travel, as they did in the years 1897–1915. Those who came may have ranked socially well below the Raymond tourists of the 1880's ("it was 'Main Street' that went to the Fair—the 'best people' had a slight disdain for it" [1]), but their insistence on urban comforts seemed almost inversely proportionate to their gentility. Further, in the era before transcontinental automobile trips, they necessarily came by train and could not easily move beyond the rails. And the urban chambers of commerce, which generally footed the bills for the fairs, hoped to reap the return.

---

son P. McElrath: *A Press Club Outing. A Trip Across the Continent* . . . (New York: International League of Press Clubs; 1893); *Sunset*, Vol. III (May 1899), p. 29; *Report*, Denver Civic and Commercial Association, Vol. II (1917), p. 4.

[1] *Sunset*, Vol. IX (May 1902), n. p.: Mark Sullivan: *Our Times*, Vol. I (New York: Charles Scribner's Sons; 1926), p. 189 n.

By the late 1920's and early thirties a shift in strategy, long under way, was clearly visible. Convention and exposition traffic was still large and even increasing, but no longer accounted for the drastic increases in the volume of Western travel over the early years of the century. Now the tourist came in his own car, bringing his family, who had interests that extended outside the city hotels and who cost too much to keep there. Often he wanted to settle, for if agricultural settlement projects dropped along with agricultural prices, still there was a good chance that he had sold out in Iowa when prices were still good, or had joined the growing ranks of pensioners. To the extent that he drew a pension, he was likely to be elderly and indisposed to adventure as well as limited in means. But by the twenties it was the fashion for even elderly pensioners to insist that they were still young, and they came west talking of mountains, desert, and beaches, even if they ended in some well-urbanized suburb. Perhaps the elastic meaning of the word *ranch* in the West (e.g., poultry ranch = suburban back-yard with more chickens than the family eats) is token of the widening vogue of the idea of the West as a place of open spaces and the outdoor life. The shift in the character of tourists was evident in the experience of the All-Year Club of Southern California, which had been founded in 1921 largely to attract visitors in the summer as well as the winter months, traditionally the season of the Raymond tourists, and which by 1932 found the summer visitors ahead in both numbers and expenditures.

There was still room for more people in the West in the thirties; actually the greatest influxes of population still lay ahead. And those who advertised the West still attended to the immigrant and home seeker, among others, casting a broad net boldly. They should have a large plan, said a member of the San Francisco Real Estate Board in 1921. "Pericles created a large plan for selling Athens two thousand years ago and Athens still is drawing interest on his investment." Californians, Incorporated, which shortly appeared (1922) to carry out a plan for the part of California dominated by the cities along San Francisco Bay, has continued to regard tourists as potential settlers ("The cream of the transplantable population in the United States today is the tourist tide," said its director in 1937), although by 1929 it knew enough about them to describe the tourist trade as a primary source of revenue, an end in itself.[2] In justifying their work the promoters pointed to profits that had not been clear even to those who reaped them, and thus magnified their own reputation and their power. But there was no thought of ceasing to attract newcomers when there was no longer a shortage of population, or when the bonanza of transients had clogged the parks and beaches: the economy of the region would not be satisfied with natural increase, and promoters who had been resourceful in serving their original purpose were no less resourceful in discovering new and further purposes.

The tourists and vacationers who surged through the West had long reflected and personified the tastes, follies, and aspirations of Americans both Eastern and Western. Swiss villas enclosed impartially both Rocky Mountain

[2] *San Francisco Chronicle*, February 18, 1921, p. 2:1; John Cuddy, unpublished address before San Francisco Advertising Club, October 27, 1937, pp. 4–6.

spas and New York elevated railroad stations. By the 1920's and thirties tourists were many enough to account not only for a substantial part of the permanent movement of population from East to West but also for a substantial part of the living of those who moved there. They were also many enough clearly to reflect, not merely by their temper but in the gross fact of their numbers, revolutionary changes in American society and in the American economy. The hordes that came west told much about what Americans thought of the West; they also told much about Americans' incomes, which supported a few thousand travelers after the Civil War and millions after the two world wars. By the second quarter of the twentieth century the numbers were so great that the tourist industry was becoming as representative of American mass production techniques as hog butchering, newspaper publishing, or automobile manufacturing. It was on such an assembly line, perversely enough, that the American tourist turned with increasing interest and enthusiasm to the shadows of the frontier and the wilderness.

5. AMERICANS
MOVE OUTDOORS

For generations Americans were so busy civilizing a wilderness, transforming it in the pattern of Europe, that they had little time for vacations, and when they had time the West was one of the last places they wanted to visit for pleasure. Then as the nation became stronger and the people came to have more money and more leisure, they also became more self-assured, less conscious of inferiority to the Old World; and the West, both because it had changed with the rest of the nation and because the eyes that looked at it had changed, became less formidable to American eyes. By the nineties the West was no longer physically dangerous, nor was it psychologically so disturbing as it had been; it was on the way to becoming civilized enough so that Westerners need not insist on the point. For many years to come it was no less eager to attract Eastern visitors than it had been in the pioneering years, but what it wanted of them changed, and what could best attract and hold them changed also. Together the East and the West discovered the West, although much that they discovered was past, and some had never been, outside of a book.

The shift in American habits and attitudes was comparable to the shift that had occurred in Europe in the eighteenth century, and may have had a similar social and psychological basis. "Precisely at this moment," Lewis Mumford has written of the retreat to nature that followed the triumph of classicism in the Augustan age, "when a purely urbane convention seemed established forever, a grand retreat began. In the Middle Ages such a retreat would have led to the monastery: it now pushed back to the country, by valiant mountain paths, like Rousseau's, or by mincing little country lanes, like that which led Marie Antoinette to build an English village in Versailles. . . . Nature was the fashion: 'every one did it.' " [1] America had begun to discover nature well before the Civil War, through Thoreau and his collaborators, but it lagged behind Europe, and not merely because it was not yet urbane, or even urban, but because it was still so Western. America was the West, the Western opportunity, and yet it writhed as it digested its riches; so many Americans were vicariously Westerners that not until the West accepted itself could many Easterners respond to it. While the paths by which Americans retreated to na-

[1] Lewis Mumford: *The Golden Day* (New York: Boni and Liveright; 1926), p. 49.

ture eventually were of all lengths and altitudes, at the beginning the least impressive were those that Westerners built.

A minor, subsidiary tradition of appreciating the outdoors goes far back into Western history. Many of the forty-niners had enjoyed life in the diggings, which may prove little, since most of them were too young to know better, and in every generation boys and young men enjoy escaping home-town mores. They would have looked more foolish than they were if they had taken no pleasures, since few could boast of profits. But apart from the gold seekers, some of the earliest Westerners amused themselves on local camping trips, perhaps to the coast near Santa Cruz to pick berries or near Newport to fish and eat rock oysters. Before there were roads they went on horseback, later by wagon. Oregon farmers took to moving their families to the mountains in the late summer or autumn, passing several weeks before harvest time in hunting and fishing, berry picking, and making jams and preserves. Young men sometimes welcomed assignments to pasturing horses and mules in the Sierra Nevada.[2]

By the eighties Westerners were camping on an impressive scale. Many families visited the Yellowstone with their own tents and equipment, said a writer in *Overland*, "for nowhere is rough-and-ready gypsy camping on the simplest scale more thoroughly appreciated as a family

[2] Eliza W. Farnham: *California, In-doors and Out . . .* (New York: Dix, Edwards & Co.; 1856), 213–47; A. N. Armstrong: *Oregon: Comprising a Brief History and Full Description of the Territories of Oregon and Washington . . .* (Chicago: C. Scott & Co.; 1857), pp. 77–9; Nash: *Oregon*, pp. 122–4; John B. Tileston: *Letters . . .* (n. p.; 1922), p. 85.

play than in the Western States." Some traced the habit
to the experience of sleeping outdoors while prospecting,
lumbering, or emigrating. When the governor of Colorado
Territory arranged a camping excursion for young lady
members of Speaker Colfax's party in 1865, they learned
that the practice had developed in early days when there
were no taverns.[3] In later years it was commonplace to
trace outdoor activities generally, including organized
sports, to the frontier heritage.

Yet the Western States were not always famous for their
athletes; there is substantial evidence that taste for the
outdoors moved west along with the indoors and had
arisen, in fact, far from the frontier. "I learn with pleasure," said Lord Bryce to the students of the University of
California in 1909, "that you have here kept within reasonable limits that passion for athletic sports and com-
petitions which has been pushed to excess in England
and Australia, and which in some American universities
goes so far that the only kind of distinction that students
value is that which attaches to proficiency in these com-
petitions." The Greek theater in which he spoke had not
yet found its destiny as a vessel for football rallies. Well
past pioneer times San Franciscans had had a reputation
for not relaxing, for overworking throughout the year.
"We are apt to forget about a vacation in California," said
a San Francisco journalist in 1880. "Nature does not

[3] C. F. Gordon Cumming: "The World's Wonderlands in
Wyoming and New Zealand," *Overland*, 2d series, Vol. V (Janu-
ary 1885), p. 8; Samuel Bowles: *The Switzerland of America;
A Summer Vacation in the Parks and Mountains of Colorado*
(Springfield: S. Bowles & Co.; 1869), p. 51.

remind us of it. . . . ." "There are no useful avocations rendered necessary by a long spell of hot weather, as on the Eastern coast," noted an English visitor. Most of the early Californians, moreover, had no time to relax, to let mere climate tempt them into the mountains or drive them from the city. They "do not live here to enjoy life," wrote John S. Hittell in 1863, "but to make money, so that they may enjoy life in some other country." And summer camping became popular in the East in the same years as in the West. The first organized private boys' camp in the United States was held on Lake Asquam, New Hampshire, in the early eighties, the first Y.M.C.A. boys' camp on Orange Lake, New York, in 1885; probably the most conspicuous campers in the West in the seventies were Easterners, not all of them tubercular, in Colorado. "Many refined Eastern States families do this," observed an English traveler.[4]

Outdoor recreation, in fact, became popular all over the United States within a few years; the West followed the East, and the East in turn, according to a writer in *Outing*, followed Europe, where the British had developed intercollegiate sports before the American Civil War. In

[4] James Bryce: *University and Historical Addresses* (New York: Macmillan Company; 1913), p. 240; John S. Hittell: *Bancroft's Pacific Coast Guide Book* (San Francisco: A. L. Bancroft & Co.; 1882), p. 197; "Summering has Commenced," *Californian*, Vol. II (July 1880), p. 86; Boddam-Whetham: *Western Wanderings*, p. 147; Hittell: *The Resources of California . . .* (2d ed.; San Francisco: A. Roman and Company; 1866), p. 442; Ralfe D. Miller: "Municipal Family Vacation Camps in California . . ." (unpublished M.A. thesis, University of California, Berkeley; 1939), p. 2; S. N. Townshend: *Colorado*, p. 41.

the seventies travelers were still commenting on American
backwardness in athletics, which some attributed to the
absence of a leisure class as well as to extremes in climate.
Billiards had seemed to take the place of field sports, even
in the West: "I saw billiard tables set up in wooden shanties on the plains of the North Platte," wrote a British
visitor in 1868, "and beyond the plains at the foot of the
Rocky Mountains." Even baseball in the first years after
the Civil War was open to the charge of professionalism;
it had its greatest following as a spectacle rather than as a
game. And then the college athletic clubs and teams began
to form, and outdoor sports spread from East to West; in
the eighties Americans began to replace British winners in
the records. Polo had appeared in 1876 at the Westchester
Club, by 1885 in Iowa, and by 1886 in Colorado Springs.
Canoe sailing, which was introduced from England in the
late sixties or early seventies, had spread to the West
Coast by 1886; and the next year the Oakland Canoe
Club astonished the country people by taking ten boats
to Clear Lake for its first cruise. The British Alpine Club
had organized in 1857, preceding the Swiss by six years,
the French by seventeen; the Appalachian Mountain Club
appeared at Boston in 1876, when Westerners generally
still considered mountaineering "to be a visionary, if not
a foolhardy, pursuit." The Far Western clubs appeared
late, the Oregon Alpine Club in 1887, the Sierra Club in
1892, under the presidency of John Muir, the Mazamas in
1894. Cycling went west in the same years: the San Francisco Bicycle Club organized in 1879, and in 1884, when
an Englishman, Thomas Stevens, made a celebrated trip
"Across America on a Bicycle," bumping part of the way

along railroad ties, groups of organized cyclists greeted him at Cheyenne and Laramie.[5]

By the nineties the whole character of tourism in Western America, so recently established, was clearly in flux. The indoor American, sedentary and dyspeptic of disposition, as he had seemed in the seventies, was giving way to a new American whose taste for outdoor amusements made Englishmen compare him to the Parisian and the Viennese. Some thought San Francisco more devoted to the outdoors than New York, and attributed the difference to southern European immigration to the West Coast, though more often the change seemed nationwide. If the Thames were American, said Maurice Low in 1905, it

[5] J. R. Dodge: "Rural Recreations," *Outing,* Vol. VII (December 1885), p. 303; Zincke: *Last Winter in the United States,* pp. 73–4; Boddam-Whetham: *Western Wanderings,* pp. 341–2; C. Turner: "The Progress of Athletism," *Outing,* Vol. XIII, (November 1888), pp. 112–13; Phil Weaver, Jr.: "Inter-Collegiate Foot-ball on the Pacific Coast," *Overland,* 2d series, Vol. XXI (February 1893), pp. 115, 130; J. B. Macmahan: "Polo in the West," *Outing,* Vol. XXVI (August 1895), pp. 385–7, 391; ibid., Vol. IX (January 1887), p. 387; William G. Morrow: "The Mosquito Fleet," *Overland,* 2d series, Vol. XX (July 1892), pp. 1–10; Kirk Munroe: "Modern Canoeing," *Wheelman,* Vol. III (December 1883), pp. 217–24; Engel: *La littérature alpestre,* pp. 220, 249; *Appalachia,* I (June 1876), p. 1; E. T. Coleman: "Mountains and Mountaineering in the Far West," *Alpine Journal,* Vol. VIII (August 1877), pp. 233–42; W. G. Steel, *The Mountains of Oregon* (Portland: D. Steel, Successor to Himes the Printer; 1890), pp. 67–84; *Sierra Club Bulletin,* Vol. I (January 1893), p. 23; *Land of Sunshine,* Vol. III (June 1895), p. 38; *Outing,* Vol. VIII (May 1886), p. 217; Myrtile Cerf: "The Wheel in California," *Overland,* 2d series, Vol. XXII (October 1893), p. 292; Thomas Stevens: "Across America on a Bicycle," *Outing,* Vol. VI (June 1885), p. 300; "Bicycling in Montana," ibid., Vol. V (December 1884), pp. 216–17.

would be dotted with excursion steamers.[6] The interests, fears, and compulsions that had produced the Raymond and Del Monte as European or Eastern transplants on the Pacific Coast were giving way to new interests in the outdoors and in the West; and meanwhile changes in transportation and in the national economy were enormously widening the clientele for Western vacations, and in turn affecting what tourists did and wanted to do.

The railroad had brought many Americans to the outdoors, especially when it learned to carry tents and duffle bags as well as steamer trunks, and when the branch lines pushed to the sites of beach and mountain resorts. The automobile did still more; it has been a major factor in a reorientation of tourists' activities and interests that goes beyond mere convenience and cheapness of access, and that long preceded the day when automobile travel meant immunity from delays, jolts, and dust. "In a little more than twenty years," said a writer in *Outlook* in 1924, "the automobile has revolutionized the average American's vacation, it has brought about a renaissance of the outdoors, and it has firmly planted a brand-new outdoor sport." The highway led into the outdoors even when the railroad still excelled in mere speed and comfort. "To possess a car is to become possessed of a desire to go far afield," said a writer in *Outing* early in the century; and even *Sunset*, the promotional organ of the Southern Pacific Railroad, recommended the automobile for the man "who thrills in an

[6] William Shepherd: *Prairie Experiences in Handling Cattle and Sheep* (London: Chapman & Hall; 1884), p. 121; A. Maurice Low: *America at Home* (London: G. Newnes; 1905), p. 157.

elemental contact with the reality of nature. . . . There is more than 'scenery' to be complacently inspected; there is the life and atmosphere of the West to be lived." [7] There were at least wider choices of camping places than the railroads offered, and great physical conveniences at low cost. Automobile enthusiasts were conspicuous in organizations such as the Save the Redwoods League, whose campaign began as an adjunct to the Pacific Auto Show of 1920.

Corollary to the automobile was the auto camp, which was common enough by the 1920's so that one might undertake a long trip in the West with fair assurance of finding a suitable place to pitch a tent within reach of the main highways. Middle Western farmers had invaded the Rockies in 1914, their cars piled high with tents and "everything but their own scenery." Denver looked on them as potential customers for groceries and gasoline as well, and opened Overland Park in 1915 as the first of the municipal campgrounds. Eventually it had a three-story clubhouse and a thousand camp-lots, where visitors might stay two weeks, or more if the park was not crowded. By 1923 there were 247 Colorado camps with a total of 643,015 campers during the year, and the camps were rapidly extending westward. "I had a few days after I got my wheat cut," said a Kansas farmer in Pueblo, "so I just loaded my family in the old bus and lit out." Fif-

---

[7] Frank E. Brumner: "Autocamping—the Fastest Growing Sport," *Outlook*, Vol. CXXXVII (July 16, 1924), p. 437; G. B. Betts: "The Rediscovery of America by the Automobile," *Outing*, Vol. XLII (May 1903), p. 171; "Main Traveled Roads in the Sunset Country," *Sunset*, Vol. XXXIX (July 1917), pp. 43, 82.

teen million Americans were making motor tours, said a
reporter (1924) who called them "the modern Argonauts."
"Their nightly habitat is the motor-tourist camp. They
are more or less consciously remodeling our civilization." [8]

In their early years the municipal camps were free, providing space, water, wood, electricity, laundry and sani-
tary facilities, lounging and dancing rooms, police pro-
tection, and sometimes even daily newspapers in the hope
that the visitors would stay long enough to spend some
money or decide to establish themselves permanently;
later there was a feeling that the free camps attracted undesirable itinerants; and by 1925 most were charging
around fifty cents a night. "The boosters who are backing
the advertising campaigns are appalled at the results of
their labors," said the New York *World* of the flood of
"tin-can tourists" on the West Coast, who had learned to
see "the California of Bret Harte" before them in "shining
pictures of their triumph out where even the 'persecuted
Chinamen became wealthy in a few years.' " Soon most of
the municipal camps disappeared under pressure from the
owners of hotels and private camps, but camping itself
continued to grow. Automobiles designed for camping—
such as the Reo "speed wagon bungalow" or the Hudson-
Essex "Pullman coach"—were already on the road in the
middle twenties, and camping trailers had made a modest
beginning. By the thirties the heirs to the municipal

[8] Arthur Chapman: "Among the Peaks of Colorado," *Travel*,
Vol. XXV (May 1915), p. 57; *Report*, Denver Civic and Com-
mercial Association, Vol. VIII (1923), p. 5; Albert Britt:
"Colorado Discovered," *Outing*, Vol. LXXVI (July 1920), p.
244; Earl C. May: "The Argonauts of the Automobile," *Saturday
Evening Post*, Vol. XCCVII (August 9, 1924), p. 25.

camps seemed to be the state and national park campgrounds on the one hand and on the other the more popular commercial tourist camps, already called motor courts or motels, and ranging from rude shacks or tents with common bath to luxurious hotel cottages or housekeeping bungalows. In 1950 a third of all tourists were using motor courts while en route, more than stopped at hotels and resorts.[9] There were still more courts in the West than in any other section, though the motorist who stopped in an Eastern or Southern tourist camp was no longer suspect of immorality.

What the motor cars and the motorists did to the outdoors would be long debated, but there is no doubt that the age of the automobile was the age in which the average American vacationer first found the West within his reach. "The automobile and the municipal camps," said *Sunset* in 1924, "have so cheapened travel that the wonders of the West's national parks today are accessible to hundreds of thousands who ten years ago had as much chance to see them as Hobson has of becoming admiral of the Swiss navy." "The closing of the pioneer age in America," pronounced *The New York Times*, "is really the opening up of an era of unprecedented mobility." Within one short decade trips that had been worth a book depreciated to

[9] *San Francisco Chronicle*, May 14, 1926, p. 18:4; William R. Mulvane: "Tenting on the New Campground," *Sunset*, Vol. LV (July 1925), pp. 12–13, 58; " 'Tin Can Tourists' Terrifying California," *Literary Digest*, Vol. LXXXV (May 16, 1925), pp. 73–6; Norman S. Hayner: "Auto Camping in the Evergreen Playground," *Social Forces*, Vol. IX (December 1930), pp. 263–4; *Travel Survey #1*, Curtis Publishing Company (Philadelphia: Curtis Publishing Co.; 1950), p. 43.

the value of a newspaper item, and the dangers of the West with them. Mrs. William R. Doremus, of Mountain Lakes, New Jersey, drove alone on a circle tour around the United States in 1929: "En route Mrs. Doremus had encountered bears, foxes, buffalo, cougars and other wild animals without being harmed, but the sting of a bee caused a serious knee infection, she wrote." [1]

The national parks became popular and populated as never before during the years when tourists were learning to travel long distances by automobile, just before and just after the First World War. Yosemite had reached a density of one thousand in a season only in 1869. A group of seventeen that came in 1865 was the largest ever. "We exhausted all the horses of the kingdom of Fremont," wrote Samuel Bowles, "and created famine in our path." The increase was slow even after the first carriage roads opened in 1874 and 1875; the annual total of visitors was still averaging around twenty-five hundred a season in the middle eighties, when old friends were complaining of commercialization. "There never will be another [Yosemite] as it was. . . . Its pristine loveliness is a thing of the past. . . ." Then came the avalanche. In 1907 the railroad replaced the stagecoach, at least to El Portal; in 1913 the automobile began to replace the railroad, against the advice of Lord Bryce, who had called it the serpent in the Garden of Eden. The next year more than fifteen thousand visitors came to the park, and the following year, 1915, more than thirty-three thousand. Henry L. Stimson,

---

[1] *Sunset*, Vol. LIII (September 1924), pp. 48–9; *The New York Times*, October 11, 1930, p. 16:4; ibid., August 18, 1929, p. 11:2.

visiting Glacier in 1913 after twenty-one years' absence, found himself in an efficient sight-seeing assembly-line that had grown with the crowds: "I was whirled about in motor cars which seemed an affront to the former sanctity of those mountains; [forced] to submit to being conducted by licensed guides over trails which I had myself discovered and made; in short everything was done to make us feel that the wilderness with its Indians had gone and modern American tourism had taken its place." [2] Glacier had 12,138 visitors in 1913, almost twice as many as the year before; by 1950, the year of Stimson's death, it had 485,950.

The other parks boomed likewise in the twentieth century, especially as automobiles made it easier for tourists to get in to the mountains and the war made it harder for them to get out of the country for pleasure trips abroad. The grotesque and the picturesque continued to draw crowds. Bradford Torrey, the ornithologist, who spent two months in the Yosemite in the first decade of the century, found that even the guides thought him strange for staying so long and for repeating walks that had pleased him, while Torrey in turn was surprised that others were "contented to stare about them for a day or two, expend a few expletives, snap a camera at this and that, and anon

[2] Samuel Bowles: *Across the Continent: A Summer's Journey* . . . (Springfield: S. Bowles & Co.; 1865), p. 232; James H. Lawrence: "Discovery of the Nevada Fall," *Overland*, 2d series, Vol. IV (October 1884), p. 371; *Report of the Director of the National Park Service* . . . *1917* (Washington: Government Printing Office; 1917), p. 190; Bryce: *University and Historical Addresses*, pp. 399–401; Henry L. Stimson, *My Vacations* (n. p.: privately printed; 1949), p. 65.

be off again." A Tennesseean who left on the second day commented that he "didn't wish to lose the thrill" through further acquaintance. Torrey himself admitted having to set a destination when he walked, "for I, no less than my fellows, have yet to outgrow the primitive need of 'a place to go to,' even when I go mostly for what is to be enjoyed by the way." Yet at least some of the increase in park attendance seemed to represent greater enjoyment of the outdoors, of the atmosphere and the larger panorama of the country rather than of famous curiosities. Ray Stannard Baker, reporting on Yellowstone for *Century* in 1903, observed that he seemed to forget the objective point, the geysers, for the natural glory of the wilderness and the outdoor life. A visitor to the Grand Canyon early in the century recalled that "people stopped between two trains, stopped, looked and listened, marveled at the scene or complained of the cost. . . . Some looked on speechless until they fainted or prayed; the rest ran away to buy post-card pictures of it and inscribe them with cant phrases of approval." Ten years later the tourists seemed more appreciative and intelligent; a stay of a week or two had become more normal.[3]

Appreciation of the wilderness by the early years of the century was more than a mood; it was becoming a movement, which was to have its spokesmen and its literature; it was on the way to becoming institutionalized. It may have advanced the more rapidly through the person

[3] Bradford Torrey: *Field Days in California* (Boston: Houghton Mifflin Company; 1913), pp. 189, 201–2; Ray S. Baker: "A Place of Marvels," *Century Magazine*, Vol. LXVI (August 1903), pp. 481–2; David M. Steele: *Going Abroad Overland* (New York: G. P. Putnam's Sons; 1917), pp. 38–9.

of the President of the United States, who set a vigorous example of enjoying the outdoors, trapping White House visitors into cross-country hikes, prodding sluggish army officers out of their armchairs and into their saddles, himself sleeping under the sky at the Yosemite with John Muir while San Francisco society awaited in the valley with banquet and reception. But Roosevelt had his many collaborators at the pen and on the platform, who found that popular favor was turning to them. It expressed itself in the demand for the nature fiction of writers as varied as Gene Stratton Porter, Ernest Thompson Seton, Mary Roberts Rinehart, and Jack London; in the growth of organizations such as Seton's Tribe of Woodcraft Indians (1902), Daniel Carter Beard's Society of the Sons of Daniel Boone (1905), and the Boy Scouts of America (1910). As a magazine editor, Beard had felt that there was little response to his first efforts to make his readers love nature, "especially the primitive wilderness—unmanicured, unshaven, without a haircut." "In the beginning there were very few on my side and I felt as lonely as a warrior in a Quaker meeting." [4] Soon a whole generation of boys looked to him as their guide into the forest.

The American tourist boom of the years of the First World War roughly coincided with a new interest in pack trips and "roughing it" all over the West, even before the full impact of the war in America. Mary Roberts Rinehart told the readers of a popular monthly magazine about her experience on the first of a series of escorted pack-trips through Glacier National Park in 1915, over a route three

[4] Daniel C. Beard: *Hardly a Man is Now Alive* (New York: Doubleday, Doran & Company, Inc.; 1939), p. 357.

hundred miles long, and began to use Glacier as a setting
for some of her popular novels. "The old West is almost
gone," she urged. "Now is the time to see it—not from a
train window; not, if you can help it, from an automobile,
but afoot or on horseback, leisurely, thoroughly." [5] The
Sierra Club had inaugurated its annual outings in 1901,
exploring the high mountain country beyond the well-
known features of the Yosemite Valley, but Mrs. Rinehart,
through her articles and serials in the popular magazines,
spoke to a larger audience. The Santa Fe Railway advertised excursions "Off the Beaten Path" in the Southwest,
ranging up to thirty-day saddle-and-pack camping trips,
and set up a "Camping-out Bureau" to give information
on how "to really rough-it or camp out-de-luxe."

The wilderness continued to draw more visitors after
the war, which happily left a surplus of pack animals as
the gasoline tractor displaced the mule at the plow. Congress had authorized leases for summer-home sites and
other recreational purposes in the national forests since
1915, but the public first came in numbers when the Government began to build and pave Western highways after
the war. By 1921 Aldo Leopold, then a Forest Service
officer in New Mexico, was invoking Gifford Pinchot's
"doctrine of highest use" to justify preserving representative forest areas as wilderness; by 1928 and 1929 the
Forest Service was bold enough to set aside the first of the
wilderness areas, though uncertain enough of popular

[5] Emerson Hough: "Get Outdoors!" *Sunset*, Vol. XLI
(September 1918), pp. 16, 50; Mary Roberts Rinehart: *Through
Glacier Park; Seeing America First with Howard Eaton* (Bos-
ton: Houghton Mifflin Company; 1916), pp. 8, 12, 15–16, 85.

support so that it permitted grazing and timber-cutting on them. It used the term "primitive areas" for a few years (1930–9) because, according to conservationists, the public might find the word "wilderness" repulsive. The high priests of the wilderness movement invoked the sanction of ecology and justified the undisturbed balance of nature on scientific grounds as on æsthetic grounds. To them the buzzard, the lynx, and the coyote were as worthy as the antelope, and man's noblest ambition was to advance the works of men as little as possible. "The day is almost upon us," warned Leopold in 1925, "when canoe travel will consist in paddling up the noisy wake of a motor launch and portaging through the back yard of a summer cottage. When that day comes, canoe travel will be dead, and dead too will be a part of our Americanism. . . . The day is almost upon us when a pack train must wind its way up a gravelled highway and turn out its bell mare in the pasture of a summer hotel. When that day comes, the pack train will be dead . . . and Kit Carson and Jim Bridger will be names in a history lesson." [6]

The depression of the thirties brought further interest in the wilderness; it was a time of triumph and of despair for the nature lovers. The recreational counterpart of the

[6] Aldo Leopold: "The Wilderness and Its Place in Forest Recreational Policy," *Journal of Forestry*, Vol. XIX (November 1921), pp. 718–21; Harvey Broome: "Our Basis of Understanding," *Living Wilderness*, Vol. XIX (Winter 1954–5), p. 47; *The New York Times*, November 4, 1928, III, p. 4:1–2; L. G. Romell: "The Importance of Natural Areas to Forestry Officially Recognized," *Science*, Vol. LXIX (June 28, 1929), pp. 660–1; *Living Wilderness*, Vol. II (November 1936), p. 16; Aldo Leopold: "Wilderness as a Form of Land Use," *Journal of Land and Public Utility Economics*, Vol. I (October 1925), p. 403.

back-to-the-soil movement was a great upsurge in Western travel and especially in camping and hiking and mountain climbing. Recovery and relief programs gave the conservation agencies money and manpower as never before. The hikers had been planning wilderness trails along the mountain ranges especially since the early twenties: the Appalachian Trail Conference organized in 1925. The Civilian Conservation Corps was available after 1933, as well as private hands, and it turned to work on the Pacific Crest Trailway and other routes, which members of the Youth Hostel movement, newly spread from Europe (1934), were quick to use. The sponsors of the Pacific Crest Trails Conference looked to the Appalachian Conference as a model; their objective was to maintain and defend "a primitive wilderness pathway in an environment of solitude, free from sights and sounds of a mechanized nature." They met at Pasadena, the headquarters of different and earlier traditions in Western tourism. The Sierra Club also prospered in California, while a new organization, Trail Riders of the National Forests (later Trail Riders of the Wilderness), an offshoot of the American Forestry Association, sent out its first party by pack train along the South Fork of the Flathead River in July 1933. The first river tourist excursion party had set out in 1926 on the Green River, which generations had known only in photographs after the pioneering expeditions of John Wesley Powell in the seventies; by 1940 "the canyons were getting to be places where you held family picnics and accidentally encountered old friends." [7]

[7] Benton MacKaye: "Why the Appalachian Trail?" *Living Wilderness*, Vol. I (September 1935), p. 7; Clinton C. Clark,

Yet all was not serene in Eden. The purist school of conservationists had been grumbling at the extension of roads and trails in national forests since the twenties, and to some of them the resources that the New Deal opened up to the Forest Service and the Park Service and to the power and irrigation agencies were less boon than catastrophe. The Wilderness Society organized in January 1935, "born of an emergency in conservation which admits of no delay," and dedicated to the idea that "scenery and solitude are intrinsically separate things, that the motorist is entitled to his full share of scenery, but that motorway and solitude together constitute a contradiction." "The fashion is," it proclaimed, "to barber and manicure wild America as smartly as the modern girl." The CCC, in a "wild orgy of road-building," said *Nature Magazine*, which cheered on the iconoclasts, "bids fair to solve the wilderness problem in much the same way the Turks set about solving the Armenian problem—by annihilation." Through its organ, *Living Wilderness*, the Wilderness Society denounced truck trail and dam programs and pleaded for restraint in meeting the demands of the multitude. The newly marked trails in the national parks, wrote a correspondent, reminded him of those in Europe, with their neatly lettered signs, "*Schöner Aussicht*," "beautiful view," at the observation points. "It was all spoiled," said another, just returned from improve-

comp.: *The Pacific Crest Trailway* (Pasadena: Pacific Crest Trail System Conference; 1945), pp. 15–17; *The New York Times*, April 25, 1937, XI, p. 6:2–4; "The Pioneer Trail Riders," *American Forests*, Vol. XXXIX (September 1933), p. 401; Wallace Stegner, ed.: *This is Dinosaur* (New York: Alfred A. Knopf, Inc.; 1955), pp. 66, 69.

ments in the Tetons: "there was no mystery—no lure—
just the weary certainty that if you plodded patiently up
endless switchbacks you were *sure* to reach Amphitheatre
Lake." "The Lolo Trail is no more," mourned a contributor to the *Journal of Forestry* (1935). "The bulldozer
blade has ripped out the hoof tracks of Chief Joseph's
ponies. . . . It is gone, and in its place there is only the
print of the automobile tire in the dust." [8] The new advocates of the wilderness may have been fighting a losing
battle: their argument of vast reservations for the pleasure of the few seemed vulnerable in a democracy, and
their resistance to the development of economic resources
ran contrary to the American tradition and the pressures
of depression, war, and prosperity. Yet they were a vigorous and a growing company, capable of wielding considerable political influence when aroused.

Perhaps the most striking aspect of the changing attitudes toward nature was the new vogue of the Southwestern desert that had developed since the 1890's and reached
spectacular dimensions in the thirties and thereafter. Pioneers and early tourists alike had scorned the land and its
human heritage. It was the epitome of ugliness and empti-

[8] William C. Gregg: "Has the Forest Service 'Gone Daffy'?"
Outlook, Vol. CXXIX (February 11, 1925), pp. 226–7; *Living
Wilderness*, Vol. I (September 1935), pp. 1–2; "A New Defender of the Wilderness," *Nature Magazine*, Vol. XXVI (September 1935), pp. 178–9; *Living Wilderness*, Vol. III (December
1937), p. 10; Elers Koch, "The Passing of the Lolo Trail," *Journal of Forestry*, XXXIII (February 1935), pp. 78–104, quoted in
"Three Great Western Wildernesses . . . ," *Living Wilderness*,
Vol. I (September 1935), p. 9; James P. Gilligan: "Wilderness
in a Democracy," *Living Wilderness*, Vol. XX (Spring–Summer
1955), pp. 25–9.

ness at a time when Westerners were straining to find some
faint shadow of Switzerland on one side, in the Colorado
Rockies, of Italy on the other, on the California seacoast.
Clarence King's friends later recalled how King had described the wonders of the region of the fortieth parallel
so glowingly that a senator "confessed strong desire to
see 'those marvelous isothermal lines,' " but even King's
literary powers were slow to sell the land itself; as his
valet said of the Grand Canyon: "It is no place for a
gentleman, sir!" [9] Those who were ill-advised enough to
spend a summer in California, when the dry breath of the
desert reached out toward the coast, warned of the consequences—twenty pounds lighter, "skin like a chip, juices
dried in me, nerves tense, and brain on fire"; most winter
and spring tourists tried to escape to the East not later
than June. Then people began to discover the desert, many
of them Easterners or Europeans rather than Westerners,
and what they found was the most authentic claim to
æsthetic merit in all of the United States.

Anthropologists on the trail of prehistoric Indian civilizations were among the first serious students of the desert
country: Adolph F. A. Bandelier, a Swiss, and Gustaf E. A. Nordenskiold, a Swede. By the time they reported
their investigations, in the early nineties, more romantic
spirits were calling attention to the Southwestern Indians:
the New Englander Charles Lummis and the Englishman
George Wharton James. Then the artists began to discover

[9] *Clarence King Memoirs*, Century Association, New York,
King Memorial Committee (New York: G. P. Putnam's Sons;
1904), pp. 382, 348; Anna E. Dickinson: *A Ragged Register*
. . . (New York: Harper & Brothers; 1879), pp. 30–1.

the Southwest. Bert G. Phillips, a New Yorker who had studied art in Paris, went to New Mexico in 1898; he was one of the first of the Southwestern artists, and became known as founder of the Taos art colony. Meanwhile the desert was finding a place in literature, not only in the romantic California novels of Gertrude Atherton, as later in the Southwestern cowboy epics of Zane Grey, but in the essays and poems of Mary Hunter Austin, the young schoolteacher from Illinois who found unhappiness and then refuge in the Mojave, and told readers of the *Atlantic Monthly* of "lotus charm," "deep breaths, deep sleep, and the communion of stars." [1]

The new charm of the desert seemed to be not only the circumstance of its not having seemed charming long enough to be familiar—Santa Fe is "the only picturesque spot in America yet undiscovered by the jaded globe trotter," said Agnes Laut as late as 1911—but also the stark, harsh quality that had repelled an earlier generation, and that persisted even in the desert cattle-country, long after more intensive uses in moister climates had made the prairies into pastures and farmyards. To the wilderness lover, the desert sometimes seemed a last refuge, especially before airplanes and air conditioning made it a suburb of the metropolis. The "practical men," having destroyed the forests and prairies, have turned to the desert, said J. C. Van Dyke (1901), but "reclaiming a

[1] *A Scientist on the Trail; Travel Letters of A. F. Bandelier, 1880–1881*, George P. Hammond, ed. (Berkeley: University of California Press; 1949); Gustaf E. A. Nordenskiold: *The Cliff Dwellers of the Mesa Verde, Southwestern Colorado . . .* (Stockholm: P. A. Norstedt & Söner; 1893); Mary Austin: *The Land of Little Rain* (Boston: Houghton Mifflin Company; 1903).

waste may not be so easy as breaking a prairie or cutting down a forest. And Nature will not always be driven from her purpose." The austerity of the dry country seemed to repel the impious hand of the cultivator, and so it seemed in a sense wilder than the Pacific shore. Yet it had a clean, uncluttered quality that somehow attracted the æsthetic mind of the early years of the century. Ray Stannard Baker found that the spacing of the bushes and cacti gave "the desert in many places a veritable park-like appearance, and one can hardly believe that men have not had the care of these wild denizens of the dry soil." "After all," he said, "there is no desert," nothing "more pitifully forlorn, more deserted, more irreclaimable, and more worthless than the man-made deserts of northern Wisconsin and Michigan, where fire has followed the heedless lumberman. . . ." In 1952 Joseph Wood Krutch spoke also of how the desert had "a curious air of being a park rather than a wilderness," but the idea must have been especially striking half a century earlier, when in general men had not yet begun to spoil the Southwest nor to repair the damage they had done in the East and Middle West. "No part of the United States," Baker told the readers of *Century*, "is less generally known than the Southwest, and none is better worth knowing. Of no other part of the United States is so large a proportion of the unpleasant and unattractive features known so well, and so small a proportion of the beauties, wonders, and utilities known so little." The desert's bad reputation, he thought, was "chiefly founded upon the hasty observations and reports of dusty transcontinental travelers, car-weary for three or four days, the edge of their interest quite blunted with longing for the green wonders and soft sunshine of California." [2]

Desert-country motifs soon became picturesque around the turn of the century, acceptable as interior decoration and as architecture. A new school of tastemakers who included Elbert Hubbard, the sage of East Aurora and editor of *The Philistine*, and Gustav Stickley (Stoeckel), of Eastwood, New York, editor of *The Craftsman (An Illustrated Monthly Magazine for the Simplification of Life)*, rebelled against the decorative façades of industrial America and against industrialism itself. They looked to English advocates of craftsmanship, as Ruskin and Morris; and in justifying the handicrafts and the return to simplicity that they preached, they were delighted to find a native American tradition of honest craftsmanship, functional and close to the soil. Stickley had begun by following Colonial models in his chair factory; then, about 1900, he turned to his own designs, angular and naked of ornamentation, and to Indian, Spanish, and "mission" themes. Visiting Arizona, he found himself entranced at Yuma, a spot that most travelers left with enthusiasm appropriate to one of the warmer circles of hell, and engaged in a spirited argument with the superintendent of the Government Indian school over the preservation of native basketry and pottery. The first Craftsman house, which Stick-

[2] Agnes C. Laut: "Through Our National Forests," *Travel*, XVII (July 1911), p. 441; John C. Van Dyke: *The Desert* . . . (New York: Charles Scribner's Sons; 1918), pp. 60–1; Ray Stannard Baker: "The Great Southwest," *Century Magazine*, Vol. LXIV (May–June 1902), pp. 5, 213, 216, 221; Joseph Wood Krutch: *The Desert Year* (New York: Sloane; 1952), p. 23.

ley presented early in 1904, recalled the California missions. Lummis and his associates in Los Angeles had preceded him, but Stickley, among others, conferred the sanction of Eastern authority, and the "mission" style caught on rapidly, especially among newcomers to the West. "Oddly enough," said one of Stickley's followers, who built a mission-style house in Pasadena, "it is the Westerner who demands and admires European 'style' of architecture and wants his house built out of a book, while it is the tourist from the East who seeks out and admires every bit of native and every bit of Mission architecture. . . ." No other American style seemed so well to satisfy "the instinct for home and for some tie that connects us with the land." [3]

Eventually, by the late twenties, the Southwest was host to some of the most advanced forms of American experimental architecture, and Frank Lloyd Wright, scorning the more literal translations of Mexican and Indian forms only somewhat less than he scorned conventional Middle Western building, looked to southern Arizona not only as a place of remarkable natural beauty but as refuge and emancipation from tradition: "here came opportunity, ideal site unspoiled." Meanwhile Western and outdoor forms and Eastern refinements and comforts were already fused in the forms of tourist architecture that began to

[3] Gustav Stickley: "The Colorado Desert and California," *Craftsman*, Vol. VI (June 1904), pp. 239, 245; Stickley: *Craftsman Homes* (New York: The Craftsman Publishing Company; 1909), p. 9; Arthur Jerome Eddy: "A California House Modeled on the Simple Lines of the Old Mission Dwelling . . . ," *Craftsman*, Vol. XI (November 1906), p. 211; Stickley: *Craftsman Homes*, p. 198.

appear early in the century. The new hotels of the 1890's were still Georgian or Swiss Gothic palaces, larger than the original Del Monte and Raymond rather than different in style or inspiration, efficient conduits of the "hotel-civilization" that Henry James found in Florida as in New York. In the first years of the new century, however, the Hispanophilia of Charles Lummis's Landmarks Club had sufficiently infected the Riverside hotelman, Frank Miller, to prompt him to begin building the almost unbelievable Mission Inn. By 1905 the Santa Fe Railway boasted of El Tovar, the new Fred Harvey hotel at Grand Canyon, built of "native boulders and pine logs," the interior woods mainly peeled slabs and roughhewn beams. The Glacier National Park Hotel a few years later was in a transitional phase, mingling Old World and New World themes: the guests arrived in jinrikishas, entered through a Chinese pagoda and imitation cherry blossoms, and chose between Swiss-costumed waitresses in the dining room or Geisha-girl waitresses in the grillroom, but on the other hand they ate to the sound of tom-toms beaten by Blackfoot Indians (educated at Carlisle), and the furnishings included bear-skins and Navajo rugs on the floors and pelts and skulls on the walls. By the twenties Indian themes seemed conventionally joined to high prices in luxury hotels such as the Ahwahnee, in Yosemite (1927), or the Wigwam, near Phoenix (1929), although in the Arizona Biltmore (1929), Wright introduced a new approach to desert architecture. The new Jackson Lake Lodge in the Grand Tetons, opened in 1955, displeased some of its patrons because the architecture was not properly "rustic" or Western, as well as because it lacked swimming pools, tennis courts, and golf courses.[4]

Even some of the smaller resorts that catered to mountain climbers carefully synthesized luxury and simplicity: outside, simple log cabins; inside, complete bathrooms, electric lights, box springs, and steam heat, though with furnace and radiator concealed, in deference to the traditional grate fire. The permanent tent-camps that grew up in the national parks (at Yosemite after 1899) soon boasted not only wooden flooring, hotel-type furniture, and maid service, but dining rooms and nightly entertainment—"every comfort consistent with 'roughing it de luxe.' " For further color they annexed, when they could, some relic of pioneer days such as John Hance, the old prospector who lived on the rim of Grand Canyon, or Galen Clark, the patriarch of the Yosemite campfire. The leading hotels were no less luxurious and expensive than they had been, but their façades had changed, and from year to year, their advertising. The Santa Fe Railway, which as late as 1908 referred to the "great resort hotels" of California as places "where you meet persons of refinement and wealth," represented a general trend by omitting those words from a revised edition of the same pamphlet that it issued three years later.[5]

[4] Frank Lloyd Wright: *An Autobiography* (London: Longmans, Green & Company; 1932), p. 302; Henry James: *The American Scene* (London: Chapman & Hall; 1907), pp. 438–9; David M. Steele: *Going Abroad Overland* (New York: G. P. Putnam's Sons; 1917), pp. 95–5, 100; *The New York Times*, August 7, 1955, II, p. X27:3–6.

[5] Chauncey H. Vivian: "The Dude Invasion of the Once

The railroads likewise tried to bring the West into the limited trains. Whereas tourists in Mexico in the eighties were warned to be on their guard at each stop against the natives, who to one anxious lady seemed "ready to take advantage of the least relaxation of vigilance," [6] by 1929 the Santa Fe, which had already called trains The Navajo and The Chief, introduced a train courier dressed in a Navajo blouse and belt, with turquoise and silver necklaces and thunderbird emblem on her hat, who had been through "intensive training under recognized authorities on Southwestern history, archaeology and Indian lore"; in 1954 her successor on the westbound El Capitán was an Indian guide in full tribal costume. In lieu of draped Victorian parlors on wheels, in 1941 the Union Pacific Railroad boasted of a "Frontier Shack" tavern-car on its streamliner City of Denver, with rough-board ceiling and walls, decorated with posters and kerosene lanterns; the Southern Pacific's new Sunset Limited (1952) had, along with a "French Quarter Lounge" car with white wrought-iron grillwork, a "Pride of Texas Coffee Shop": "Here leather walls bear authentic pioneer Texas brands, applied with a hot iron. Antique silver longhorns and spurs accentuate the Texas motif." The Great Northern called its coffee-shop car on the new Empire Builder "The Ranch," and adorned it with livestock brands, branding irons, and beamed ceilings.

Wild West," *Touring Topics,* Vol. XVIII (February 1926), pp. 15–16, 32; *California Limited . . . ,* Santa Fe Railway (n. p.; 1908).

[6] Mrs. J. Gregory Smith: *Notes of Travel in Mexico and California* (St. Albans, Vt.: Printed at the *Messenger and Advertiser* Office; 1886), pp. 23–4.

Perhaps the most characteristic institutionalization of the new era in Western recreation and vacation travel was the dude ranch. Nothing else symbolized so well the changed attitude of twentieth-century Americans toward the idea of the West, and toward Western life as distinguished from the climatic or geographical curiosities that had attracted tourists in an earlier time to live the good life of Saratoga or Atlantic City in a transplanted Eastern resort hotel.

The ranch country was still new when it began to take in paying guests. Easterners in search of health were renting cheaply built cottages on Colorado ranches during the summers in the 1870's, boarding with the owner's family or doing their own housekeeping; some simply pitched tents. And young Englishmen, attracted by newspaper advertisements that promised agricultural training, and by their own "visions of 'broncho-busting' and rope-swinging," came as boarders or unpaid apprentices to ranches and farms in Minnesota, Dakota, and Wyoming, usually to their own bitter disappointment when they suffered the hardship and monotony of a winter on the plains.[7] The first ranchers to make a living systematically out of tourists rather than livestock, however, were the Eaton brothers, Pennsylvanians who had been in Dakota for two years when they induced Theodore Roosevelt to come west in 1883, and who in 1904 moved to a new location near Sheri-

[7] Anna Gordon: *Camping in Colorado, with Suggestions to Gold-seekers, Tourists and Invalids* (New York: Authors' Publishing Company; 1879), pp. 95–7; F. W. Grey: *Seeking Fortune in America* (London: Smith, Elder & Co.; 1912), p. v; "A Glimpse of the West," *Blackwood's*, Vol. CXXXV (June 1884), pp. 762–6.

[167]

dan, Wyoming. Many a rancher went into "dude wrangling" only gradually and informally, reluctant to admit
that it was more than a side line or a kindness to friends;
it was not until the early 1920's, when many a Westerner
made on dudes what he lost on cattle, that the West generally awoke to realize that it had a new industry. By 1924
the ranchers were enough awake to form the first of the
trade associations, and to begin to try to define what they
were.

The dude ranch's atmosphere in time became fairly well
standardized as a judicious mixture of comfort and color.
The clientele apparently was a little like Mary Garden, the
opera singer, who said that she wanted to marry a Western rancher. "But he must be a gentleman rancher. I would
not want to have to work . . . to wash dishes or do house-
work." The associations bravely compiled their bluebooks
and approved lists, excluding establishments that were
primarily gasoline stations and roadhouses, and debating
whether a genuine dude-ranch took overnight trade or
operated on the European plan, but sometimes it was hard
to say whether the stagecoach or buckboard that met the
train was much more synthetic than the ranch animals
themselves. The handsome cowboys who gave female guests
the titillating illusion of being squired across the pages of
Owen Wister or Zane Grey often were college students on
vacation, whose background might be a five-credit course
in "recreational ranching" offered through the school of
commerce. Actually the old-type cowhand, who wrangled
four-legged rather than two-legged stock, often failed to
deliver the kind of authenticity that the customer wanted,
even if there had been enough of him. After the Rocky

Mountain ranches, following the lead of their Eastern
competition, began opening for winter sports in the middle
thirties, the secretary of the Colorado Dude Ranchers' Association bluntly recommended hiring professional skiers:
"An old cowhand on a pair of skis usually looks as
if he were about to play London Bridge . . . is falling
down." [8] Often the guests outnumbered the cattle as well
as the cowboys, and the cow ponies would have disappeared from some areas if they were not essential to atmosphere.

Dude-ranch advertising was heaviest in "quality" pub-
lications, such as *Country Life, Town and Country, Vogue,*
and the *Junior League Magazine;* and in reaching their
more expensive prospects the railroads and the ranchers
stressed the authentically rough and natural features
rather than swimming pools and golf courses. The industry did not want highways into the ranches, said a railroad
representative at an association session; rather it wanted,
as it were, to destroy good roads in its advertising, to preserve the idea of the wilderness. On the other hand, the
market was not afraid of airplane fields, and those reposi-
tories of frontier atmosphere with good airline connections
or even fields of their own had a real advantage. In the
1950's Frontier Airlines, which connected Billings, Salt
Lake, Denver, and El Paso, proudly advertised itself as
"The Dude Ranch Airline." The ranchers had to sense out
the conflicting desires of the "dudes," who wanted to escape from the artificiality of city life but usually not com-

[8] *San Francisco Chronicle*, October 21, 1923, p. 2:2; *The
New York Times*, November 15, 1936, XII, p. 1XX:1–2; ibid.,
February 28, 1937, XII, p. 4XX:5.

pletely. "They want to wear overalls and a loud shirt and a pair of cowboy boots and rough it (not too roughly, of course, for to many of them wearing overalls is roughing it and they still want baths, nicely served meals and clean pleasant surroundings)." [9]

By the mid-twenties the ranches were frankly locating for climate and scenery; by 1928 even the Eaton brothers bought a ranch in Arizona for winter-season operations; and "ranches" in the desert, in areas where fodder and stock had to be imported along with the guests, began to compete seriously with the hotels of Florida and southern California. Pressure of population in desert country suddenly became a major concern to nature lovers who only a few years before had implored passers-by to stop and look, and so reservations like the Joshua Tree National Monument (1936) had to be created so that visitors would not wear the desert out and carry it away. One used to camp freely without trespassing, said a botanist (1954), but "every desirable spot, every spot with a seep or trickle, is now filed on and has signs 'Keep Out.' " Land that was overgrazed at ten head of cattle per square mile blossomed out in the highest concentration of ranches that the West had ever seen. The new long drives followed the sun twice a year, the cowhands at the wheels of trucks and the livestock in trailers along with other tourist equipment, and with the alfalfa that the stock ate. Arizona cities had begun to feature city-type amusements early in the century, such as tennis, golf, and automobiling (in 1910 Tucson, soon to become the center of a ranch area, boasted of a

[9] *Minutes,* Dude Ranchers' Association (1931), pp. 55, 61; *The Dude Rancher,* VI (April–May 1938), p. 12.

" 'speedway' or boulevard thirty-five miles long") ; [1] these
continued but became subordinate in advertising to the
newer appeal of the frontier. Increasingly the ranch moved
to the market, not only to the land of winter sunshine but
to the states of heavy population: by the thirties there
were dude ranches as far west as the Philippines and as far
east as New England, where a local taste for rural life had
appeared before the First World War in the migration of
wealthy city-dwellers to abandoned farms; by the later
forties Western riding clubs within New York City itself
were drawing on the dude ranches' clientele. If social sanction for ranch life seemed to be lacking, it came with the
visit of the Prince of Wales to his ranch in Alberta in the
fall of 1923.

Actually the dude ranch, for all its humors and inconsistencies, was less impressive for its artificiality than for
representing the shift in the interests of the well-to-do
tourists who had once made headquarters at the Del Monte
or the Broadmoor, and who now seemed to seek out the
kind of Western life, and those parts of the West, that once
they had taken great pains to avoid. There is a necessarily
synthetic quality in most attempts to recreate or preserve
the old West, and if the dude ranches were notably more
synthetic than the primitive areas that public authority
tried to maintain or develop, such as the Theodore Roosevelt National Memorial Park in North Dakota, yet the
better representatives of the type were less synthetic than
what the tourist often found in Western towns. Perhaps

---

[1] *History of Joshua Tree National Monument,* U. S. National Park Service (Washington: Government Printing Office;
1955), p. 47; *Tucson, The Sportman's Paradise* (n. p.; [1910?]).

they represented the most acceptable alternative to the heat and tensions of the East for Americans who had grown up among grain fields rather than cattle ranges, and to whom there was something painful in the memory of their real pioneer or rural past. If the dude ranches seemed sometimes to represent a kind of re-creation of the Western dime novel or radio serial-program, as the pseudo-Hispanic-American pageantry of some of the California towns corresponded to Mrs. Jackson's *Ramona*, nevertheless there had been a cattle country, there still was one (though of a somewhat different kind), and it would have been more difficult to amuse resident tourists on miniature versions of Western wheat, sheep, or sugar-beet ranches, or in the copper mines of Butte, the lumber camps of western Oregon. The tourist had, as the American tourist had always had, a desire for action and sociability, and the routine of the dude ranches, centering around horses and cowhands, satisfied it reasonably and healthfully along with the new taste for the outdoors. Over the years more than a few dudes, acquiring a taste for ranch life more genuine than the contrivances of summer entertainment, became ranchers themselves, and were proud to register in New York hotels as visitors from Wyoming or Montana. Some of them might raise few cattle except by proxy, but at least in the bad times they lost no more than those who were there for a living rather than for a life. Old-timers who looked at their new neighbors to scoff soon learned that the profits of renting horses held up better than the profits of selling beef, and themselves moved into an industry where the traffic was regular and the overhead was low.

The symbolism of tourists' interests in the West, and of

what Westerners thought tourists' interests were and ought to be, took sometimes more extreme shape in the festivals that become traditional in the tourist country, and in their by-products, than in the typical dude-ranches. The Western fairs of the 1870's and eighties, and even into the nineties, stressed mainly the productivity of Western farms and mines; if they reached beyond the ideas of natural riches and local enterprise, it was to the traditions of the Old World rather than to the local color of the New. The Colorado territorial fair of 1872, rejoiced the editor of *Out West*, gave "evidences of taste and refinement": "remnants of the old days of lawlessness, and drinking, and gambling" were declining. Most chambers of commerce were eager to forget those who had occupied the ground before them. Fandangos were a thing of the past in the Pajaro Valley, near Monterey, noted a local booster with satisfaction: "They were resorted to by ambitious politicians some years ago to conciliate the Spanish vote, but the real genuine article has been defunct some time. . . ." [2] When the Western States and railroads planned their exhibits for the fairs at Atlanta in 1881 or at Chicago in 1893, they apparently strove to attract settlers rather than tourists, and the most popular arrangements seemed to be no more Western than the obelisk, which appeared in such materials as apples, wheat, and bottled olive-oil. Los Angeles County displayed forty-five hundred oranges at Chicago, in the form of the "Old Liberty Bell."

[2] *Out West*, I (October 3, 1872), p. 3; *Directory of the Town of Watsonville, 1873* . . . (Watsonville: C. O. Cummings; 1873).

In the nineties frontier themes began to intrude, but only gradually. The San Francisco Midwinter Fair of 1894, a kind of adjourned session of the Chicago World's Fair, boasted of the achievements of "Intellectual California" and went on to offer a forty-niner mining camp, where each night someone was killed at a *baile*. "At last," said *Harper's Weekly*, "the Eastern visitor may realize his ideal of California." Los Angeles, which for several years had held flower festivals, burst out that spring with "La Fiesta De Los Angeles," including a historical parade. But the Pasadena New Year's Day Tournament of Roses, which began in 1889, was featuring Roman chariot races between 1904 and 1915, complete with drivers in togas; Portland followed several months later with its own first rose-show (May 1889). (A generation later an Oregonian attributed the rejection of local traditions for a floral display to a sense of inferiority, as if Cinderella, accepting the criticisms of her stepsisters, had painted her face for the ball. "The inferiority complex entices [Portland] from what she could do supremely well into a competition where at best she can only be second or third rate.") Leadville's pride in 1895–6 was an ice palace, built to resemble a medieval castle. Santa Cruz went to a grand extreme by holding a five-day Venetian Water Carnival in 1895, in "strictly first-class and lavish manner." Gondolas bearing Japanese lanterns glided under a "grand triumphal arch . . . built on the lines of the columns in the Cathedral of St. Mark and the Rialto bridge. . . . At the top of each gilded column sits a lion with his tail uplifted to the sky." The frontier was still a little too close to be altogether acceptable. What San Francisco prided herself

on most at the Midwinter Fair was the evidence of cultural
and material progress: the Greek temple overshadowed the
log cabin. "It has startled the world," said *Overland*, "into
a realization of the fact that the land of the sluice-box and
the rocker has become the land of the plow and the
pruning-hook." [3] The time was approaching, but had not
yet arrived, when the West would be so clearly beyond the
pioneer stage that some pioneer type, particularly the
cowboy, would be standard equipment in every Western
midway.

While William F. Cody and his imitators were touring
the East and Europe as early as the 1870's and eighties,
and sometimes it seemed that every Western railroad station had its Buffalo Bill ready to hoodwink the tourists,
the West did not, in general, turn to playing wild West
until the new century, that is, until it realized that it was
through living the real thing. The historian of the rodeo
traces the first annual rodeo back to the Frontier Days
Celebration at Prescott, Arizona, in 1888, when the old
range-life was already disappearing. "The whoops and
yells and whirling lariats of the cowboy fade farther and
farther into the distance," said a writer in the *Fortnightly
Review* in 1887. Cody's Wild West Show, featuring Indians and horsemen, was billed first in 1883 in Omaha, where
it was not a financial success; by 1887 it was in London,

[3] *Harper's Weekly*, Vol. XXXVIII (February 24, 1894),
pp. 185–6; Lon F. Chapin: *Thirty Years in Pasadena* ([Los
Angeles]: 1929), pp. 304–6; Charles H. Chapman in Ernest
Gruening: *These United States, A Symposium* (New York: Boni
and Liveright; 1923), p. 289; *Traveler*, Vol. VI (July 1895),
pp. 4–5; *San Francisco Chronicle*, June 11, 1895, p. 1:3; *Overland Monthly*, 2d series, Vol. XXIV (July 1894), p. 107.

where it was. But Denver's Annual Festival of Mountain and Plain (1895–1902, and since 1912), which the passenger agent of the Denver and Rio Grande Railroad suggested to match Rocky Ford's Watermelon Day and Colorado Spring's Fruit Day and Flower Carnival, got along without a rodeo until 1901. By the time Cheyenne, inspired by Greeley's Potato Day and by liberal donations from the Union Pacific Railroad, held its first Frontier Days Celebration in 1897, the end of the frontier was still so recent that some citizens objected that the tone was "not elevating in character," but the motif was already strongly nostalgic: the plan was to "get all the old timers together, and have the remnant of the cow punchers come in with a bunch of wild horses. . . ." As the Union Pacific passenger agent at Denver said, it was "something that few people here have ever seen"; therein lay its attraction. Only a few years before, in the eighties, the Cheyenne Club had required formal dress. "The Frontier has become conscious of itself," said Frank Norris, "acts the part for the Eastern visitor; and his self-consciousness is a sign, surer than all others, of the decadence of a type, the passing of an epoch." [4]

In the heyday of the cattle country holidays had often brought riding talent to town more or less spontaneously;

[4] Clifford P. Westermeier: *Man, Beast, Dust; The Story of Rodeo* (n. p.; 1947), pp. 35, 375, 390–4, 396; John Baumann: "On a Western Ranche," *Fortnightly Review,* n. s., Vol. XLI (April 1887), p. 533; Robert D. Haneworth: "Early History of Cheyenne 'Frontier Days' Show," *Annals of Wyoming,* Vol. XII (July 1940), pp. 199–204; Ray B. West: *Rocky Mountain Cities* (New York: W. W. Norton; 1949), p. 116; Frank Norris: *The Responsibilities of the Novelist and Other Literary Essays* (New York: Doubleday, Page & Company; 1903), pp. 72–3.

such displays declined with the open range. "We may keep alive for many years the idea of a wild West," said Norris, "but the hired cowboys and paid rough riders of Mr. William Cody are more like 'the real thing' than can be found today in Arizona, New Mexico or Idaho." "If any traveller expects to encounter the traditional 'cow boy' aspects of life," warned Lilian Whiting (1906), "he will be very much disappointed." A writer in *Out West* admitted sadly that "the big tournaments are things of the past." But actually the rodeo as a spectacle, as a representation of what the West wanted to recall of its youth and to show to the East, was just on the threshold of its great popularity. Pendleton had its first Round-Up in September 1910, and others soon followed as Pendleton succeeded. "The Round-Up," proclaimed the sponsors, "is a celebration to show the world that life on mountain and plain has not lost its picturesqueness, that the cowboy has not vanished with the invasion of the farmer. . . . Only a few years and the frontier will have passed, but today the cowboys from ranch and range are challenging the world to equal their marvelous achievements." [5] What had been past, then, now was still contemporary, and in a few years more there were probably more skilled roughriders than there had been in the 1870's. The townspeople who solicited their attendance, and promoted the rodeo as a family entertainment and pioneer festivity, had had time to forget the ancient rivalry of homesteader and cattleman,

[5] Norris: *Responsibilities of the Novelist*, p. 72; Lilian Whiting: *The Land of Enchantment* . . . (Boston: Little, Brown & Company; 1906), p. 10; Sharlot M. Hall: "Fourth of July in Cowland," *Out West*, Vol. XXVII (July 1907), p. 19 n.; *Pendleton Round-Up*, 1911 program (Oregon Historical Society).

and how the authentic cowboy had been the terror of the town when he came in for a lark.

By the twenties the rodeo seemed to be in many a Western town only the most climactic feature of a system of pageantry in which not only the "cowboys" but the whole population acted, and that continued after the principal actors in the rodeo proper had moved on for their next professional engagement. Sometimes residents rode and roped, as when polo players from the expensive Monterey peninsula country-clubs appeared under pseudonyms in the Salinas Rodeo of 1925; more often they simply wore what passed for riding clothes under threat of discipline by a local vigilance-committee, and stopped shaving for a few weeks. Then eventually, recalled an old resident of Salinas, "the professionals moved in and it became 'show business.' A working cowman hasn't time to attain the circus perfection of the professionals and soon even the wild horses and the Brahma bulls were imported. . . ." "Half the cowboys are cowgirls," complained an Oregonian of the celebrations at Pendleton, "incredible monsters that never rode the range, and the other half out of dime novels." It was not long, however, before some began to take such displays seriously, like the man who after several years of playing the part in the Days of '76 parade, climaxed by a visit to the White House, came to believe that he was, in fact, Deadwood Dick. As the annual festival and the seasonal resorts proved more and more lucrative, the market for "Western" clothing extended; Westerners began buying what they had imported to sell to the tourists, and wore it after the tourists had left; in the years after the Second World War, when cowboy costumes for preschool children reached unprecedented popularity, the fashion seemed to filter, like the habit of reading comic books, into older generations as well. "There are more cowboy clothes worn in Arizona now than during the peak of the cowboy days," said a Phoenix reporter. "In the old days when a cowboy came to town, he usually dressed in a blue serge suit from Sears Roebuck." "Only the imitation cowboys," as Frank Norris had observed when the new style was just getting started, "the college-bred fellows who 'go out on a ranch,' carry the revolver or wear the concho." [6] Today one encounters middle-aged businesswomen in some Rocky Mountain cities sporting buckskin jackets and skirts such as only a fancy woman in her cups would have been willing to be seen in, dead or alive, three quarters of a century ago.

In general the pioneer, wild West theme has tended since the twenties to surpass the French and Spanish and Spanish-Indian themes in Western festivals, and the mission towns of California no longer have a monopoly in trading on the past. Meanwhile older traditions have persisted for many years. The early dramatic pageants that sprang up all over the United States under the auspices of amateur theatrical groups in the years following the first of them, at Sherborn, England, in 1905, had been as slow to embrace the American period as the parades that

[6] John Steinbeck: " 'Always Something to do in Salinas,' " *Holiday*, Vol. XVII (June 1955), p. 59; Chapman in Gruening: *These United States*, p. 290; Robert J. Casey: *The Black Hills and Their Incredible Characters; a Chronicle and a Guide* (Indianapolis: Bobbs-Merrill Co.; 1949), pp. 202–4; Debs Myers: "Arizona," *Holiday*, Vol. XIII (January 1953), p. 28; Norris: *Responsibilities of the Novelist*, pp. 72–3.

preceded them in the nineties. When students at the University of North Dakota presented "A Pageant of the North-West" in 1914, they brought Chippewas from Turtle Mountain Reservation to grace the scene, but they commemorated Radisson, La Salle, La Vérendrye, and Lewis and Clark rather than the homesteaders or the cowboys. The older Spanish mission pageants, as the Ramona Play at Hemet (1923–   ) and John Steven McGroarty's Mission Play at San Gabriel (1912–   ), have had their many imitators on the scale of municipal festivals: Old San Rafael Fiesta Days (1934–   ), the Spanish Trails Fiesta at Durango (1937–   ), and De Anza Days at Riverside (1940–   ), although only Durango had significant Spanish remnants. But rodeos are frequent adjuncts to the lesser Spanish and Indian fiestas, and the pioneer caravan follows on Spanish mission and army even in communities established nearer to 1949 than to 1849, and whose most authentic gold-seekers were real-estate speculators.[7] Old Ezra Meeker, who had crossed the plains to Oregon in 1852, aroused more pity than enthusiasm when he began to retrace the route eastward by oxcart in 1906, but before his death in 1928 he had made the trip by automobile and airplane as well, sold thousands of copies of books by and about himself, founded the Oregon Trail Association (1926), and established himself as a professional pioneer and ornament to pioneer celebrations. Perhaps the most striking signs of the times appeared in 1939 and 1940, when the Colorado Springs Chamber of Commerce began serving chuck-wagon dinners every Monday, Wednesday,

[7] Louis Ziegler: "A Cahuila Fiesta . . . ," *Touring Topics,* Vol. XXIII (January 1931), pp. 50–1, 53.

and Friday during the summer season in the Garden of the Gods, and Tucson held its first Old Tucson Days in a discarded motion-picture set. The West had forgotten Italy.

The strength of the new traditions of pageantry proved itself dramatically in the course of two presidential visits in the mid-twenties. When Theodore Roosevelt had gone west in 1903 as president, and in 1911 as ex-president, mending his political fences and greeting old-time cowhand friends among the remnants of "the golden days when the men of the vanishing frontier still lived in the Viking age," he appeared in tails and top hat, and on speakers' platforms, according to his station. But when President and Mrs. Harding stopped at Meacham, Oregon, to see the Oregon Trail pageant in 1923, on their way to Alaska, the crowds saw them riding in the Concord coach, Mrs. Harding seated beside the driver on the return trip. It was Calvin Coolidge who achieved the ultimate. Four years later, in 1927, he wore a ten-gallon hat at the Belle Fourche roundup and an Ogalala Sioux headdress at The Deadwood Days of '76 Show. Six thousand people watched his adoption into the Sioux as "Leading Eagle," and then a representation of Custer's last stand. The press reported that the West had taught the President how to play and how to enjoy the wide-open spaces, that he enjoyed wearing boots and ten-gallon hat in the living room, after dinner, which at least was no more incongruous than the stories of presidential golf on greens that all sloped toward the cup, and liver-fed hatchery fish planted between weirs across Squaw Creek, and all but fastened on his hook. Most people in South Dakota, said a *New York Times* correspondent, "fail to see anything incongruous in it at all. The Black Hills are really as tame and conventional as the Green Mountains. The cowboy stuff is just scenery." Still it was a new setting for presidential relaxation, and it was news that conformance to the conventions of Western touristdom was politically convenient when conformance to the conventions of Eastern society was not. The sombrero outranked the silk hat. The President both followed and confirmed the style, presenting a minor tourist bonanza to the promoters of Rapid City, who had invited him out. Twenty-five years later tourists were visiting the game lodge at Custer State Park at the rate of 100,000 a year, most of them curious to see where the Coolidges had stayed, where New England had surrendered to the West.[8]

By the time of the Coolidges' summer trip, the Dakota country had changed drastically from what it had been when Howard Eaton first introduced vacationers to it nearly half a century earlier, and since Roosevelt fled out to his ranch to forget political disillusionment and domestic tragedy. The cattlemen had retreated, and the tourists had advanced, to the extent that it was altogether natural that the reporters should suspect that Coolidge wanted not

[8] Roosevelt to John Hay, August 9, 1903, in Roosevelt: *Cowboys and Kings; Three Great Letters* (Cambridge: Harvard University Press; 1954), p. 1; *San Francisco Chronicle*, July 4, 1923, pp. 1:3, 2:5; ibid., July 6, 1927, p. 6:1; ibid., July 10, 1927, p. 10A:1; ibid., August 5, 1927, p. 2:15; *The New York Times*, August 5, 1927, p. 1:6; ibid., August 8, 1927, p. 3:6; ibid., July 3, 1927, II, p. 1:8; Robert J. Casey: "Magic Mountains," *Holiday*, Vol. I (July 1946), pp. 48–50; Casey: *The Black Hills*, pp. 96–7, 202–4; Phil Stong: "The Magic of Mountains," *Holiday*, Vol. XIV (July 1953), p. 132.

to escape the crowds but to seek them out, to put his fingers on the people's political pulse. If the little Vermonter seemed ridiculous in his hat and boots, and a far cry from the young rancher from Manhattan and Chimney Butte, he represented a far more numerous type, one that was becoming more numerous still. In 1883 a young man from the city might still find his future, and opportunity and high adventure, too, in the open spaces of the West, as Roosevelt had done, or tried to do; by 1927 opportunity was clearly enough concentrated in the city, but men—and women, too—from Plymouth and Northampton and Boston and all the other towns and cities of the East and Middle West were turning for a summer holiday to the outdoors and to a section that offered not so much opportunity as the living museum of the nation's past, and the casual kind of relaxation that most museumgoers seek. It was news to have the President recognize and share the common taste, but it was already common.

6. FILLING UP
THE WIDE–OPEN SPACES

THE WEST has always been as elusive as the sunset, though perhaps it was never so hard to find as it is now that so many have gone to look for it. In the 1860's and seventies most of the plains and mountains were as they had been before the white men came, but most Americans found the cost of going there too much, their own capacity to accept the outdoors too little. By the second and third quarters of the twentieth century the nation was industrialized and urbanized enough to pay the price of admission and to enjoy the show. Cities in East and West were supporting traffic on rails and highways, and in the air, that carried the westbound traveler more easily and more cheaply than ever before, and moreover they were storing up appetites for the outdoors that Americans had never had when so many more of them had lived close to the soil. Yet the efficient engines that gave Americans the incomes, the automobiles, the leisure time, and the hunger that they needed for the West, also took the West away. The Western cities not only spread out from the rail ends and river mouths as cities have done in the East, so that Santa Barbara and San Diego became almost contiguous with Los Angeles, San Jose and Walnut Creek with San Francisco, but by a kind of social metastasis they transformed parts of the West whose charm had been that they were least urban. On the one hand the cities that had tried to seem Eastern when they were small tried to seem Western when they were large; on the other hand the city-bred techniques of the huckster penetrated into the hinterland. Those who made it their business to sell the West sometimes tried to preserve it, when they did not have to create it; inevitably they transformed it.

Among the most patently commercial Western charades that snare the tourist are those of Nevada, which is to say Reno and Las Vegas. Nevada is distinct from other desert areas in its development as tourist country: the tourists came there, or through there, because the railroad did, before they came to Palm Springs, Phoenix, Santa Fe, and Taos, but for half a century or more their purpose was to get through as quickly as possible. The state boasts no celebrated Indians, aboriginal or Spanish ruins, canyons, writers, or artists' colonies. Even sin has shallow roots, historically speaking. San Francisco is and always has been "the city" to most of Nevada, and any Nevadan who wanted to sin expansively knew that wider choice awaited him at the end of an overnight railroad-trip than in the paddocks of Reno. An irregular traffic came in for prize fights, which Nevada made legal (1897) a few years after California suppressed them in 1890, the visitors often sleeping in parked Pullman cars for lack of hotel space; and a regular if minor traffic came in for divorces; but Nevada, like its neighbors, strove to forget much of its past, such as it was. An antigambling law of 1909 confined the gleanings from the visitors largely to hotelkeepers and lawyers. The West was wide open ten years ago, said *Sunset* in 1914. "Today there is not a single open gambling place in the West. He who would Dame Fortune woo must go to Indiana." [1]

Meanwhile the larger cities of California cleaned up in the name of progress, without much regret for their less reputable pasts, and without setting off a major exodus to areas off limits. Even San Francisco had prepared for the Panama-Pacific Exposition of 1915 by taking scrubbing-brush to its past in singularly unsentimental spirit: "They have known us as the 'Paris of America,' and we want to prove that we are not, that we are going to be one of the cleanest cities in the world." [2] Paradise Alley became Maiden Lane, the Barbary Coast was never the same after the fire of 1906 and the progressive movement, and altogether San Francisco night life was almost as disappointing to later-day visitors with visions of plumbing the modern Sodom and Gomorrah in the style of

---

[1] "The Swing of Morality's Pendulum," *Sunset*, Vol. XXXIII (September 1914), p. 458.

[2] *Transactions*, Commonwealth Club of California, Vol. VIII (June 1913), p. 297.

the Reverend Mr. Parkhurst as Salt Lake City had been
to studious inquirers into polygamy some years earlier.
Los Angeles had little to forget or be forgiven for outside
the Spanish-speaking districts, which did not count; southern California as a whole before the First World War was
still devoted to small-town amusements. A New York
journalist referred to Los Angeles as the "chemically
pure" city; it was there that the California prohibition
movement had its stronghold. The exceptions to the pre-
cepts of Middle Western morality that southern California
permitted were likely to be in favor of the "right elements,"
as when the city fathers of Pasadena had abstained from
enforcing the local prohibition ordinance in the Raymond.

Perhaps in the long run repression in California corresponded to expression in Nevada, which certainly serves or
shears out-of-state visitors more than its own residents,
but the Nevada tourist-trade in its now distinctive variants
was slow to develop. Divorce as a major Nevada industry
dates approximately from Mary Pickford's suit against
Owen Moore in 1920, though Mrs. William Ellis Corey,
wife of the president of United States Steel, had brought
Reno into the headlines by establishing residence in 1906
and bringing accusation against Mabelle Gilman, the
singer, as corespondent. When Earl Russell came to the
Nevada side of Lake Tahoe to prepare for a divorce in
1899, the idea was quite novel: "The hotel-keeper [at
Glenbrook] greeted us with more surprise than enthusiasm, and could not be got to realize that we meant to stay
not only one night but many nights." In 1927 the hotel-
keepers lobbied through a law cutting the residence re-

quirements from six to three months, and in 1931 the legis-
lature dramatically scooped its competitors by establishing
a six-week limit and legalizing gambling.[3]

Actually the gambling provisions of 1931 probably had
more effect on Nevada's atmosphere, and perhaps on its
economy as well, than those affecting divorce. Las Vegas,
which was virtually a new town, profited when the new
law coincided with an influx of workmen and then of
sight-seers to the Hoover Dam area, somewhat as Phoenix
had profited by its proximity to the Roosevelt Dam. Early
in 1939 Harold Ickes, come to inspect the public works
under his jurisdiction, found it "an ugly little town where
gambling dens and saloons and prostitution run wide open
day and night. We visited several of these establishments,
but we found nothing colorful or romantic about them—
just intent-looking people losing their money at various
gambling games and giving the impression that they didn't
have any money to lose." More energetic enforcement of
laws in Los Angeles, wartime prosperity, and the good
fortune of fast railroad transportation during gasoline
rationing boosted it along further in the forties, when the
first of the big hotels opened: El Rancho Vegas in 1941,
the Last Frontier ("The Old West in Modern Splendor")
in 1942. Fremont Street proclaimed its offerings in neon
signs insisting on the Westernness of a commercial development that was one of the youngest of the suburbs of Los
Angeles: the Boulder Club ("Enjoy the Old West—Craps
—Faro Bank—Bar—Cocktail Lounge"), the Frontier

---

[3] John F. S. Russell: *My Life and Adventures* (London:
Cassell & Co.; 1923), p. 239; *San Francisco Chronicle*, March 19,
1927, p. 2:4.

Club, the Western, the Horseshoe, the Pioneer, the Golden Nugget, the Last Frontier, Frontier Village. The Silver Slipper, adjoining the Last Frontier, was a miniature Western museum, splendid in red damask walls; ancient mechanical pianos adorned a reconstructed ice-cream parlor. Each spring (after 1935), as if anything had to be added, the town staged its own Western festival at Helldorado Village. Yet, as if to demonstrate the depth of its Western foundations, it turned in the fifties to African and European and other themes: the new hotels were such as the Desert Inn, the Sahara, the Riviera, the Steamboat, the Moulin Rouge, the Tropicana, El Morocco, and the Dunes, which advertised "Magic Carpet" extravaganzas in the Arabian Room, the Sinbad Bar, the Aladdin Room, the Caliph's Court. Spectacularly high salaries drew the most expensive theatrical performers from New York, London, and Hollywood, in turn to draw the crowds or to assure them that Las Vegas had "class." [4]

The older part of Nevada, in the area tributary to Reno rather than Las Vegas, lagged somewhat in its excrescences of luxurious hostelries, but it was here that the Western theme reached a kind of zenith. In Reno, Harolds Club,

[4] Harold L. Ickes: *The Secret Diary of Harold L. Ickes*, Vol. II, *The Inside Struggle, 1936–1939* (New York: Simon and Schuster; 1954), p. 581; Oscar Lewis: *Sagebrush Casinos; The Story of Legal Gambling in Nevada* (Garden City: Doubleday; 1953), pp. 138–41, 191–6; Paul Ralli: *Viva Vegas* (Hollywood: House-Warven; 1953); Lucius Beebe: "Las Vegas," *Holiday*, Vol. XII (December 1952), p. 107; *Saturday Review*, Vol. XXXVIII (February 5, 1955), pp. 29, 30; "Las Vegas: Dice, Dollars and Doom Town," *Fortnight*, Vol. XVIII (June 1955), pp. 36–8; Gilbert Millstein: "Mr. Coward Dissects Las Vegas," *The New York Times Magazine*, June 26, 1955, pp. 18, 41–2.

established in 1936, began during the war to post the West, and eventually some of the East as well, with its covered-wagon trademark ("Harolds Club or *Bust*"). By 1944 it was publishing a series of "historical" advertisements in newspapers, which it made available in reprints and in two bound volumes for schools and libraries, and shortly it developed the pioneer theme in the museum exhibits of departments called Roaring Camp, Fort Smith, and the Covered Wagon Room (where Western paintings appeared on illuminated glass, and whiskey falls cascaded behind a silver-dollar bar). "See the History of the Old West . . . the Indian wars, the fighting peace officers, the Vigilantes, the famous bad men. . . ." At Harolds all of this was at least as authentic as most of the Western history that is served out of a book rather than out of a bottle, and more authentic by several degrees than the assorted and rootless oddities that pulled in the tourists all over the West: the alligator farm in Los Angeles, the alleged mysteries and freaks of nature among the coastal redwoods, the omnipresent boardwalk concessions and motion pictures. Nevada might be in large part a tourist stop on the way to the coast, or a safety valve for San Francisco and Los Angeles, but at Harolds Club and at Virginia City, which made a living out of restoring the atmosphere of the Comstock Lode, the West seemed to exist for local veneration as well as for export. It might be as incongruous for a former New York society columnist to preach the cult of the frontier (and at that in a "gee-whiz style reminiscent of Bonanza times") as for the agents of the cattle- and silver-barons to apostrophize rugged individualism and state rights, but Lucius Beebe

[190]

seemed to strike a representative note when he revived the *Territorial Enterprise and Virginia City News* in 1952, as "an expression of wish-fulfillment, a wistful recollection of better things and lost times. . . ." It was good business, and yet it served spiritual as well as economic need. As Beebe said: "In Nevada, because we have no industrial civilization and a very little agrarian influence, we have maintained a small oasis of individualism in an encroaching conformity." While watching the tendencies (the "obscenity") of the national Government with "dismay and apprehension," [5] Beebe seemed to revive the historic mood of outrage against the "Crime of '73" more at some new threat to a narrow-gauge railroad than at the problems of silver prices and grazing rights, and the importation of sheepherders and other immigrants. And even as the miners and stockmen scoffed at some of the newcomers and their foibles, they seemed to welcome the image of Nevada and Nevada's heritage that Beebe and his associates drew.

By the time Beebe moved from a Madison Avenue hotel to a private car on the Virginia and Truckee Railroad, Virginia City and its neighbors had awakened into a new life. Hardly anyone had ventured into the old mining-districts before the First World War unless he came on business, and the ghost towns of Nevada, as the "Bret Harte country" of California, survived largely because no one cared enough to pillage them for souvenirs and they were too far away to use for firewood. The movement

[5] *Territorial Enterprise and Virginia City News*, May 2, 1952, p. 4; Betsy Rose: "The West's Livest Ghost Town," *Fortnight*, Vol. XVIII (August 1955), p. 19.

to preserve them dates chiefly from the twenties, when tourists were beginning to pay more, and beef and wool less. The tourists in effect returned, two or three generations late, some of the gold and silver that had drained out to San Francisco. But whereas the silver bonanzas of the 1860's and seventies had made it possible for the West to bring the East into the mountains, even to opera houses and brownstone mansions, the tourist bonanzas of the 1940's and fifties financed restoration of the West that had passed, or was supposed to have been.

The larger cities of the Far West in the main were too busy with the present to go as far as Reno and Las Vegas went in shaping themselves after the past, or what they labeled as the past; nor could they recapture the authentic flavor of pioneering as easily as Virginia City, which had only to dust off the past to put it on display. Yet the Los Angeles area probably achieved as complete a change of old attitudes toward pioneer themes as any part of the West, including its colonies in the desert. No other section of the Pacific Coast, at least, had insisted so loudly that it was Eastern in the eighties and nineties; and indeed it had had very little pioneer history of its own, relative to the environs of Denver or San Francisco. When Charles F. Lummis first began building the Landmarks Club and the Southwest Museum in Highland Park, his was a voice crying in a Middle Western wilderness. But by the time Lummis died, in 1928, Los Angeles had become, more or less posthumously, the capital of Spanish California, and through the miracle of the silver screen, capital of the cow country as well. There was further token of the new era in the care taken to create, or "restore," a Spanish market

place adjacent to the new railroad station in mission style
(1939), where tourists disembarked instead of in the very
grounds of transplanted New England resort hotels; and
no tourist attraction in the neighborhood of Los Angeles
developed more spectacularly in the forties than Knott's
Berry Farm at Buena Park. Here the proprietors of what
had been a fruit stand and roadside tearoom built a wild
West town such as might have been in Nevada or the
Mother Lode Country or any of several places four hundred miles or more distant from Los Angeles, and they
even furnished it with a narrow-gauge railroad from the
Colorado Rockies. There was little doubt that tourists
saw more than they were likely to see (or to have seen)
in any one of several mining towns built to be lived in
rather than looked at, and no doubt at all that more tourists did the seeing. At Arcadia the Pony Express Museum,
started in 1923—commemorating a brief episode in Western history whose chief importance was that it concerned
not Los Angeles and the southern transcontinental route
but San Francisco and the overland route—displayed a
spectacular array of relics, including the inevitable narrow-gauge locomotive from the northern mountains; near
Anaheim the ten million dollar ultimate in monuments to
the past, Disneyland, displayed "Frontierland" as one of
five "fairyland worlds," where citizens with twentieth-
century incomes might satiate themselves on a nineteenth-
century narrow-gauge railroad and (supreme restoration
of restorations for southern California) a river side-
wheeler.[6]

[6] Thomas Welles: "The Pony Express Museum," *Overland*,
2d series, Vol. XCI (March 1933), pp. 44–5; John Hughes:

The frontier trappings of Los Angeles corresponded, on a properly gargantuan southern California scale, to artificialities and inconsistencies throughout the wild West that the tourist saw. The peculiar dilemma of southern California was that it was trying to be all things to all men, Western and yet Eastern, urban and yet rural; it had so recently become the fourth largest city in the nation that it still could not quite believe it, and automatically shouted that it stood not fourth but third, which shortly it was, as if by incantation, and yet it clung to small-town banalities amidst metropolitan congestion. It attracted by its youthfulness, by what Hamlin Garland called "the vacation psychology of the region," but it had to insist that it was not young but old. "It all seems temporary," wrote Garland when he visited Los Angeles in 1928, "a kind of fair built for pleasure and not for the business of living"; [7] it was its good fortune, as far as the tourist industry was concerned, that it continued to seem temporary even when it had achieved the shoddiness of the Loop area of Chicago and the atmospheric pollution of Pittsburgh. Perhaps it was blind, and unconscious of its vagaries; perhaps it wisely accepted them as useful stock in trade and as the inescapable consequence of varied ancestry and divided purpose.

The humors of Los Angeles may amuse because they are the humors of the nation, which goes there to do as it

"Pony Express Museum," *Pacific Pathways*, Vol. I (June 1946), p. 38; *The New York Times*, May 8, 1955, X, p. 37XX:1–5.

[7] Hamlin Garland: *Afternoon Neighbors; Further Excerpts from a Literary Log* (New York: Macmillan Company; 1934), pp. 480, 557.

wishes, and finds there the ultimate satisfactions and frustrations when it thinks it wants the West. Nowhere else in the West can the traveler find the reassurance of so many fellow onlookers, or so much assistance in interpreting and appreciating what he sees; and what he sees is typical of much of Western tourism, if not of the West before the tourists came. All over the West it is the beaten path that draws the crowds, and those who come to the wilderness demand the luxuries of home and hotel life: "the masses will not come to worship until cushions are ready for their knees." "A paradise on a bad road will never achieve popularity," warned an outdoors magazine. Pack trains had color in themselves, and therefore figured in the offerings of dude ranches and helped to maintain the mule population far beyond any justification in agriculture; yet by the forties and fifties they were giving way to jeeps and airplanes as they gave way earlier, on easier roads, to automobiles. Enthusiasts for the Hopi and Navajo country held out the spell (1920) of "a vacation that is different from any that you have ever had; or if you are seeking something new—an unexplored land where white men seldom go and where you will meet unknown dangers—then go to the desert. . . ." Yet the Santa Fe's Indian detours did not draw many patrons until Packard sedans with courier-hostesses replaced the mules in the twenties. The drivers were cowboys skilled in singing around the campfire and in appealing to ladies "of uncertain age but certain bank accounts." The Southern Pacific's Apache Trail offered not only cliff dwellings but the Roosevelt Dam on "a wonderful motor trip." And this was only the beginning. On the whole the desert had æsthetic acceptability, but few visitors and still fewer residents before the thirties, and the real boom came in the fifties, to parts that seemed as urbanized as the metropolis that supported them, and certainly were far more luxurious. Frank Lloyd Wright, who looked forward gloomily in 1935 toward the crowds that would "set Arizona backward a decade or two," said that even then "the remarkable beauty peculiar to this . . . region is quite undiscovered by the grand-average American, or for that matter, by the upper American." [8] Then came air conditioning and the airplane, and the deluge.

The great vogue of the high mountains, beginning some years before, had coincided with the growth of conveniences and luxury accommodations. Yosemite in the years of its great growth just after it first admitted automobiles had become, said one visitor, "a Palace Hotel turned into a 1,000-square mile public park." "Marie Antoinette, who would unquestionably have been fashionable and popular in New York," remarked a writer in *Harper's* (1914), "would as unquestionably have had an Adirondack camp." Earl Russell noted the extravagance of private vacation-houses comparable to suburban residences at Lake Tahoe in 1899, and was "annoyed . . .

[8] Theodore S. Solomons: "Unexplored Regions of the High Sierra," *Overland*, 2d series, Vol. XXVII (May 1896), p. 486; R. C. Rockafellow: "Better Roads to Playgrounds . . . ," *Outdoors Pictorial*, Vol. IV (April 1926), p. 31; Earle R. Forest: "Desert Camps and Trails," *Outing*, Vol. LXXV (February 1920), p. 276; *The New York Times*, August 18, 1935, X, p. 12:2–3; *Frank Lloyd Wright on Architecture; Selected Writings, 1894–1940*, Frederick Gutheim, ed. (New York: Duell, Sloan and Pearce; 1941), p. 196.

by its air of fashion and by the absurd way in which the
women dressed themselves in smart clothes and the men
in brown boots and other things, obviously preferring
parading up and down wooden side walks and verandahs
to enjoying the country life in the country." The reign
of fashion in the Sierra resorts even some years later was
still general enough to explain in part why the public at
large reacted so passively to plans to dam the Hetch
Hetchy Valley during the Taft Administration. It was
possible for the power interests with designs on the waters
of Tahoe itself to picture a contest between simple irriga-
tionists and a few San Francisco millionaires interested in
preserving a choice preserve for summer resorts, whereas
a high official had clearly made a mistake in 1954 when
he said that he opposed using the parks "for a selected
few, who, through education and special training, are best
able to understand and enjoy the grandeur of scenery."
Even then the hikers and riders who ventured more than
an hour away from the camp cafeteria were still relatively
few, although the hiking clubs and the pack-train parties
grew rapidly, so much that jeeps began to replace mules
in "mountain safaris" in the fifties. Primitive areas such
as the Olympic rain forest and the Grand Tetons were
still far from crowded, although their visitors were increasing far more rapidly than those who went to the more
popular parks—by more than ninefold in the Tetons
from 1940 to 1955. Even Dinosaur National Monument
was attracting, at the peak of the controversy over the
Echo Park Dam, no more than a tenth the one million
tourists a year that the Interior Department said would

come when it had been improved and modernized, although tourists had increased by almost two hundredfold in the three years that the prospect of improvement had kept it in the headlines.[9]

And in Alaska, which thrilled to the prospect of hordes coming from the States to see what Alaskans liked to call the last real frontier (perhaps by airplane on a seventeen-day trip out of Seattle, at ten per cent down and the balance in twenty months), most of the visitors to Mount McKinley National Park at mid-century were staying at the railhead rather than at the older camp-sites in the heart of the park; instead of traveling by dog team, they rode with Charley Porter in the bus from Fairbanks to Whitehorse. Hank Monk had been dieselized. It was possible on such retreats to nature to salvage some of the amenities of civilization, as well as to move farther into the wilderness: a group of Colorado businessmen, Roundup Riders of the Rockies, who set out each year on a week's mountain pilgrimage, maintained an entourage that included portable hot showers, a masseur, and beer trucks on a twice-daily schedule. The football coach at the University of California complained that college students'

[9] David M. Steele: *Going Abroad Overland* . . . (New York: G. P. Putnam's Sons; 1917), pp. 163–4; Harrison Rhodes: "American Holidays: Springs and Mountains," *Harper's Monthly Magazine*, Vol. CXXIX (September 1914), p. 547; Russell: *My Life and Adventures*, pp. 241–2; Elizabeth Kent: *William Kent, Independent* (Kentfield, Calif.: privately printed; 1950), pp. 321–2; *The New York Times*, May 13, 1954, p. 28:7; ibid., July 31, 1955, II, p. X25:2–5; "U. S. is Outgrowing its Parks . . . ," *United States News and World Report*, Vol. XXXVIII (June 10, 1955), pp. 78–9; *The New York Times*, May 8, 1955, X, p. 39XX:3–6.

leg muscles were loose, and blamed the decline in hiking and walking.[1]

The friends of the parks, as most Americans, were never quite sure of how rugged they wanted to be. The Park Service, under the vigorous leadership of Stephen T. Mather, who directed them 1917–29, insisted and continued to insist that its function was to stimulate patriotism and foster knowledge and health rather than to advance recreation, which it left chiefly to others, but the people shared the views of one of Mather's chiefs as Secretary of the Interior, who referred to the national parks as the people's playground; Mather himself loved to see the crowds pour in, and Congress listened best to requests for money when its constituents came in force. The occupational hazard of park administrators was that they tended to assume that statistics measured success, even when they tried to stand against making the parks into mountain broadwalks and frantically urged state authorities to develop recreation areas near the parks to drain off some of the crowds. "To the very extent that we save these places *not* commercialized," said a park official (1953), "to that very extent will we succeed in saving also their *commercial* value in terms of travel." Yet the crowds did not always seek the wilderness. "From a record of travel in our parks," reported one of Mather's predecessors, "it may be shown that the finest scenery without accommodations will not receive so large a travel as an inferior character of

[1] *Alaska Recreation Survey,* Part Two, National Park Service (n. p.; 1955), pp. 2, 5; Edward A. Herrion: "Hungry Highways," *Holiday,* Vol. I (May 1946), pp. 85–8; *Life,* Vol. XXXIX (August 15, 1955), pp. 85–91; *The New York Times,* April 1, 1955, p. 29:1.

scenery which has a better type of accommodation." It was noteworthy that by far the largest crowds at the parks came in the years of the great Western expositions, at Portland in 1905, at Seattle in 1909, at San Francisco in 1915; Yellowstone was a way station on the route to the midway. The popularity of excursions to Canada coincided with the drought that followed the Eighteenth Amendment ("Four and twenty bottles packed in a car; / When the lot we've opened we'll all begin to sing: / 'O, Uncle Sam, I love you, but God save the King.' ")[2]

The American vacation was moving into the West, and more into the Western outdoors, but it was by no means clear what sent it there. In an age when the wilderness had recently ceased to be oppressive, some began in the nineties to talk of yearning to touch mother earth like the giant Antæus, a yearly urge "to flee the haunts of men and take up and live the life of a savage in all of its most primitive simplicity and naturalness," or of the "call of the cave man," "those primitive instincts in man manifested in the longing for the freedom of a forest life." Henry L. Stimson, who began to go west regularly in the late 1880's, later wondered whether what had attracted him was the heritage of his ancestors three generations earlier who had fought in northern New York with bears and panthers and wolves, or perhaps jealousy of an earlier generation of Americans who had vented their youthful energy in conquering a continent. Old John Muir, no

[2] Conrad L. Wirth: "What are National Parks?" (typescript address, October 1953; San Francisco: National Park Service); Superintendent of National Parks: *Annual Report* . . . (Washington: Government Printing Office; 1916), p. 2; *San Francisco Chronicle,* May 13, 1923, p. A3:3–4.

longer an eccentric hermit or bearded wood-spirit but an indispensable fixture of Sierra Club trips, benevolently surveyed the change in his lifetime: "Going to the woods is going home; for I suppose we came from the woods originally." And in the thirties T. K. Whipple, a Princetonian who had discovered the West while teaching English at the University of California, mused on the land as one of three terms in the American equation, to which Americans escaped in body, on hunting- and camping-trips, or in fantasy, as in reading of cowboys and trappers. All of these interpretations implied that natural man naturally loved the outdoors; yet the interpreters themselves contributed to a new appreciation of nature among men and women who, if not cultivated, had at least achieved that level of literacy that demands the approval of recognized tastemakers. It was they who wrote the books about the West that gave it a certain literary and historical sanction that only Europe and the East once had had. The early promoters of Rocky Mountain tourism had been baffled, as one of them complained, by the lack of precedent and sanction: "The trouble . . . is not the absence of vistas, but that some person of taste, genius and imagination . . . has not preceded these befogged tourists, and discovered and described them. Had there been, then it would be fashionable to follow in his footsteps . . . for if they did not, it would be evident that these bell-weather-led tourists were people without any taste." [3]

[3] *Yosemite Valley via Big Oak Flat Route* . . . (n. p.; [1901?]), p. 12; Rufus Steele: "In a Friendly Outdoors," *Sunset*, Vol. XXXIII (July 1914), p. 61; James Weir: "A Little Excursion into Savagery," *Outing*, Vol. XXVI (July 1895), p. 305; Clarence Pullen: "A Camp in the Woods," *Harper's*

Meanwhile a Muir might go on foot to the Sierra Nevada, and make his bed in a hollow tree and his dinner of tea and a crust of bread, but early in the twentieth century the unspoiled masses, in general, still lacked the time and the means to reach the open spaces. And those of their betters who cared to leave the hotels spent freely as they enjoyed the wilderness, though there was still so much of it, and there were so few of them, that they could cut firewood, tent poles and bed supports without spoiling it for others and, indeed, without seriously risking intrusions into their own privacy. Camping had much in common with yachting, a writer in *Harper's Weekly* had observed in 1911, when campers were still not much more numerous than yachtsmen: it offered freedom and comfort, and the camper could spend even more money than the yachtsman if he chose, allowing for the size of his outfit. In Colorado in the nineties, General W. A. J. Palmer of the D. and R. G. Railroad was taking guests on picnic- and camping-expeditions that brought the comforts of the city into the wilderness, only a few years before the population of the city came as well: "The most idyllic, yet luxurious life beside that singing stream" in a private compound of nearly 700,000 acres, wrote Hamlin Garland, "feasting at night on turtle soup, and steak and mushrooms, drinking champagne out of tin cups," attended by "a platoon of cooks,

Weekly, Vol. XXXIV (July 26, 1890), p. 582; Stimson: *My Vacations,* p. 1; John Muir: *Our National Parks* (Boston: Houghton Mifflin Company; 1901), p. 78; T. K. Whipple: *Study out the Land* (Berkeley: University of California Press; 1943), pp. 39–40; John H. Tice: *Over the Plains, on the Mountains* . . . (St. Louis: Printed by the *Industrial Age* Printing Co.; 1872), pp. 192–3.

valets, maids, and hostlers." On a more modest scale, *Country Life* magazine, which began in 1901 to describe gentlemen's comforts in estate and field, told of "Camp-keeping as a Fine Art" in the California redwoods, two miles from a railroad but with a Chinese cook in attendance; and some campers brought carpets, canopies, and rocking chairs. Theodore Roosevelt, by contrast, had lived a life at Elkhorn Ranch that was primitive enough so that he did not take his womenfolk there until 1890, when its days were numbered. "I don't believe I will be able to keep the ranch house open much longer," he wrote to his sister, "and you ought to see something of the life." [4]

The introduction of women and family groups to outdoor camping probably did much to civilize and refine it, and tame it down, and reduce it to a conventional average, though there was scarcely any kind of outdoor ruggedness that remained a male monopoly. The introduction of the masses probably did still more, though the aristocracy was quick to take fright and retreat before common clay, and sometimes fled into the remote wilderness. "Vacationing having ceased to be aristocratic and exclusive," observed a Californian in 1929, "it becomes more and more difficult to find an exclusive place in which to practice it." "The automobile made traveling possible for vast numbers of people," commented a correspondent of *The New York Times* (1930), "but did very little to make it fashionable.

[4] Thaddeus S. Dayton: "Camping Out with an 'Auto,'" *Harper's Weekly*, Vol. LV (September 2, 1911), p. 12; Hamlin Garland: *Daughter of the Middle Border* (New York: Macmillan Company; 1929), pp. 233–7; Henrietta S. Breck: "Camp-keeping as a Fine Art," *Country Life*, Vol. II (October 1902), pp. 217–20; Roosevelt: *Letters*, Vol. I, pp. 186, 233.

The very fact that all the mechanics, the clerks and their wives and sweethearts were driving through the Wisconsin lake country, camping at Niagara, scattering tin cans and soda pop bottles over the Rockies, made those places taboo for bankers and the chairmen of the board." It would have been difficult under any circumstances to keep much primeval atmosphere where the new density of sylvan population demanded asphalting to hold down the dust, plumbing to limit stream pollution, and fencing to protect the very roots of the trees underfoot. Further, whereas those of the elite who came to camp had come, in general, because they had some taste for it, and chose the wilderness rather than some more conventional and expensive pleasure within their means, the whole people came to the people's playgrounds, including those who merely sought cheap transportation in their own cars and cheap housing on Government land. Many of the new converts to camping, commented a salesman (1927), were people who used to stay at hotels. "The same interest they used to devote in getting together a lot of fancy clothes for the resorts they now put on camping equipment. . . . They're as comfortable in camp as they would be in a hotel, and they have the same urge to dress up, though fashion calls for a different sort of dress. . . . Where is the camper who now splits his own wood and blows his own fire? Not many of his kind are left." The improvements that the majority wanted forced improvements on others, and seemed to leave less room for extremes of either luxury or austerity, for the privacy that the Palmers had needed for their champagne picnics or that John Muir had needed for his hermitical communion with the mountaintops. In the parks, the Palmers would have had to submit to hotel accommodations more suited to railroad employees than to railroad owners, and a ranger might have told Muir to register for camping privileges and make his tea at a public campfire site, his toilet at a public comfort-station. "The trouble with our national parks," one of their friends is said to have remarked, "is that there is no place in them for a man of means." Yet there was also less place in them, year by year, for the man without the price of a hotel suite or an "outfit," and without a taste for public improvements, especially if he wanted to see the major tourist attractions and a stretch of open landscape from where he slept. Even in 1921 the campers at Mammoth Hot Springs gave the impression of "a great army bivouac," [5] and far greater armies were mobilizing.

Meanwhile the low-priced internal combustion motor supported a tourist invasion and transformation of Western lakes and inlets as well, although more slowly and on a smaller scale. The more prosperous families of Seattle were just beginning to spend their summers exploring the islands of Puget Sound in the years before the First World War, islands whose virgin forests were only an hour or two from a dock in Seattle or Port Angeles. "It is decidedly cheaper than staying at home," said an enthusiast, who enumerated the costs of a cruiser with skipper, cook, and deck hand at about five hundred dollars a month. The

[5] R. L. Duffus: "America Works Hard at Play," *The New York Times Magazine*, September 1, 1929, V, p. 21:1; Mildred Adams, "Now We Are Discovering America Again," ibid., July 13, 1930, V, p. 11:2; *The New York Times*, August 7, 1927, VII, p. 12:1; Horace A. Buker: "You Mustn't Molest the Bears . . . ," *Outing*, Vol. LXXIX (January 1922), p. 172.

enormous growth of boating came a generation later, when few mountain- or desert-lakes seemed too far from civilization to salute the sunrise with the hornet's buzz of the outboard motor, and the Upper Colorado River Commission hopefully advertised "tomorrow's playground for millions of Americans" on the dammed-up waters of Dinosaur.[6]

So many tourists went to some parts of the West that there was scarcely room for them to see it. Whether because they demanded "conveniences," as most of them did, or because sheer numbers required asphalt pavement, toilets, and garbage cans, the bloom of the wilderness was ever fugitive. "To discover some spot where nature is yet unadorned and then to adorn it is the occupation of the resorter," remarked the *Independent*. Sometimes there seemed to be a kind of law of improvement, or deterioration, or progression toward the shape of civilization, by which the tent pitched beside a stream became the campground and ultimately the motel, complete with air conditioning and television; or by another line of evolution, the trailer, at first little more than an extra wheel or two under camping gear moved from the running board, was soon a young apartment larger and more expensive than the car that pulled it, and so cumbersome on all but the widest highways that it became more familiar on blocks, or with wheels entirely removed, and within reach of 110-volt current, than on the road. Its tenant left each morning for

[6] Walter V. Woehlke: "The Puget Sound Country," *Sunset*, Vol. XXXII (June 1914), p. 1234; *Tomorrow's Playground for Millions of Americans*, Upper Colorado Commission (Grand Junction: 1954).

college class or factory job rather than for the trout stream. The first house trailer apparently was a homemade model, in 1929, whose owners pulled it from Florida to Los Angeles. By 1931 one could buy a factory product, and during the depression and wartime and postwar years, more and more Americans did so. In 1955, according to the Mobile Homes Manufacturers Association, two million persons were living in trailers, and ninety-five per cent of sales were for permanent residences.[7] The trailer was simply cheap housing or escape from the responsibility of housekeeping; the great outdoors was the wooden slatted path to the common bathroom, or a paved "patio" where retired couples from Indianapolis played canasta in the afternoon.

Some of the Western municipal vacation camps, which began in quite a different tradition, became hardly distinguishable from commercial resorts. When the city of Los Angeles established the first of them, Camp Seeley, in the San Bernardino National Forest in 1912, it was to be for the benefit of poor children, and on a Spartan scale, with the campers cooking and washing dishes themselves, to hold down costs to about three dollars a week. By the thirties the campers were chiefly from professional and salaried rather than laboring families, the co-operative feature had disappeared, and most of the camps had developed elaborately organized recreational and social programs, with campfire performances and intramural ath-

---

[7] "Summer Resorters," *Independent,* Vol. LV (August 27, 1903), p. 2070; Lloyd Wendt: "Home on the Road," *Holiday,* Vol. II (December 1947), pp. 113–14, 122; *Eugene Register-Guard,* February 3, 1955, p. 3B:1–2.

letics under professional direction. A study published by
the University of Colorado in 1953 showed that tourists
overwhelmingly preferred scenic spots developed with
private concessions, such as the Royal Gorge, to those
without, such as the Black Canyon of the Gunnison (by a
ratio of nearly ten to one) ; and that more wanted to swim
than to ride.[8]

Tourists also were pouring literally by the millions, and
to the consternation of Army Engineers, into reservoir
areas not originally intended for recreation, and as inferior to the wilderness in the authentic flavor of nature
as they were superior in accessibility and in convenience
for boating, swimming, and fishing; eventually the Park
Service recognized popular demand and attempted to keep
up with it in housekeeping facilities. The Forest Service
likewise had to welcome visitors to its province, although
its forest camps seldom seemed to have the drawing power
of the national and state parks, where the camp sites were
closer to each other and to commercial improvements; and
in turn the true wilderness areas lagged far behind the
camps. At least some in the crowds that came to the favorite outdoor scenic and recreation areas seemed to share
the herd instinct of those who filled the huge university
football stadia built just before and after the First World
War rather than any deep feeling for the outdoors or even
for sport. In their queues of automobiles winding on the

[8] Wallace Hutchinson: "A Dollar-a-Day Vacation," *Sunset,* Vol. LIX (July 1927), pp. 36–7, 62–3; Miller: "Municipal
Family Camps," pp. 8–11, 16–17, 72–4, 84; *1953 Statewide Colorado Summer Tourist Survey,* University of Colorado Bureau of
Business Research (Boulder: University of Colorado Press;
1953), pp. 38–9.

highways, or deposited at row-house auto courts or in parks laid out like military encampments, they may have advanced somewhat in individual freedom of movement—the choice of one auto court over another—but their regimentation was different in kind rather than in degree from that embraced by the railroad tourist of an earlier generation. If they were seeking a rugged, individualistic West, their numbers seemed to preclude their finding it.

The ultimate in the mechanization of the outdoors for the multitudes by mid-century seemed to be skiing, once the sport of the solitary in the remote wilderness, but now the most glamorous of roadside concessions. While winter sports in the Western mountains have attracted tourists since about 1912, they did not become popular on a large and profitable scale until after the first American-made rope tow appeared, in Vermont in 1934. Two years later, in the fall of 1936, the Union Pacific Railroad opened Sun Valley, near its station at Ketchum, Idaho. Since then visitors who come to the ski resorts simply to wear the latest in ski clothing from Abercrombie and Fitch, ride the chair tow, and recuperate from the trip over hot buttered rum or moose milk have sometimes exceeded the skiers. "New mountain-climbing machines have made skiing one of the fastest growing sports in America," said a writer in *Holiday*. Squaw Valley, which he described, had the lift with the largest capacity in the world, convenient to both the lodge and a main highway across the Sierra Nevada to Reno. The phenomenal success of skiing became a major worry for conservationists after 1945, as resort operators trying to lengthen their seasons and enlarge their clienteles looked for ski sites in wildernesses such as the

White Mountain Primitive Area of New Mexico and the San Jacinto Primitive Area of California, or perhaps in Rocky Mountain National Park, where the completion of the Colorado-Big Thompson Water Diversion Tunnel left an uncomfortable vacuum in tradesmen's pockets. "Mount Rainier is on the way to becoming a 'Sun Valley,'" said a conservationist when the Secretary of the Interior rejected a proposal for a tramway but permitted ski tows and a T-bar lift nearly a mile long.[9]

The automobile, which made the ski camps possible, opened many and conflicting opportunities to the vacationer, but sometimes it seemed to contribute numbers and velocity rather than appreciation. It brought him into the wilderness, but it also brought him out again in a hurry, and in a cloud of dust. "The huge and aggressive business known collectively as *Travel*," wrote a member of the Sierra Club, "is a more dangerous adversary than all the oil, lumber, cattle, and mining interests combined." The interest of the automobile and gasoline companies, which did much to project good roads and to advertise Western travel, was more in keeping the traveler moving than in letting him stop to look, and often he needed no persuasion. "The psychic nature of the motor tourist or camper is to take all and want more," said an advocate of the wilderness

[9] *The New York Times*, January 21, 1953, p. 37:1–2; Ray Duncan: "California's Snow Boom," *Holiday*, Vol. XV (February 1954), pp. 64–5; *The New York Times*, February 6, 1955, II, p. X29:4; Harry C. James: "The San Jacinto Winter Park-Summer Resort Scheme," *Living Wilderness*, Vol. XIV (Winter 1949–50), pp. 4–16; "That Sacred Trust," *National Parks Magazine*, Vol. XXX, No. 124 (January–March 1956), pp. 3–6; *Living Wilderness*, Vol. XIX (Winter, 1954–5), p. 32.

idea (1925). "To the auto camper, distance lends enchantment; to the true wilderness lover, wildness exerts the mystic influence." The National Park-to-Park Highway, projected amidst much fanfare in the middle twenties, was the goal of those who cared more for where they had been than for what they might see and feel: to ride six thousand miles and through twelve parks, said a contributor to *Outdoors Pictorial* (1925), will be the ambition of every motorist. "Post cards written home," said an auto-camp owner in southern Oregon (1930) to an inquiring sociologist, "show that the main topic is how many miles were covered for the day and how many they expect to make the next day. A comfortable clean place to stop is of secondary importance, and very seldom is any mention made of scenery passed through. They did not see it, traveling 40 to 50 miles per hour." [1]

Many of the major tourist attractions in the West, it should be noted, were not merely the wilderness gilded and cushioned, but displays that might as well have had any other natural and historical setting. There was no reason why Gutzon Borglum should have carved the faces of four presidents on Mount Rushmore (1927–39) except that South Dakota was willing not only to interpose no objection but to help raise the money in order to attract tour-

---

[1] Ansel Adams: "Problems of Interpretation of the Natural Scene," *Sierra Club Bulletin*, Vol. XXX (December 1945), p. 49; "Comment on the Wilderness Plan," *American Forests*, Vol. XXXII (January 1926), p. 45; H. O. Bishop: "The National Park-to-Park Highway," *Outdoors Pictorial*, Vol. II (July 1925), p. 13; Norman S. Hayner: "Auto Camps in the Evergreen Playground," *Social Forces*, Vol. IX (December 1930), p. 257.

ists; and yet the tourists detoured from the main line of westward travel at the rate of 913,808 a year by 1953 (seeing the mountain even at night, by artificial lighting), more than visited the Grand Canyon or Sequoia or Mount Rainier and almost as many as visited Grand Teton, and the greater part of those who entered the state. Likewise there was no specific historical justification for such spectacularly successful tourist attractions as the Black Hills Passion Play, which came from Lünen, Germany, in July 1938, to Spearfish, South Dakota; the Bach festival at Carmel, California (1935–   ) ; the Institute for Humanistic Studies, which followed on the Goethe Bicentennial Festival at Aspen, Colorado, in 1949; or the Shakespearean festival at Ashland, Oregon, where a prize fight shared the program with *Twelfth Night* in the first year, 1935, except in the hunger that many frontier communities had had for drama and music such as their people had known in the East.[2]

Thus as the twentieth century wore on, the outdoor West was making new and wider appeals, even as the open spaces filled up. It seemed to gain most strikingly in the twenties and thirties. A nostalgically rural and Western spirit stirred as more Americans went to live in the city: a generation whose folk heroes were Henry Ford and Charles Lindbergh and whose political leaders were Calvin Coolidge and Herbert Hoover was not undivided in its respect for Wall Street. Meanwhile the very decline of

[2] Gilbert C. Fite: *Mount Rushmore* (Norman: University of Oklahoma Press; 1952), pp. 231–2; Robert Meyer: *Festivals U.S.A.* (New York: Washburn; 1950).

agricultural opportunity led those whose business was to sell the West to offer it on some other basis. Railroads that just after the war were still exhorting potential settlers to look to a smiling land of Canaan switched to extolling "the 'Far West,' a fabled land, a story land, still a country of pioneers, still a frontier. Here are cowboys and Indians" (1927). The West was poor enough so that it needed no more farmers, but rich enough so that it need not be ashamed of itself; and so Americans who after the war no longer felt inferior as nationals found in the West Americans who no longer felt inferior as Westerners, and who had lost with their feeling of inferiority their old compulsion to insist that the West was more Eastern and more European than it was in fact. Indeed, they sometimes acquired a new compulsion to insist that the West was more Western than it was or ever had been. It was easy for them to adopt a new image in a time when American incomes were growing along with cities and factories, when more Americans were able to ride west in their own automobiles. Perhaps the new image appealed most of all because of changes that were world-wide as well as American and Western, changes toward urban life and toward greater interest in hiking, camping, and outdoor sports, which were escape from urban industrialism and which were possible on a large scale only with the incomes and leisure of an industrial society.

It was easy to look westward also in the decade of the great depression of the thirties, when Americans turned away from the ruins of their faith in technological and financial wizardry to seek the reassurance of fundamentals, when many of them left the city to return to the soil (if only to an FHA house in Westchester), and when more of them had leisure for week-end recreation than they had known before. This was the decade of the rural American themes of painters like Grant Wood and Thomas Hart Benton, the decade of municipal golf-courses and ski trains. An assistant to the Secretary of Agriculture wrote poetically of the historical antecedents of Western recreation as well as of new departures in government, mooring it back in the eighteenth and nineteenth centuries: "in a manner of speaking the whole American settlement from coast to coast was an adventure, a grandiose outing, a burst of escape from overcrowded, overdriven civilizations that were not working any too well in Europe." [3] "Back to the soil" made psychological sense if not economic or historical sense in a time of agricultural overproduction, and as recreation rather than farming it was good fun besides, at low cost if necessary for those who had to amuse themselves cheaply. And yet the extent and volume of outdoor recreation were such, in one form or another—suburban gardening, touring the West, fishing, and hiking—that it was one of the few phases of the American economy that continued to prosper reasonably well in unprosperous times. It was especially easy for Westerners to believe in the new image of the outdoor West when the promoters that they had hired told them that more tourists were pouring into parks and national monuments and national forests than was safe for themselves or for the remnants of wilderness that they presumably came

[3] Russell Lord, ed.: *Forest Outings by Thirty Foresters* (Washington: Government Printing Office; 1940), p. 20.

to see; that more tourists were going to Mount McKinley during the bad times of the 1930's than had gone to Yosemite in the good times of the 1870's.

The wider tourist-market of the twentieth century thus had swallowed up the synthetic, transplanted imagery of the era of the early Raymond excursions. It had been easier to maintain the illusion for the few than for the many. In turn, by the middle of the century, the crowds that were going west were too large to share wholeheartedly in the newer imagery of the outdoor West. Ansel Adams complained in 1945 as one might have complained in 1875 of obsession with the curious and the picturesque: "Our weakness in our appreciation of nature is the emphasis placed upon scenery, which in its exploited aspect is merely a gargantuan curio. Things are appreciated for size, universality and scarcity more than for their subtleties and emotional relationship to everyday life." A handful of conservationists defended the wilderness, and the people preserved it, or some of it, but without achieving understanding and integrity of experience. They had learned, said a Western forest officer, "to take to the open road in a closed car and return to the breast of Nature and litter it up with banana peels and beer cans." So great a fraction of the population as went west could not easily be expected to be deeply interested in an active life, or in contemplating nature otherwise than from the windows of a moving automobile; the flesh was too often weak and the spirit unwilling, especially as Americans generally seemed to be less interested in exercise even while they were more interested in sports, and as the tourist himself came to be the elderly pensioner. In 1953 more than a fifth of the

[215]

tourists in Colorado were seeking places where they might retire, despite the incompatibility of snow and altitude with aging circulatory systems. Increasing numbers of tourists had too little time or imagination or money, perhaps, for the simple life; in 1948 the most popular form of vacation recreation in southern California, according to the All-Year Club, was going to the motion pictures, which outranked spectator sports, while spectator sports in turn outranked participation sports (including golf, bowling, and billiards as well as hunting and camping).[4]

As regular vacations became increasingly general and real incomes rose, it was within the means and habits of many Americans to regard a trip to the West not as a single great adventure but as an extended week-end automobile tour or visit to the wife's relatives. By 1952 ninety-five per cent of labor-management agreements provided for vacations with pay, and the average wage earner covered had three weeks or more. Improved highways—and the Western states had some of the best—might make it easier to reach the wilderness, but they hardly seemed wild themselves, and they were a temptation to many visitors to try to see so much of the West that they saw very little indeed. Thomas Wolfe, touring the national parks at high speed in 1938, saw his fellow travelers " 'making every national park' without seeing any of them—the main thing is to 'make them'—and so on and on tomorrow." [5]

Perhaps the tourists had been oversold; perhaps the

[4] Ansel Adams: *Sierra Club Bulletin*, Vol. XXX, p. 47; Russell Lord: *Forest Outings*, p. 9; *U. S. Travel*, National Park Service (Washington: 1949), p. 3.

[5] Thomas Wolfe: *A Western Journal* . . . (Pittsburgh: University of Pittsburgh Press; 1951), p. 3.

brightly colored representations of Western scenes in the promotional pamphlets of mid-twentieth century were so different from what they were likely to see with mortal eyes and within a summer that they turned in disillusionment to other and more accessible synthetic images and pastimes, as their ancestors had turned to the images of the West enshrined in the early tourist-hotels. "Our expectations of the Parks are largely formed by the resort-colored interpretations of the travel folders," said Adams; "the pleasures of the day overshadow the eternal pageant; the great mountains and parks become mere backdrops for a shadow play." "These professional enthusiasts are ruining travel for us," complained J. B. Priestley of an American tour in the thirties. "No reality can hope to compete with their purple eruptions. . . . What is this real world after those shiny folders . . . ?" [6] The desert might seem no emptier to one who had read that there was nothing there to see than to one who tried to reconcile photographs of a congestion of desert blooms and rabbit and prairie dog villages with the alkali dust stretching along either side of a four-lane highway. The outdoor West that some tourists found was little more than the open spaces between gasoline stations and a species of decoration and advertising in neon fluorescent tubing.

[6] Ansel Adams: *Sierra Club Bulletin*, Vol. XXX, p. 48; J. B. Priestley: *Midnight on the Desert* . . . (London: W. M. Heinemann Ltd.; 1937), p. 92.

7. THE VANISHING
TOURIST

THE GREAT day of tourism in Western America, at least in a quantitative sense, may still lie ahead. The tourist traffic almost surely will have to increase more slowly, for to continue the trend of the last seventy years would soon make commuters out of all of us. Southern California, which had 658,594 tourists when it began to count them in 1928, had 3,944,860 a quarter of a century later, in 1953; Yellowstone National Park increased from 19,542 in 1908 to 460,619 in 1928 and 1,326,858 in 1953. In 1916, just after the automobiles entered the national parks, one of three hundred Americans was a visitor; by 1954, one of three. Yet no decline was in prospect; the parks were serving more visitors with smaller staffs, and no one counted those who turned away for lack of accommodations.

As he increases, the tourist changes, and our interest in him changes. In the main it declines, although we cannot ignore the social and economic importance of the mass of him, and when we read the statistics of the mass we know that we are reading about ourselves as well. We lose the tourist as a personality; we do not find him individually or his observations in the books about the West, nor do we find books that he has written.

The decline of the tourist as witness to the West represents something more than the uselessness, from the contemporary point of view, of writing about what everybody already knows or thinks he knows, whether by his own travels or vicariously in full color, on a large screen. It reflects also changes in the West and in the tourist himself.

Once the tourist was very much the outsider, wealthy and as urban in his background as the West was rural. As an outsider he enjoyed some real advantages. He was alert to what he had not seen at home and so recorded it with interest, which he transmitted to his reader. Sometimes coming from afar means that he had a special claim to Western hospitality and so moved beyond railroad station hotels into homes as other travelers could not.

Yet the tourist as outsider also had his troubles and his limitations. Aside from such rare exceptions as the members of the Japanese mission who came to Washington in 1860, he was seldom as much an outsider as the Greek Herodotus in Egypt, or the Venetian Marco Polo in China. Most Easterners felt in some way the burden of the West as their own national inheritance, which they must defend militarily if not verbally, and civilize, and make to pay dividends, or in which they must prove their own virility and their own Americanism. Consciously or unconsciously, they were likely to be at least potential or vicarious settlers and investors. Europeans were freer from such burdens, except when they were investors, but to many of them America still had some of the fascination of a glimpse into their own country's future, as it had had still more in the more troubled atmosphere of revolutionary Europe in the 1830's and forties: the Far West was Canada or Australia of the next generation, and the democracy of the frontier was the cataclysm that awaited their aristocratic institutions at home, for better or for worse. Whether Easterners or Europeans, they were likely to be almost as ignorant of rural East as of rural West, and so confused what was merely rural American with what was peculiarly Western; the Englishman might be due for a special shock if he knew rural England and came, therefore, from the stronghold of aristocracy and deference to aristocracy to the spawning grounds of opportunity and equalitarianism. The great English economist, Richard Cobden, complained in 1859 that "writers and travellers fall into a great unfairness in comparing the middle and upper classes with whom alone the tourists and book-writing class associate in Europe with the *whole people* whom they meet at the tables d'hotes and in the railway cars in the United States." [1] Many came thinking that they knew what to expect, and their expectations misled them.

Now, while tourists' incomes still run well above the national averages, their range narrows as their numbers

[1] Richard Cobden: *American Diaries* . . . , Elizabeth H. Cawley, ed. (Princeton: Princeton University Press; 1952), p. 208.

increase. A higher percentage of bondholders travel than of wage earners, but the wage earners outnumber the bondholders on the highways, even while television and a new home in the suburbs lay heavier toll on wage earners' incomes. Rural America also goes increasingly on vacation, and the people of the rural states; increasingly, in fact, the westbound tourist moves literally from rural to metropolitan America, reversing the pattern of an earlier age, as Iowa and Kansas find that they can afford to visit Denver and Los Angeles. The tourist merges into the average American as the places that he tours merge into the average of America. The tourist likewise, as Easterner, comes to affect what pass for Western or outdoor habits when he is at home, or in his own section. He and his wife enjoy "outdoor living" in Western-cut denim jeans; they learn to broil steaks over open fires (perhaps using electrically operated spits on their apartment balconies); they patronize Eastern rodeos and dude ranches. Even in the early 1920's *Sunset* found that "the principal occupation of many rural Eastern sections is now that of being as wild and rough as possible in order to attract the campers, hikers and outers generally. In fact, the decayed hinterlands of the east, with their stony soils, which succumbed to the competition of the fat Western lands, are now coming back as local wild wests, and many a once disconsolate remnant of the colonial families is riding into prosperity on the wilderness that has returned whence his forefathers drove it." [2]

If the tourist sometimes feels that he is meeting himself

[2] "When the Far West Goes to the Wild East . . . ," *Sunset*, Vol. LI (November 1923), p. 45.

and old friends and neighbors as he heads west, it may be in part because the Westerner also has become a tourist and has shaped himself to the patterns of tourism, even while he, the tourist, has become a Westerner. There was a time when the Westerner stood apart. An Englishman who visited California in 1877 found that everyone in a group of San Franciscans urged him to go to the Yosemite, but, on cross-examination, that only one in six had been there himself. The statistics of the twentieth century reveal an entirely different disposition. By 1950 more than half of the tourists entering the state of Washington came from other parts of the Pacific Coast, and the proportion was increasing. This may have been so in part because of the increase in the number of persons who took trips of several days' duration, but not entirely. The Rocky Mountain and Pacific Coast areas exceeded all other sections in percentages of families taking vacation trips, the range extending from well under half for the east-south-central area to nearly three fourths for the mountain area. The Far Westerner was traveling abroad more than the Easterner, and he was also seeing more of the West than the Easterner saw of the East. Perhaps it was so because the Westerner had had to learn to travel when he came west and has had to take distances in stride ever since in a section where the big metropolitan areas tend to be farther apart than they are in the East (Boston and Washington, all of twelve senators apart, are closer by rail than San Francisco and Los Angeles); perhaps it was so because the appeals that first brought him west continue to work on him after he has become a Westerner, or because in the West he was losing the wilderness so rapidly that he, more than others, sensed the loss. It may have been so because Westerners have more automobiles relative to population than Easterners do (there have been more automobiles registered in California than in New York since 1940), and more cities within reach of attractive vacation areas. Even as early as 1929–30 California cars outnumbered all others in the national parks except cars locally registered; more Californians were traveling (two thirds more) in other states than residents of other states were traveling in California.[3]

As tourist travel of local and Western origin mingles with and in fact overwhelms Eastern travel in the West, the tourist loses the sense of isolation that he often had had in the 1870's and eighties, when London and Boston sometimes dominated the cars and the hotels. The wealthy tourist of those early years lived a sheltered life on tour, as he did when at home in the East, and the cultural impact of his visit fell chiefly on the resident Westerners who were inspired or demoralized by his displays of wealth and idleness, their respect for his manners quickened by their hopes that he would invest his capital. His presence, or the prospect of his presence, justified the hotels that local aristocracies frequented. When he came in larger numbers and in more modest circumstances, joining rural and small-town society for a season or a series of seasons, he some-

[3] Wallis Nash: *Oregon*, p. 70; Robert F. Lanzellotti: *The Washington Tourist Survey, 1950* (Pullman: State College of Washington; 1951), pp. 5–6, 9; *Travel Survey #1*, Curtis Publishing Company, p. 57; Peter B. B. Andrews: "New Peaks for Vacation Travel Expenditures," *Printer's Ink*, Vol. CCXXXIX (May 23, 1952), p. 49; *Touring Topics*, Vol. XXIV (August 1932), p. 6; ibid. (September 1932), p. 9.

times lost some kinds of influence and gained others: he
wanted to ride and drive, and so contributed to demand
for roads; often he attended church or camp meeting and
so strengthened the rural parishes, although on the other
hand he was likely to undermine Sabbatarianism, as when
Pasadena, even when an advertised feature of the Raymond tour was that every Sabbath was a day of rest, swallowed its principles in permitting Sunday band concerts;
mingling informally with his neighbors, he cut down differences of interest and cultural level between city and country, between East and West.[4] But eventually, while press
and radio and motion picture took over more of the task
of explaining Americans to each other, the visitor, who
under the most advantageous circumstances can bring
only a small part of his environment in his trunk, so much
more nearly approximated the common levels of economic
and social achievement and aspiration that there was no
natural flow of ideas downhill from East to West; the
Easterner, at once far outnumbered and bereft of the prestige of the traveler from afar whose opinions carry weight
proportionate to the difficulty of his journey and the dis-
tinctiveness of his caste, carried away more than he
brought. Now the typical tourist-party has become a
family from Spokane or San Francisco out for a long
week-end rather than a family from New York out for a
winter. The big market is the local market, which knows
the country already (or feels that it knows it) and is out
to enjoy a swim, a picnic, or a hike—perhaps a merry-go-
round and a Ferris wheel, too—rather than the great ad-

---

[4] Edward Hungerford: "Our Summer Migration. A Social
Study," *Century*, Vol. XLII (August 1891), pp. 574–6.

venture. Inevitably its tastes affect the Easterner, who is now in the minority, and him who caters to the Easterner.

Meanwhile, though the West entertains vastly more Western tourists than Easterners, it dresses up like a wild West show at increasing numbers of its tourist places, with trappings that would have impressed only the greenest of new arrivals seventy or eighty years ago. It may have formed the habit in some places when tourists stepped out of their Pullmans looking for Buffalo Bill to escort them; it may be catering to an Eastern tourist market that is small but spends heavily in the 'more fashionable dude-ranches and gambling-houses, more heavily than a larger market spends in the more typical vacation-places.

More fundamentally, the West plays West, and acts out a kind of Easterner's view of the West based more on the testimony of television than of history, because the West has become Eastern; the Westerner has become an Easterner, and not merely host to Easterners. The Far Westerner always has been an Easterner in some sense; he is still more likely to have been born east of where he lives than any other American, though the percentage of native sons necessarily rises above the level of the first years of settlement. He is an Easterner in some newer senses now; much of the Far West, which has always lived much under the shadow of cities like Portland, San Francisco, and Denver, has become more urbanized than the Mississippi Valley and the South. The tourist with Western license-plate who camps in the Yellowstone, scans the roadside markers in Montana, or reviews the battle of the Little Big Horn, may live in the third- or fourth-largest city in the United States.

[225]

The Westerner learned to behave like an Easterner, and to look at the West somewhat as an Easterner does, even before Los Angeles became a city, and even after he left the East for the West. When he came, he had to justify the change to himself and to those he had left behind; the need was both economic (since he had staked his labor and his savings on a new land) and psychological. Inevitably he learned to talk like a promoter, and even to think like a promoter, when harsh reality peered around the palm trees and boulevard markers. It was because reality (or what he feared was reality) looked so grim, and the distance from the old home was so great, that he insisted, in effect, that the new home was the best of the East in a kindlier climate, with some of the rougher elements of society as well as of weather left behind. These were the days when Pasadena tried to transplant Back Bay and the White Mountains, when Manitou tried to be Saratoga, and Del Monte could not make up its mind between Hampton Court and Lake Geneva. Even then, however, pride demanded that the new country should offer something distinctive, to match the distinctive antiquities of the older states. Having moved the greatest distance from home, the Westerner was already more interested in the distinctive superiority of his section than most other Americans are, aggressively proud, as if always conscious that those yet to be convinced were passing by and might stop to build with him or to undermine his own faith in himself, whereas the Southerner reassures himself without trying to convert others. When the West ceased to be frightening, and to his surprise began to fulfill and even exceed the Westerner's predictions of wealth and population, he retained something of the old promotional spirit, whether from what he heard about the West at his mother's knee as a native son or from what he read about the West in a lithographed pamphlet as an immigrant. It may be that he exchanged an old sense of insecurity for a new one when the desert began to bloom like a southern California real-estate advertisement and the land that he had been afraid to buy before for a pittance came to sell at Eastern prices. At this stage he grows sideburns before the annual rodeo and affects a big hat, without quite knowing whether he does it out of civic spirit, because others expect it of him, or because he, as a transplanted Easterner, expects it of himself. He may not dare to do otherwise, if he realizes how precariously he lives, how much he depends on the tourist trade. In the land of the cowboy, running a motel may be the most obvious alternative to working for a beef, oil, or irrigation trust: dude wrangling in its various shapes has succeeded prospecting and homesteading as the great individual opportunity in a section that has had to "attempt to balance its economy by capitalizing on its myth." [5] There is pathos and poetic justice in the spectacle of Arizona businessmen doing snake dances in Indian costumes; there is also sound economic instinct.

The old West is at once undiscoverable, and in other respects, almost indestructible. Some of its spirit remains, though Western optimism is more than the hope that springs before the slot machine, and Western equalitarianism is more than a gaucho shirt. Likewise much of nature remains, and seems large enough to withstand for some

[5] West: *Rocky Mountain Cities*, p. 22; Donald Wayne: "The Wild West," *Holiday*, Vol. III (March 1948), p. 60.

time the forces of civilization: the peat mulch of the San
Joaquin Valley, the coal furnaces of Salt Lake City, the
wood-pulp mills of the Willamette, the factories and diesel
buses of Los Angeles still leave the air over the West as a
whole chiefly unpolluted, and most of the mountains and
the desert are as they were. But the very desire to find the
wild West, to live through something like the pioneer experience, recalls that they are gone. The essence of the
Western experience is not in seeking out, for a week end
or a summer, hardships that authentic pioneer Westerners
submitted to out of unqualified necessity. The tourist in
the West may find nature, but he cannot recreate history.
He is out of touch with it whether he sleeps in a motel or
in a tent, on a plastic air-mattress or on balsam branches.
In the fifties New Yorkers by the thousand were hunting
deer with bow and arrow, and Western river guides, who
had begun by taking parties down the rapids of the Yampa
and the Green, were organizing treks by boat and plane
down the Yukon and to the North Pole.[6] The families that
made such trips did more than John Wesley Powell or
John C. Frémont or Jedediah Smith had done, and they
also did less.

The twentieth-century tourist who tries to recapture
some of his pioneer heritage as his pioneer ancestors lived
it is beaten before he starts. If they did not ignore the
wilderness, they tried to destroy it. Perhaps they ignored

[6] A New York law of 1948 established a two-week archery
hunting-season. *The New York Times,* November 8, 1954, p.
23:3; and cf. Saxton Pope: *Hunting with the Bow and Arrow*
([San Francisco: The James H. Barry Co.;] 1923), p. 38; *The
New York Times,* March 6, 1955, II, p. X21:2–3.

a part of it—the relatively inaccessible and unrepresentative part that remains to us today—because they were too busy destroying another part, or because they wanted to forget that it might destroy them if they did not destroy it, or even if they did. Many of the early Western tourists, on the other hand, those who were essentially uninterested in nature, kept the wilderness more beautiful than Americans of mid-twentieth century do, not only because they were so few but simply because they let it alone. No one had told them that they ought to breathe it, climb it, live in it, let it tan their skins and turn their fat into muscle, soak up its flavor as another way of life rather than glimpse it as a curio or spectacle. Most of them did not even try to carry away parts of it as trophies. Perhaps there were other thrills and challenges that served them, directly or vicariously; perhaps they needed the wilderness less because they knew that it was there in abundance. Now the wilderness has scarcity value, and if those who go west do not rest content with the substitutes for it that have come on the market, then they must learn to experience it without using it up. If they do learn, they will have departed from the spirit and practice of their pioneer ancestors and their tourist ancestors as well; and if they do not, Americans will have the opportunity of observing what happens to man when he has completely mastered the wilderness, of finding whether man completely civilized, completely de-Westernized, can escape, on a spiritual as well as physical level, the fate of the too protected deer that die off when we destroy their natural enemies. "Recreational development," said Aldo Leopold, "is a job not of building roads into lovely country, but of building receptivity into the still unlovely human mind." [7] It is a new and subtler form of civilization, rather than mere atavism, that nature lovers like Leopold preach, and that the Western tourist may have to learn if the West is to continue to be worth touring as more than a series of widely spaced recreational enterprises.

Likewise it is not easy to recapture the shape of Western democracy in the West and in the wilderness, although nearly everyone knows that the West is where democracy came from and where undemocratic inequality wears away in the outdoors. Americans grew up in the tradition of giving a quarter section, one hundred and sixty acres, to each man as a homestead, perhaps more if the land was dry; this was what Lincoln said a free government should do to make freedom mean more to free men. Who is to say that we can best preserve the spiritual value of the wilderness to the republic if we say that only a few may use it? We do something like that when we say that only a few cattle may use grazing land, but it is easier to tell when livestock damage grass than to tell when people destroy beauty. The wilderness lovers may succeed in keeping out the airplanes of the few, but what can they do when the many say: "We, the people, want roads further into the wilderness, a ski lift, motels, and cafeterias; this is the highest use of wilderness for us"? Forest Service officials some years ago ascribed the popularity of forest retreats to differences in noise: "Thus we find that the tired busi-

[7] Aldo Leopold: "Conservation Ethic," *Bird-Lore,* Vol. XL (March–April 1938), p. 109.

ness man whose nerves are frayed by the noise in his office, with its volume of fifty-seven decibels . . . hies himself off to some woodland dell and there . . . finds peace and content in an atmosphere of only twelve decibels." [8] Why not, then, some simple, objective test of a limit of so many square yards, or so many decibels? There would be more resistance to such a solution now than three quarters of a century ago, but there also would be more pressure toward it.

There are parts of the West where one can hardly sit on the beach for the tourists, or hardly see the scenery for the billboards and drive-in stands that are supposed to catch the tourists' eyes. At such places old residents—that is, those who were there the year before—sometimes meditate on the virtues of tidal waves and the Black Death. Yet tourists are an essential part of the West, the West that is, the West that was, and the West as Westerners like to think it was. They are essential to quality as well as to economy. They are no less essential than old residents, who in their time were also tourists and have not altogether lost their former character. Even members of old families —those who can trace a grandparent who came west when a man could still expect to raise a family on a rising real-

[8] *The New York Times,* September 13, 1931, II, p. 12:8. Robert Marshall had an answer: "It would be possible to have thousands of people see the original of the Mona Lisa if it were divided into a thousand fragments, and if one of the fragments were sent to each of a thousand museums, but in doing this the value of the painting would be destroyed for everybody." "Maintenance of Wilderness Areas . . . [1936]," *Living Wilderness,* Vol. XIX (Summer 1954), p. 31.

estate market—were, if not tourists, at least the benefici-
aries of tourism. If there were not tourists, would it be
much worth while to be a member of an old family? Could
members of old families have thought, independently, of
being what they are and want to be? Would El Dorado be
as golden?

A NOTE ON THE SOURCES

THE MATERIALS for further reading on the history of tourists and tourism in the West extend over the bulky stack-areas of libraries and archives that are concerned with history, exploration, travel, description, transportation, literature, and much more besides. Because I want my text to be longer than my footnotes, in general I have not cited advertisements, railroad timetables, and the like, which are voluminous and important, and I have slighted newspapers. Historians arrive at many of their conclusions by slow cumulative processes, building up impressions from masses of scattered ephemera. This book took shape while I examined sources of Western history that included, I think, practically every extant volume of Western memoirs, travel, and description, and every magazine published in a Far Western territory or state. Anyone who wishes to retrace my steps may arrive at some different interpretations—the West is large enough to contain a good many; he is almost certain to find the means of enjoying himself.

INDEX

INDEX

A Note on the Author

EARL POMEROY was born in Capitola, California, in 1915. He received a B.A. degree from San Jose State College in 1936 and completed his studies at the University of California at Berkeley, where he was awarded an M.A. degree in 1937 and a Ph.D. in 1940. He has taught history at the University of Wisconsin, the University of North Carolina, the Ohio State University, the University of Oregon, and the University of California, San Diego.